19.25

KU-533-304

4 0

Mental Illness in the Community

Mental Illness in the Community

THE PATHWAY TO PSYCHIATRIC CARE

David Goldberg and Peter Huxley

Foreword by Michael Shepherd

Tavistock Publications
LONDON AND NEW YORK

First published in 1980 by
Tavistock Publications Ltd
11 New Fetter Lane, London EC4P 4EE
Published in the USA by
Tavistock Publications
in association with Methuen, Inc.
733 Third Avenue, New York, NY 10017
© 1980 David Goldberg and Peter Huxley
Typeset by Red Lion Setters London WC1
Printed in Great Britain by
Richard Clay (The Chaucer Press) Ltd,
Bungay, Suffolk.

ISBN 0 422 76740 9 (hardback edition)
ISBN 0 422 76750 6 (paperback edition)

British Library Cataloguing in Publication Data
Goldberg, David
Mental illness in the community.
2. Family medicine
I. Title   II. Huxley, Peter
616.8'9'075   RC469   80-40943

ISBN 0-422-76740-9
ISBN 0-422-76750-6 Pbk

Contents

Acknowledgements

We wish to thank many friends and colleagues who have sent us details of their research which are relevant to the viewpoint put forward in this book. Professor John Wing and Professor George Brown patiently answered our questions as they related to their surveys of depression among Camberwell women, and Dr Darrel Regier and Mr Irving Goldberg of the Division of Biometry and Epidemiology of the National Institute of Mental Health, Washington, very kindly provided us with detailed documentation about the exciting research now being carried out in primary care settings in the United States as a result of their leadership. Dr R. Layton MacCurdy and Dr Hiram B. Curry of the Medical University of South Carolina made facilities available for the research reported in Chapter 4, which lies at the heart of our argument: without their help, and the facilities of the library at Charleston, this would have been a much thinner book. Dr Janet Hankin of the John Hopkins University, Baltimore, made available a copy of her annotated bibliography of the literature concerning mental disorder and primary care some eighteen months before publication and so made our search through what has become a vast literature much easier than it would otherwise have been.

Professor Michael Shepherd of the Institute of Psychiatry of the University of London has kept us informed about the research programme carried out under his supervision at the General Practice Research Unit, and provided the facilities for the development of the General Health Questionnaire. Our conviction that those who wish to study psychological disorder in community settings should concentrate their attention on events in the family doctor's office, and our interest in social variables as determinants of the course of minor psychiatric disorders can both be traced to research carried out by the GPRU.

We make no apology for having seized the opportunity of writing this book to set forth the programme of research carried out in the past decade in the Department of Psychiatry at the University of Manchester. It is not easy for readers of our various publications to see how one study relates to another, or to appreciate the viewpoint which informs our research strategy. We have tried to give a reasonably comprehensive account of the context in which our research has taken place, but inevitably we will have omitted many studies and given very brief descriptions of others.

We are indebted to the family doctors in Philadelphia, Manchester, and Charleston who collaborated with us on the three surveys reported in Chapter 4, and to the many patients who have completed questionnaires and allowed us to interview them, and we would like to thank M.E. Sharpe, Inc. for permission to reproduce the portion of Chapter 8 originally published in the *International Journal of Mental Health* in 1979.

Manchester 1979

Foreword

The term 'community psychiatry' has gained increasing acceptance in recent years. While its precise meaning has been disputed, most workers in the field would probably subscribe to the view expressed at a recent symposium devoted to its critical appraisal, namely that it be '. . . identified as the best possible clinical care delivered to individuals and to population groups in community settings. Services are delivered in communities and their institutions rather than within the setting of total institutions (state hospitals, asylums etc.).'[1]

The emphasis here is on the major psychiatric illnesses, particularly the schizophrenias and the affective disorders. In line with this opinion the principal concerns of community psychiatrists have been with the extramural fate and management of psychotic patients who were formerly regarded in largely institutional terms. Paradoxically, most community psychiatrists have seemed unaware of the fact that the bulk of mental illness in any community never comes to their attention at all. The reason, as Professor Goldberg and Dr Huxley point out in this book, is 'that psychiatrists base their concepts of mental illness on the highly selected sample of patients who are referred to them'. As they rightly argue, 'this selection process is therefore important in determining what will be thought of as a psychiatric case'. Accordingly, they subject the selection process to a detailed scrutiny by bringing together and reviewing much of the relevant published work, including their own, which relates to the pathways of psychiatric care. The evidence clearly establishes the major role of the primary care system in the detection and management of mental illness in the community, confirming the conclusion of a World Health Organisation report that 'The primary medical care team is the cornerstone of community psychiatry'.[2] In their further discussion of the types of disorder encountered and of their treatment, the authors deal with some of the practical implications of these studies, including the importance of associated social factors and the significance of the findings for the training of primary care workers.

In the light of this information it is apparent that a new perspective must be brought to the concept of community psychiatry if it is to survive. The primary health care team rather than the psychiatrist occupies the centre of the stage; the patient-population comes to be dominated by a large group of so-called minor psychiatric disorders which rarely confront the hospital-based physician. In defining the issues and presenting the facts, Professor Goldberg and Dr Huxley have not only helped clarify the role of psychiatry within the broad framework of public health to which it rightly belongs; they have also provided a pointer to future developments in the rational development of a discipline which has still to demarcate its own territory and delineate its own boundaries.

MICHAEL SHEPHERD
Professor of Epidemiological Psychiatry
Institute of Psychiatry
University of London

NOTES

1. Astrachan, B. (1977): In *New Trends of Psychiatry in the Community*, edited by G. Serban. Cambridge, Massachusetts: Ballinger. p. xviii.
2. Report of Working Group (1973): *Psychiatry and Primary Medical Care.* Copenhagen: WHO.

CHAPTER 1
Introduction

Knowledge about mental illness and its social correlates has until recently largely been derived by studying those treated by the psychiatric services. This is reasonable for major disorders which are relatively rare and which are likely to reach the psychiatric services, but it is unreasonable for common conditions which often do not reach them. For example, a study that is based only on those under treatment by psychiatrists cannot possibly demonstrate the importance of a possible social correlate which may itself be associated with a reduced chance of receiving treatment.

Although there have been notable attempts to define psychiatric illness on theoretical grounds,[1] there is a more prosaic sense in which psychiatric illnesses are those disorders that occur among the clients of psychiatrists. These illnesses are enumerated in the World Health Organisation's *Glossary of Mental Disorders* (World Health Organisation 1974). Since people consult psychiatrists for a variety of reasons, it is hardly surprising that the classification offered by the Glossary is strikingly inclusive; so that the clinician is even able to use ratings keys for classifying those with long-standing traits, such as lesbians, eccentrics, and stutterers. If only psychiatrists were in the habit of saying to their patients, 'You don't have a psychiatric illness, go away', they might be said to have some part in the definition of mental illness: but such behaviour is very rare. Until quite recently psychiatrists did not *define* psychiatric illness, they *described* it. The descriptions which have resulted from their efforts are systematic and intelligent, but they are based on a study of a small subset of patients who present themselves – or who are presented by others – for psychiatric care.

What a given society understands by psychiatric illness is effectively defined by the characteristics of the referral pathway to the psychiatrist's office. Paradoxically, psychiatrists have very little to do with the decisions which must be taken before a patient comes to see him, although naturally psychiatrists collectively contribute to the climate of ideas which will influence non-psychiatrists in their decisions concerning referral. Once a patient arrives in his office, the psychiatrist will typically concur with lay judgement and assign a diagnostic label, since his client has defined himself as psychiatrically ill by occupying the formal patient role.

Countries where there are large numbers of psychiatrists, and where members of the public can refer themselves directly to psychiatrists without the necessity of using a primary care physician as an intermediary, are therefore likely to have patients referred to psychiatrists with relatively minor disorders and life problems and to use rather over-inclusive criteria for deciding what constitutes a psychiatric illness. There is a real sense in which such psychiatrists are functioning as specialized primary care physicians, and it is hardly surprising that their colleagues in countries where patients are typically referred by primary care physicians have developed more conservative notions of what constitutes a psychiatric case.

In recent years an important development has occurred which allows psychiatrists to play a decisive role in the definition of what constitutes a psychiatric illness. The arrival of standardized psychiatric interviews and psychiatric screening questionnaires has allowed researchers to study systematically the distribution of symptoms among patients receiving psychiatric care.[2] It has become clear that, with certain interesting exceptions, most psychiatric patients have a common core of symptoms which relate to mood disorders – notably anxiety, depression, fatigue, irritability, and sleep disturbance.[3] The exceptions fall into two groups: on the one hand, major disorders such as hypomania, certain forms of schizophrenia, and some organic states which can readily be diagnosed by the possession of other florid patterns of psychopathology; and on the other hand, various kinds of abnormal personality which may occur without the critical symptoms of mood disorder, and which therefore fail to meet the criteria for a psychiatric illness.

The most elaborate attempt to specify a psychiatric illness in operational terms is John Wing's Index of Definition derived from the Present State Examination (see Wing *et al.* 1977; Wing 1980), the latter being a 140 item research interview developed at the Institute of Psychiatry and now used throughout the world by the World Health Organisation. An alternative, rather cruder attempt to define a psychiatric illness is represented by psychiatric screening questionnaires such as the General Health Questionnaire.[4] In order to satisfy the Index of Definition, one must have more than a critical number, type, and severity of PSE symptoms, while in order to be considered a 'probable case' on the GHQ a respondent must endorse more than a critical number of symptoms from a checklist offered to him. It is worth noticing two rather arbitrary characteristics of both these ways of identifying a psychiatric illness. In the first place, the 'psychiatric patients' who were used to generate the calibration groups on which each system depends were produced by a particular health care delivery system: in both cases, the British National Health Service. From a British viewpoint this may seem very reasonable, but it might seem less reasonable viewed from Washington DC, or New York, where the copious availability of analytically trained psychiatrists taking direct referrals from the community may result in many patients failing to meet the Index of Definition. The second point is that either measuring instrument will produce distributions of patients without a clear division between 'cases' and 'normals'; so that the decision as to where subclinical disturbance ends and being a psychiatric case begins is, in the last analysis, arbitrary. For example, the concept of a 'case' which was used in the validation studies of the GHQ had regard to a degree of psychological disorder which was 'just clinically significant' in relation to a patient's visit to his general practitioner. Several studies have shown that this is equivalent to a 'Borderline Case' in Wing's scheme; if one required the two instruments to produce similar rates one would need to raise the threshold score used by the GHQ.

The same arbitrary standards are used by the rival American scheme, the Research Diagnostic Criteria of Spitzer, Endicott, and Robins (1975). In order to be diagnosed as, for example, a 'major depression' a patient must possess certain key symptoms and then at least five out of a shopping list of eight associated symptoms. Naturally, some patients just fail to make it to the criterion. This sort of procedure is perfectly reasonable; but it is also completely arbitrary.

In the past few years these research instruments have been used to measure rates for psychiatric illness in the general population in order to arrive at estimates of prevalence independent of the illness behaviour of the patient or the ability of his medical attendants to detect and treat any disorder that may present. When this is done the concepts of psychiatric illness which have been derived from those patients seen by psychiatrists are being back-projected onto the general population in order to assess the numbers of those with similar patterns of symptoms who have not sought psychiatric care.

Despite the somewhat different theoretical underpinnings of the various methods of psychiatric case findings now in use, two conclusions are unmistakeable. First, there is far less variation between recent estimates for rates of illness in random samples of populations than there were in the studies reported up to the early 1970s;[5] and second, it is quite clear that even in the developed countries of the world, most mentally disordered patients are not being treated by the psychiatric services.[6]

AIM OF THE BOOK

We will attempt a summary of research findings that have used the case-finding techniques which have recently become available, with particular emphasis on research which deals with the detection and management of psychiatric disorders by family doctors. As we shall show, the greatest share of the burden falls on their shoulders both in England and the United States. The book has three aims:

1. To describe the *selection processes* which operate on psychologically disordered individuals which determine which of them will seek care; having sought care, which will have their disturbances detected; having been detected, which will be treated in a primary care setting and which will be referred for psychiatric care. A schematic model will be used to illustrate these steps.
2. To describe the *kinds of psychiatric disorder* commonly encountered among patients at each stage of the help-seeking process, and to summarize what is known about *social factors* associated with psychological disorders at each level.
3. Since most psychologically disordered patients who seek care will continue to receive treatment in primary care settings, our third aim is to describe the forms of treatment which should be available in such settings, and the training which primary care physicians and other health professionals should receive to enable them to provide such care.

THE MODEL TO BE USED

A simplified model will be presented with five levels, each level representing different populations of subjects. In order to pass from one level to another it is necessary to pass through a filter.

Level 1 represents the community: at this level, our knowledge is derived from surveys of psychiatric morbidity which have either screened entire populations or which have been based on random samples of a particular population.

Level 2 is represented by studies of psychiatric morbidity among patients attending primary care physicians, irrespective of whether or not the physician has detected the illness. The first filter is between the first and second levels. The factors which determine whether or not an individual passes through the first filter are often referred to as 'illness behaviours' of the patient.

Level 3 consists of those patients attending primary care physicians who are identified as 'psychiatrically sick' by their doctor. These patients collectively represent psychiatric morbidity as it is seen from the vantage point of the primary care physician, and they will be referred to as the 'conspicuous psychiatric morbidity' of general medical practice. The second filter is represented by their doctor's ability to detect psychiatric disorders among patients in the second level. It will be shown that passage is through this filter is determined by characteristics of both doctor and patient.

Level 4 is represented by patients attending psychiatrists in out-patient clinics and private offices. In England, the primary care physician is critically placed to determine who will be referred for psychiatric out-patient care, and he will therefore be thought of as the third filter. In the United States it will be shown that in addition to patients being referred to psychiatrists by primary care physicians, there is a considerable 'short circuit' of the second and third filters, in that a substantial number of patients are self-referred and thus pass directly from the first filter to level 4. However, even in the United States, many patients enter psychiatric care by referral from primary care physicians and thus passage is through the second and third filters (detection and subsequent referral).

Level 5 is represented by patients admitted to psychiatric hospitals and mental hospitals. They form the population most commonly referred to in national statistics of mental illness. The psychiatrist now appears for the first time, as the gate-keeper to in-patient beds. Even here, his powers are not absolute, since the number of patients he allows through the fourth filter depends on the number of beds made available to him by the health authorities. In all countries it is possible for an acutely psychotic patient to short-circuit the entire system and pass directly from level 1 to level 5, pausing only to be vetted by the psychiatrist acting as the fourth filter. However, these patients typically display major psychotic syndromes and once more the psychiatrist usually plays little part in deciding that a patient is referred to him in this way.

It will be seen that 'psychiatric illness' proper begins at level 4; yet psychiatrists do not define such illnesses, since they seldom send patients away undiagnosed. However we choose to define a psychiatric illness in theory, in practice it is defined by the process of passing through the first three filters. Each of the filters is selectively permeable, so that some individuals are more likely to pass through than others. And we can already see that the key people deciding who shall pass through are the patient and his family doctor.

MEASURES OF PSYCHIATRIC MORBIDITY

If one wishes to study the distribution of a disorder in a human population, it is necessary to distinguish between the inception and prevalence. Inception refers to the *rate* at which new cases occur per unit time, and prevalence to the *level* of disorder, either at a point in time, or over a period of time. Generally speaking, surveys of illness in random samples of the general population will report point prevalence, while surveys in consulting populations will report period prevalence and sometimes inception rates. The definitions of each will be given so that the relationships between them may be more readily understood:

Annual inception rate (Synonym: Incidence rate)

This refers to the number of individuals with a new episode of a given disorder each year, per 1,000 of the population at risk. If the disorder only affects a particular age group, it is permissible to adjust the population at risk to take this into account.[7] The decision as to what is to be considered a 'new' episode is of course arbitrary; where psychiatric morbidity is concerned, it is usual to define it as one for which the patient has not previously consulted for at least one year.[8]

Point prevalence

This refers to the number of people with a given disorder in a population at a point in time. It can obviously be expressed either as a percentage or as a rate per 1,000 at risk. If the age of the population surveyed is known, one can use point-prevalence data to calculate 'morbid risks' or disease expectancies in populations.[9] In a large survey it is often impracticable to assess everyone on the same day unless the condition is very easy to count. Provided that each member of the population is only considered once, it is usual to allow such surveys to continue over a short time-period.

One-year period prevalence (Synonym: Annual patient consulting rate)[10]

This refers to the number of people who suffer from a disorder during the course of a calendar year on at least one occasion, per 1,000 population at risk. Individuals may be seen on numerous occasions during a year, and they will be counted as cases if they display the condition at any time during the survey year.

It is always possible to calculate one of these parameters if one knows the other two, since: One-year period prevalence = Point prevalence + Annual inception rate, and it is possible to calculate the mean duration of a disorder if one knows period prevalence and inception, since: Point prevalence = Annual inception × Mean duration of episode.

It will be noticed that both the prevalence and the inception rates are expressed 'per 1,000 population at risk' rather than as a percentage of all those attending doctors. In countries where people are free to shop around for medical care – going perhaps to one primary care physician when their child has a rash, but to another for a gynaecological complaint – such measures are almost impossible to calculate. In Britain, where as part of the National Health Service, every member of the population is registered with a single general practitioner, it is relatively straightforward matter, and estimates have been available for many years.[11] In the United States it has only recently become possible to calculate similar rates by studying populations registered for care with Neighborhood Health Centers and various forms of Health Insurance Plan; but even recent estimates suffer from the disadvantage that the populations receiving care from such schemes may not be fully representative of the general population.

We will not be concerned in this book with the numerous studies which report that 'x per cent of a particular physician's patients are emotionally disturbed', since such estimates tell us nothing about the population at risk, and indeed the size of the estimate tells us more about the physician making the assessment than it does about the level of symptomatology among his patients.[12] However, if we have a large representative sample of primary care physicians, and we know what percentage of their patients are thought sick, then we can make a rough estimate of treated sickness by multiplying this percentage by the proportion of people in that population who seek care each year. This procedure was used by the National Institute of Mental Health in order to estimate the period prevalence of conspicuous psychiatric morbidity in the USA,[13] and it will be used in this book to estimate the prevalence of morbidity at level 2.

It is now time to put some flesh on the skeleton of the model. Where the established psychiatric services are concerned (levels 4 and 5), the existence of psychiatric case registers allows us to examine prevalence and inception rates on both sides of the Atlantic. It is possible to add to these measures data from studies in primary care, notably Shepherd's study of seventy-six London general practitioners, and the more recent estimates made by NIMH for American primary care and out-patient medical practices: these are shown in *Table 1*.

Despite the major differences in the health care systems, the similarities between the two countries are more striking than the differences. The NIMH estimates that the ratio of total (level 1) inceptions to inceptions

Table 1(1): *Britain and the United States compared: Rates per 1,000 population at risk for the inception and prevalence of psychiatric morbidity*

	annual inception rate		annual period prevalence	
	Britain	United States	Britain	United States
level 5: psychiatric in-patients only	3.3 (Salford) 3.8 (Camberwell)	not known	6.3 (Salford) 6.8 (Camberwell)	7.0 (de Facto) 7.5 (Monroe County)
levels 4 and 5: *all* psychiatric patients (case registers)	9.0 (Salford) 12.5 (Camberwell)	10.0 (Monroe County)	14.6 (Salford) 20.1 (Camberwell)	29.0 (de Facto) 27.0 (Monroe County)
level 3: conspicuous psychiatric morbidity (primary care)	52.0 (Shepherd)	(not known) level 1 estimated to be 50.0 (de Facto)	102 (Shepherd: formal psychiatric) 139.4 (Shepherd: total psychiatric)	90 (de Facto) 93.4 (Pasamanick)

Note: For references see Note 14 to this chapter.

treated by the psychiatric services is 5:1, and it can be seen that this is the approximate ratio of Shepherd's inceptions in general practice to those reported to the Camberwell Register. Although inceptions are no more frequent in Monroe County than in Britain, it can be seen that one-year period prevalence is substantially higher in the United States, indicating that cases stay longer in treatment.

It has already been admitted that the model presented in this book can to some extent be bypassed in the United States since patients can refer themselves to psychiatrists directly. It is impossible to calculate the size of this bypass with available data, but there are two reasons for supposing that it is not so great as to invalidate the model completely. First, of the 24.0/1,000 patients in treatment, only 4.0 are being seen by psychiatrists in private offices, and only 2.0 by private practice psychologists: the remainder are seen in hospital and community health centres. Secondly, of the 2.1 million new patients seen by office-based psychiatrists in 1975 and 1976, 30 per cent were referred by another physician, and therefore obeyed the model presented here.[15] Unfortunately, it is not known what proportion of visits to hospital-based psychiatrists are self-referrals, although a study by Horwitz (1977) showed that only 30 per cent of patients at the Connecticut Mental Health Centre had not been seen by another professional before coming to the psychiatric service. Even for those who bypass the system by directly referring themselves to psychiatrists, the fact that psychiatric care must be paid for means that the first filter will be less permeable to those in lower socioeconomic groups. A study by Fink and others (1969) showed that when psychiatric consultations became free for those registered with the Health Insurance Plan of Greater New York, the referral rate to psychiatrists jumped from 6.6 to 11 per 1,000 at risk. At this stage we can conclude that the first filter is somewhat more important in the United States than it is in Britain, but that even there the majority of patients probably pass the second and third filters in order to obtain specialist care (see p.53 'The American Bypass').

Another point to notice is that although the American prevalence rates for conspicuous psychiatric morbidity are fairly similar to Shepherd's rate for 'formal psychiatric' illnesses, the British doctors have substantially higher rates than their American counterparts when 'psychiatric-associated' illnesses are included. One probably cannot conclude that there is any true difference between the patient populations however, since different survey forms were used in the various studies, and the design of the survey form critically affects the level of morbidity reported by the physician.[16]

In order to complete the comparison at all five levels it is necessary to combine the data shown in *Table 1(1)* with data from community surveys and from consulting populations, and here a major difficulty arises. Most community surveys report point prevalence rates, yet these can never be directly observed in surveys of consulting populations at levels 2 and 3. This would not matter greatly if inception rates at level 1 were known, since this would enable us to convert the level 1 point prevalence rates to period prevalence rates, and thus affect a comparison (see equation on p.6). Unfortunately, inception rates are very hard to come by in the community, although it is to be expected that in the future greater efforts will be made to collect data in such a way that estimates of inception can be made. In order to allow a rough comparison to be made despite these problems, we have relied on point prevalence of psychiatric disorder at levels 1 and 2 estimated from responses to the General Health Questionnaire made by two samples of respondents. The first was a sample of 4,067 unduplicated consecutive attenders to General Practitioners in Greater Manchester, and the second was a random sample of 213 patients in the community in South Manchester. In order to calculate the period prevalence rates at level 2 it was assumed that 60 per cent of the Manchester population attended during a year, and that approximately one third of illnesses detected by the GHQ are new illnesses.[17] There are no data with which to compare the level 2 estimates, although the fact that the physicians studied were detecting only 55 per cent of the expected true positives fits in with it fairly well. A comparison of morbidity at all five levels can therefore be made for one-year period prevalence using recent British data, and this is shown as *Figure 1*.

The figures given here for period prevalence at level 1 are somewhat higher than one would predict from estimates of point prevalence made by Wing's PSE-ID method, to be described in the next Chapter. It must be concluded that many of the mood disorders detected by the General Health Questionnaire (GHQ) are transient, non-specific disorders which would not satisfy Wing's Index of Definition for 'definite disorders'. There are two reasons for nevertheless using estimates based on the GHQ for our present purposes. First, it will enable us to make valid comparisons between levels 1, 2, and 3 of the present model: whatever the shortcomings of the method of measurement, like will be being compared with like. Second, even if the GHQ tends to produce slightly higher rates than the PSE-ID method, numerous investigators have shown that GHQ scores correlate highly with summed severity scores based on the PSE or the Clinical Interview Schedule (for review, see Goldberg 1978).

There are several points to notice about *Figure 1*. The factors that decide which seventeen individuals are to be referred to psychiatric services

	the community		primary medical care			specialist psychiatric services	
	level 1		level 2	level 3		level 4	level 5
	morbidity in random community samples		total psychiatric morbidity, primary care	conspicuous psychiatric morbidity		total psychiatric patients	psychiatric in-patients only
one-year period prevalence, median estimates	250	→	230 →	140	→	17 →	6 (per 1000 at risk per year)
		first filter	second filter		third filter		fourth filter
characteristics of the four filters		illness behaviour	detection of disorder	referral to psychiatrists		admission to psychiatric beds	
key individual		the patient	primary care physician	primary care physician		psychiatrist	
factors operating on key individual		severity and type of symptoms psycho-social stress learned patterns of illness behaviour	interview techniques personality factors training and attitudes	confidence in own ability to manage availability and quality of psychiatric services attitudes towards psychiatrists		availability of beds availability of adequate community psychiatric services	
other factors		attitudes of relatives availability of medical services ability to pay for treatment	presenting symptom pattern socio-demographic characteristics of patient	symptom pattern of patient attitudes of patient and family		symptom pattern of patient, risk to self or others attitudes of patient and family delay in social worker arriving	

Figure 1: The pathway to psychiatric care: 5 levels and 4 filters. (For full discussion of the estimates of one-year period prevalence, see text and note 17.)

from the 250 who may experience distressing psychological symptoms are those that relate to the sick individual, the attitudes of those in his environment, and his family doctor. The psychiatrist plays almost no part at all in this process, except that he may have influenced the family doctor's concept of what constitutes a mental illness during his training. At each level in the model, severity and type of symptoms will influence the permeability of the filters. There is evidence for example, that all four filters are selectively permeable to psychotic symptoms, and the reverse is true for transient mood disorders.

The most striking thing about the figures shown is that the first filter is very much more permeable than the second or third. The predicted prevalence of disorder among attenders is only slightly smaller than the predicted prevalence in the population at large, leading one to suppose that the majority of psychiatrically disordered individuals – at least within the ambit of the British National Health Service – do consult their doctors. We shall review what is known about the characteristics which determine illness behaviour in the next chapter; but wish to emphasise at this point that the factors which reduce a prevalence of 230 at level 2, to seventeen at level 4 are those which occur in the primary care physician's office. This stark epidemiological finding is the one which caused us to give major emphasis to the processes by which psychological disorders are detected and subsequently managed by the primary care team.

A final point to make is that it should not be thought that the patients allowed through by each filter should neccesarily have been allowed through: a Venn diagram for the five populations of patients would not be a series of concentric circles. *Figure 2* shows what a Venn diagram does in fact look like and takes into account consultation behaviour at the first filter, as well as the tendency of some patients who would not meet a research criterion for psychiatric illness to pass through the second and third filters.

In this diagram, A represents the population who will attend their doctor in the course of one year: it therefore takes up to 66 per cent of the enclosing square (Royal College of General Practitioners 1979). B represents the population who will be psychiatrically disturbed during the course of the year: our best estimate is that about 80 per cent will attend their doctor during an episode of disturbance, so that it is drawn with the 20 per cent who do not pass the first filter sticking out from circle A. The population identified by their doctor as 'psychiatric' is shown as C, and although it overlaps with B there are considerable numbers of patients whose illnesses are unrecognized by their family doctor, as well as substantial numbers labelled 'psychiatric' who report very few symptoms on self-report

Figure 2: Venn Diagram showing relationship between the first 3 levels

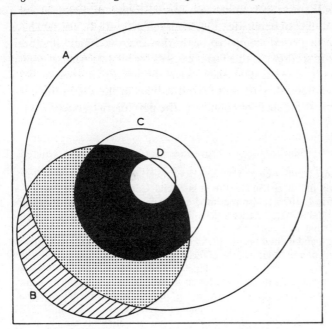

A = Consult their doctor during year
B = Psychiatrically ill during year (level 1)
C = Identified by their doctor as psychiatrically ill (level 2)
D = Referred to a ppsychiatrist (level 3)

▨ Do not pass 1st filter (ill, but do not consult)
▦ Do not pass 2nd filter (illness unrecognised by doctor)
■ Do not pass 3rd filter (not referred to a psychiatrist)

questionnaires. Even when allowance has been made for the known errors associated with self-report questionnaires, these patients remain: we shall consider why this should be in Chapter 4. Finally, the patients referred to psychiatric services are shown as D: the reason that this circle is not completely within B is that some patients are referred to psychiatrists with minor personality problems which fail to satisfy research criteria for psychiatric illness.

Now psychiatric case registers, and official statistics concerning mental illness, are wholly concerned with D. Medical sociologists have conducted much research into the determinants of 'illness behaviour' in patients – but such research is really concerned with whether or not a patient passes the first filter. If we compare D with B, the most striking thing is that failure to pass the second and third filters are more important reasons for a symptomatic patient not being identified as psychiatrically ill: yet they have been relatively neglected compared with the interest which has been lavished on the first filter. In this book, we will try to state what is known about each of the three filters which stand between the experience of distressing psychological symptoms by individuals in the community and receiving treatment for such symptoms by the psychiatric services.

NOTES

1. Easily the most lucid essay on the concept of mental illness was written by Sir Aubrey Lewis in his article 'Health as a Social Concept' (*British Journal of Sociology* 1953, 4: 109-24; also reprinted in *The State of Psychiatry*, Routledge and Kegan Paul 1967). In this article, Lewis argues that health is a single concept, and that it is not possible to set up essentially different criteria for physical health and mental health. Besides subjective feelings and the degree of total efficiency of an individual, the criterion of health is adequate performance of functions, physiological and psychological. The part-psychological functions in which there may be a disturbance for an individual to be thought ill include perception, learning, thinking, remembering, feeling, emotion and motivation. In order for illness to be diagnosed, the patient's symptoms should conform to a recognisable clinical pattern: that is to say, psychiatric illnesses are essentially syndromal in nature. The argument is taken further by Kendell in his book *The Role of Diagnosis in Psychiatry* (1975) in which he insists that mental illness is a concept, not a thing. A change in the defining characteristics of a disease may alter the population of patients embraced by the term, or even their symptoms and signs.

   'To our generation it is self-evident that diseases, tuberculosis as well as schizophrenia, are nothing but man-made abstractions, inventions justified only by their convenience and liable at any time to be adjusted and discarded. Our present outlook is so wholeheartedly empirical that we find it difficult to credit how an earlier generation could have talked of disease being "discovered" like so many golden sovereigns on a beach, or have imagined that there were a finite number of them waiting to be identified. Yet although we know these things perfectly well, we have still not rid ourselves of the old Platonic assumption. Claims are still made even now that this or that syndrome is a "disease entity", in spite of the fact that the word entity, defined in the Oxford dictionary as "a thing that has real existence", is meaningless outside its original Platonic context. . . . In fact, it is equally meaningless to assert on behalf of any abstract noun or concept either that it does or that it does not exist. The only question at issue is whether it is a useful concept, and even this question has to be asked within a defined context.'

   Wing, Cooper, and Sartorius in their book *The Measurement and Classification of Psychiatric Symptoms* (1974) write:

'our present sophisticated medical knowledge has accrued because of centuries of observation and description, in which the describers and classifiers have played as dynamic and creative a part as those concerned with the process. It is hardly helpful to tell psychiatrists that there is no need to begin at the beginning; that Kraepelin was unnecessary and that all they have to do is to look at their patients' problems. Such advice, if taken seriously is likely to be translated into a purely *ad hoc*, symptomatic approach, or one in which any theory is acceptable since none is meant to be tested'.

Where major psychiatric illness is concerned, such as organic mental states and the major psychoses, problems of taxonomy are not so great since these conditions are discontinuously distributed in human populations, and, although the matter is still not beyond controversy, a typological rather than a dimensional model better fits the facts as they are known. But there are still major difficulties concerning the most sensible way of classifying minor depressions and anxiety states, with which we will be largely concerned in the present book. Wing and his colleagues write: 'in some important conditions, such as diabetes and hypertension, the processes underlying disease are now seen to be complex and even continuous, rather than discrete, as they were in some of the simpler and more obvious disease models provided, for example, by acute bacterial or viral infection.'

It is still too early to say whether the processes underlying depressive illnesses are continuous or not. A complex model allowing for an interaction between genetic predisposing factors and environmental factors, leading to release of depressive phenomena, seems to be appropriate. At the epiphenomenal level, there is an unbroken continuum between severe, psychotic states on the one hand and minor moods swings on the other. It is possible to arrange patients in some fairly stable rank order, between cheerful individuals on the one hand and severely depressed patients on the other: somewhere on this continuum the line must be drawn between those whose mood disorder is impairing their social and psychological functioning, and those in whom normal homeostatic mechanisms may be expected to operate. Needless to say, the point where the line is drawn will depend upon the purpose of a particular investigation. If we wish to obtain an optimal discrimination between those who will, and those who will not commit suicide, we are likely to choose a different cutting point from that which will best discriminate between those who will or will not benefit from discussing their problems with another person. A third point might be needed to discriminate between those who will or will not respond to antidepressant drugs.

2. The standardized psychiatric interview most often used in international studies of psychiatric illness is the 'Present State Examination' (PSE) described by Wing, Cooper and Sartorius (1974). There are many others. Spitzer's 'Schedule for Affective Disorders and Schizophrenia' (SADS) is now being widely used in the United States. From this it is possible to make diagnoses using the Research Diagnostic Criteria of Spitzer, Endicott, and Robins; just as it is possible to make diagnoses from the PSE using Wing's CATEGO computer programme. Many of the surveys to be reported in this book have used the 'Clinical Interview Schedule' of Goldberg, Cooper, Eastwood, Kedward, and Shepherd (1970). This is a fairly brief interview designed for use by a psychiatrist in a community setting. The Dohrenwends have used a standardized research

interview called the Psychiatric Status Schedule, while the research group at Washington University, St Louis, have produced the Renard Interview. Both the Renard Interview and Spitzer's SADS Interview can be used to make psychiatric diagnoses using the research diagnostic criteria of Spitzer, Endicott, and Robins. The procedure used by Dohrenwend and his colleagues in constructing the PSS is somewhat different from that used by the psychiatrists who have constructed the other two research interviews: Dohrenwend has demonstrated that his various scales have internal consistency using a coefficient alpha (Cronbach 1951) and he then proceeds to show that patients and prisoners have higher mean scores on their scales than random community samples. The latter is not, of course, a very demanding requirement to make of a scale of psychopathology; but presumably further tests of validity will be forthcoming from this research group. The four internally consistent scales produced by the PSS are delusions and hallucinations; alcoholism; depression-anxiety; and suicidal tendencies. There are also large numbers of psychiatric screening questionnaires, some of them (like the General Health Questionnaire) aim at detecting non-organic psychiatric disorders regardless of diagnosis, while others are directed at a particular syndrome, such as depression. A fuller description of these screening questionnaires is to be found in Goldberg (1972).

3. The validation studies for the General Health Questionnaire lead one to suppose that the possession of *any* twelve from a checklist of sixty symptoms of psychiatric illness will cause an independent observer to conclude that a significant psychiatric illness is present. Although some of these sixty symptoms are more discriminant than others, it is not possible to stipulate any particular symptoms which *have* to be present in order for the respondent to be thought psychiatrically ill. If one examines the twelve most discriminant items, they consist of the sort of symptoms enumerated in the text. Furthermore, if one examines the other psychiatric screening questionnaires which have been used by other researchers, the same sort of symptoms regularly make their appearance. In his book *The Hierarchical Nature of Personal Illness* (1976) Foulds argued that psychologically disturbed individuals should be arranged in a hierarchy, with florid, psychotic syndromes at the top of the hierarchy, and less specific symptoms at successively lower levels. Individuals who have ascended to higher levels of Foulds' hierarchy are said to have all the symptoms of patients at lower levels in addition to the more differentiated symptoms. This hierarchial model has recently been tested by Surtees and Kendell (1979), who have found that about 75 per cent of the psychiatric patients examined by them using the Present State Examination obeyed Foulds' model by exhibiting symptoms at all lower levels as well as the higher levels which justify their position on the hierarchy. However, there were important exceptions. About 50 per cent of those diagnosed by conventional psychiatrists as schizophrenics or manics (and so occupying one of the upper two classes of Foulds' hierarchy) failed to exhibit the neurotic symptoms they required lower in the hierarchy. The arguments advanced in this book do not depend upon a hierarchical model along Foulds' lines, and we have always conceded that estimates of psychiatric morbidity made by the General Health Questionnaire are estimates that are prone to errors of various sorts. Even though it is not possible to say that a person with a high score will necessarily be a psychiatric case, or that a person

with a low score will necessarily be normal, it is nevertheless possible to make predictions of the likely level of morbidity in a population of respondents to known limits of error.

4. The Index of Definition (ID) is derived from ratings made by Present State Examination (PSE). The ID is based upon the number, type, and severity of PSE symptoms, and was constructed in order to find the threshold point at which sufficient information was available to allow classifications into one of the functional psychoses or neuroses (Wing *et al.* 1978). The Index of Definition does not use cut-off scores, although these are incorporated. Just as important is the presence or absence of key symptoms, both singly and in combinations. The lowest four levels are called 'below threshold'. Level 1 is defined by the absence of PSE symptoms, level 2 is between one and four PSE symptoms, and level 3 between five and nine symptoms. Level 4 is more complex, it can be determined by a total score of ten or more non-specific neurotic symptoms, or by the presence of a single key symptom such as depressed mood, autonomic anxiety, or hypomanic affect, without other related symptoms such as slowness or guilt being present as well. At this level of disorder, insufficient information is thought available to justify attempt at the clinical classification such as that embodied in the CATEGO programme. Level 5, the 'threshold level', usually provides a minimum basis for such a classification. The essence of the defining rules is that key affective symptoms (moderate in severity) are present together with each other or with certain other important symptoms. For example, a combination of hypomanic and depressed affect; of depressed affect and autonomic anxiety; or of depressed affect and psychomotor slowness or pathological guilt would be sufficient for level 5, even though a total PSE score of 10 was not reached. Levels 6, 7, and 8 provide increasing degrees of certainty that the symptoms present can be classified into one of the conventional categories of the functional psychoses or neuroses, either by clinical judgment, guided by the WHO glossary, or by using the CATEGO programme.

Whereas screening techniques such as the GHQ simply measure the mass of a patient's current symptoms and try to convert this into a probability statement that the patient is, or is not significantly psychiatrically disturbed, the ID is clearly a more subtle and elaborate system which is capable of discriminating between those symptom patterns which are thought particularly significant even though they may comprise a small number of critical symptoms. It seems likely that many patients who would be described as 'threshold' on the ID, would be declared cases by the GHQ. This is not merely because of the differences between the two which have just been mentioned, it also relates to the different concepts of a case used by ourselves on the one hand and Wing's group on the other. The GHQ was designed as a community research tool, and it was linked to a concept of a 'just clinically significant psychiatric illness' that was thought appropriate to conditions of general medical care. In the validation studies of the GHQ a respondent was deemed to have a 'mild' psychiatric illness if emotional disorder was thought to be either entirely or largely accounting for that day's consultation. Inevitably this meant that many patients with transient emotional disorders were counted as cases; as well as some who had fewer symptoms than might be expected in a psychiatric outpatient clinic of a hospital. Interested readers will find case examples in note 2, Chapter 4. Wing and his colleagues have preferred to produce operational criteria for defining 'cases' as defined by the specialist psychiatric services. In either case, the decision is sensible, but arbitrary; and ultimately depends on the nature of the primary care and hospital services in which each set of researchers develop their notion of a significant psychiatric illness. It is not intended to suggest that Wing and his colleagues have produced their criteria for a 'definite' illness by stipulating detailed criteria in such a way that a perfect discrimination is obtained between community samples and samples treated by hospital services: there is in fact no way of doing this, all one can do is to use the criteria in such a way that the overlap between the various populations is minimized. For example, in Wing *et al.*'s (1978) paper, sub-threshold (5 or below) disorders are reported in 20.8 per cent of a series of psychiatric inpatients, 33 per cent of a series of psychiatric outpatients, and 97.1 per cent of a general population sample. The last figure is of particular interest, since it is considerably higher than what one might expect from the figures reported in Chapter 2. The reason for this is that 'threshold' disorders are usually counted as cases in the studies reported in Chapter 2; if this is done, 91 per cent of the general population sample report by Wing (1979) are at level 4 or below. Duncan-Jones and Henderson (1978) have proposed a two-phase design for use in population surveys linking the GHQ with the PSE-ID and this is described further by Henderson and his colleagues (1979). The two-stage procedure used by Henderson and his colleagues in essence consists of a stratified sampling strategy using the scores of the GHQ-30 to form the strata, and using a progressively greater sampling fraction for ascending levels of GHQ scores. This is more sophisticated than the cruder practice usually used in Britain where the population is divided into two strata: high scorers and low scorers. However, it is only really suitable for large-scale surveys which would generate sufficient numbers in each of the various strata to enable realistic sampling. The Australian investigators then use methods of logit regression in order to calculate case rates from the GHQ scores in the original samples.

5. In 1969, Dohrenwend and Dohrenwend reviewed forty-four field studies of mental disorder in their book *Social Status and Psychological Disorder*. In 1974, in their 'Social and Cultural Influences on Psychopathology', they reviewed twenty-six further studies; a total of seventy studies in all. The range for reported prevalence is from 1.1 per cent to 69 per cent. The main value of such an anthology seems to us to be a scholarly one; that is to say, it is useful to have a collation of various field studies of mental disorder that have been made throughout the world. Inevitably, the various research studies gathered together by the Dohrenwends are very heterogeneous and often relate to different types of mental disorder: it seems pointless to try to build a wall with bricks of such varying quality.

6. The number of psychiatrists made available per 100,000 population at risk by different countries around the world is determined more by the given country's expenditure on health care than it is by the demands posed by the proportion of psychiatrically disordered patients in any particular country. It should therefore surprise no-one that in those countries where there are very few psychiatrists per 100,000 at risk, the majority of even the psychotic patients are not being cared for by psychiatrists. However, even in a country like the United States which spends a high proportion of its GNP on health care and which is lavishly supplied with psychiatrists compared with developing countries, a recent paper

by the Division of Biometry and Epidemiology of the National Institute of Mental Health indicates that the majority of psychologically disordered individuals in the United States are not being cared for by the specialist mental health services (Regier, Goldberg, and Taube 1978). This paper argues that the *de facto* US mental health services system is provided for by the primary care/outpatient medical sector. The division estimates that at least 15 per cent of the US population is affected by mental disorders in any one year, but that in 1975, only one fifth of these were served in the specialty mental health sector; whereas three fifths were identified in the General Medical (primary care) sectors.

7. The rate so obtained is called an age-specific incidence rate. There are problems in calculating inception rates. Where psychiatric case registers are concerned, the issues are relatively straightforward, in that the inceptions are the number of patients notified to the register the first time in a given year. Even here one must distinguish between inception from the point of view of the register and inception from the point of view of the patient: sometimes a patient has been treated elsewhere in the past, and is therefore having an inception from the register's point of view, but a readmission from his own. In Camberwell, for example, the annual inception rate of 707 per 100,000 at risk is made up in the following way: 362 first ever contact with psychiatric services; 175 not first ever contact but first on register; and 170 where previous contact was not known, although it was the first contact with the register (Wing and Fryers 1976:79). In community surveys, investigators sometimes try to estimate annual inception by asking those who are found to be disordered whether their illness began in the previous year. This procedure is bound to produce underestimates of inception, since there may well be patients who were disturbed in the previous year, but who are now functioning well and no longer remember their symptoms as vividly as they did. The best known study by a psychiatrist which has attempted to calculate inception rates was that by Hagnell (1966) where a psychiatrist visited almost every member of two adjoining parishes in South Sweden, and tried to build up a picture of each respondent's health over the previous decade. Although he had had access to each subject's full health records before his interview with them it is once more possible that his estimates of inception were lowered by a tendency of patients to forget symptoms which were now no longer troubling them. This criticism is actually not usually levelled against Hagnell's work, since his estimates of inception were so high.

8. The decision concerning what is to constitute a 'new' episode of illness of course depends upon the nature of the illness being studied. A new episode of Huntingdon's Chorea, for example, is defined by the occasion on which it is first diagnosed; all subsequent admissions are held to be readmissions. It is usual to deal with psychiatric conditions of relatively long duration, such as schizophrenia, in the same way. However, it would be absurd to deal in this way with conditions of short duration which are commonly recurrent – such as the common cold. Conditions such as this affect the entire population, and 'a new episode' of illness is a return to illness from a state of health. Minor mood disorders are somewhere intermediate between common cold and schizophrenia: they are subject to remissions and relapses, but they do not affect the entire population. Clearly, an arbitrary decision is called for. Shepherd and his colleagues (1966) defined a new psychiatric illness as one for which the patient had not previously consulted for at least one year.

9. A 'disease-expectancy' or morbid risk, means the likelihood that any individual who survives long enough to be exposed during a period of risk in life when the particular disease usually arises, will develop the disease. In the case of schizophrenia, for example, the maximum period of risk exists between the ages of fifteen and forty-five: in Weinberg's shorter method of calculating a morbid risk, the method essentially consists of adjusting the denominator of the population at risk in a prevalence survey in the following manner: those who have not reached the age of risk for the disease are totally disregarded, while all those who have exceeded the period of risk (forty-five in the case of schizophrenia) are counted, together with half of those who are still in the risk period. The rationale for this simple corrections is quite straightforward: the subjects who have been included in the survey whose age falls within the risk period but have not been found to have the disease may yet live to develop it, but those who have exceeded the risk period and not developed the disease maybe assumed to have escaped it. Weinberg's shorter method has the merit of simplicity, and gives a satisfactory approximation to morbid risks calculated by more elaborate methods.

10. One-year period prevalence is preferred to the synonym 'annual patient consulting rates' since the latter tends to be confused with a consultation rate which is by no means the same thing. A consultation rate is defined as the number of consultations during the course of a calendar year, per 1,000 at risk. It is possible to count an individual patient more than once when computing a consultation rate, whereas a one-year period prevalence will only count each person once.

11. See for example Logan and Cushion's (1958) General Morbidity Survey, and the results of the General Morbidity Survey carried out by Shepherd and his colleagues with special attention to psychiatric morbidity.

12. The immense variability between estimates of psychiatric illness made by lone general practitioners has been described by numerous previous commentators, including Shepherd *et al.* (1966), Kellner (1963), and Goldberg and Kessel (1975). Goldberg (1979) has argued that the level of morbidity reported by an individual practitioner tells one more about him than it does about the actual level of morbidity among the patients consulting him: this argument is repeated more briefly in Chapter 4 of this book.

13. Data for the National Center of Health Statistics 1974 Health Interview Survey showed that 57 per cent of the civilian non-institutionalized US population was seen in a physician's office during one year – this would amount to 119,000,000 persons in 1975. Since 60 per cent of all visits in the 1975 National Ambulatory Medical Care Survey (NAMCS) were accounted for by the primary care specialties of family practice, internal medicine, and paediatric, the same percentages of the total patients seen were attributed to these specialities. Based on multiple special surveys of general practice populations, 15 per cent of primary care physician patients were estimated by NIMH to have a mental disorder. Other non-psychiatrist physicians, however, recorded a diagnosis of mental disorder at about one third the primary care physician rate in the 1975 NAMCS. Hence, 5 per cent of their patients were estimated to have emotional disorders. Reiger and his colleagues (1978) therefore calculated that slightly over 21,000,000 persons with mental disorder were seen in the primary care/out-

Introduction 21

patient medical sector during 1975 in the United States, to be compared with 7.1
million who were seen by the specialized psychiatric services. The investigators
then estimated the number of persons with mental disorder in general hospital
in-patient nursing homes, and an allowance for duplications between these three
segments of the health services, and added a very conservative estimate of those
not in treatment: they produced a grand total of 31.9 million persons with
mental disorder during 1975, which represents 15 per cent of the total US
population.

14. For Salford and Camberwell see Wing and Fryer (1976): for Monroe County see
    Babigian (1977); for 'de Facto' see Regier *et al.* (1978); for Shepherd see
    Shepherd *et al.* (1966); for Pasamanick see Pasamanick *et al.* (1956).

15. Results of the National Ambulatory Medical Care Survey are reported by the
    National Center for Health Statistics (see Advancedata 1978). There is another,
    rather more indirect, reason for supposing that the ability of Americans to short-
    circuit this model cannot be all that great: in Chapter 6 we shall be reviewing
    evidence which suggests that the total volume of patients referred to American
    psychiatrists via American primary care physicians is roughly comparable to the
    reported rates in Britain: if there was substantial tendency for patients to short-
    circuit primary care physicians by direct referrals, we should therefore expect
    that the overall treated rates reported by American cases registers be
    substantially higher than those in Britain. However, we can see from *Table 1(1)*
    that this is not the case.

16. We shall be returning to this point in Chapter 3 (see note 1).

17. It can be seen from *Table 2(1)* on page 23 that the point prevalence of psychiatric
    illness in the South Manchester population is 18.4 per cent. If we make the
    assumption that approximately one third of the illnesses detected by the GHQ
    are new illnesses – and this has been the experience of many field surveys – then
    it is reasonable to assume that approximately a further 6.2 per cent of the
    population will suffer an episode of such illness in the course of the ensuing
    year. The one-year period prevalence therefore becomes approximately 25 per
    cent, and this figure has been shown in *Figure 1* on page 11. At level 2 we have
    followed the procedure adopted by NIMH in their 'de Facto' paper and taken
    the percentage of consecutive attenders on the very large multipractice survey in
    Manchester who were predicted to be psychiatrically disturbed by the GHQ,
    and multiplied this by the percentage of the Greater Manchester population
    who attend their general practitioners in the course of one year. The probable
    prevalence of 38.6 per cent seen among consecutive primary care attenders (see
    Goldberg 1978: 23) is therefore reduced to a probable prevalence of 23 per cent
    by taking into account the fact that only 60 per cent of the Manchester popu-
    lation attend their doctors during the course of one year.

CHAPTER 2

Level 1: Mental illness in the community

The wide discrepancies between earlier estimates of the amount of mental illness in random samples of the population were due largely to differing criteria for case identification. As recently as 1974 Dohrenwend and Dohrenwend were able to report rates which varied from 1 per cent to 69 per cent in a total of seventy studies, and advised their readers that differences in the type of rate employed – point, period, or lifetime prevalence, or ten-year inception rates – were of relatively minor importance compared with other methodological problems that arose if one survey were to be compared with another. Many of the earlier surveys arranged patients on a continuum of psychological impairment and did not attempt to base their concept of a 'case' on the direct assessment of a respondent by an experienced clinician.[1]

The famous exception to this was Essen-Moller's (1956) survey near Lund, Sweden, where trained psychiatrists interviewed 2,550 inhabitants in a defined geographical area. The observing psychiatrists not only recorded the presence of well-delineated psychiatric disorders, but also major personality deviations, normal personality variants, and the presence of certain subjective complaints. However, Essen-Moller 'left it to the reader to decide where to draw the line between the diseased and the abnormal, and the sound part of the population, and thereby let the former contain from a few percent to up to some 60 per cent of the population'.

The arrival of standardized research interviews linked to clearly stated diagnostic criteria for the more important mental illnesses has meant that there is now far less variation between the reported rates, so that interesting comparisons become possible between patient populations at different levels of the model (see Chapter 1) or between populations in different cultural settings. Despite these welcome developments, there are still considerable differences between the various diagnostic criteria, so that it is only reasonable to make a comparison if two studies have used the same case-finding method and have expressed their results in the same kind of rate.

Table 2(1): *Prevalence rates per 1000 population at risk for random samples of the general population for all psychiatric illness: results from recent surveys*

(GHQ = General Health Questionnaire; CMI = Cornell Medical Inventory; SADS = Schedule for Affective Disorders and Schizophrenia; RDC = Research Diagnostic Criteria; PSE = Present State Examination; ID = Index of Definition; CIS = Clinical Interview Schedule)

type of rate	investigators	location	case-finding method	size of sample	all psychiatric illness rates per 1000 population		
					males	females	total
rates calculated from psychiatric screening questionnaire	Goldberg, Kay and Thompson (1974)	South Manchester, UK	GHQ	213	114	233	184
	Finlay-Jones and Burvill (1977)	Perth, Australia	GHQ	2342	89	150	120
POINT PREVALENCE	Ingham, Rawnsley and Hughes (1972)	industrial Wales (Rhondda)	modified CMI	300	120	230	175
		rural Wales (Vale of Glamorgan)		581	50	155	203
clinical assessments POINT PREVALENCE	Dilling (1979)	Bavaria, W. Germany	CIS	1231	160	218	193
	Weissman, Myers, and Harding	Newhaven, USA	SADS-RDC	511	164	189	178
clinical assessments	Wing (1979)	Camberwell, London		800	59	119	90
	Orley and Wing (1979)	Ugandan villages, Africa	PSE-ID	191	194	291	241
ONE-MONTH PERIOD PREVALENCE	Duncan-Jones and Henderson (1980)	Canberra, Australia	GHQ/PSE/ID	756	70	110	90
clinical assessments	Brown and Harris (1978)	Camberwell, London	PSE	458	–	170	–
ONE-YEAR PERIOD PREVALENCE	Brown et al. (1977)	North Uist, Outer Hebrides	PSE	154	–	120	–

Generally speaking, estimates of prevalence derived from symptom inventories and psychiatric screening tests give rather higher figures than those which are based on the clinical interview. It can be seen from *Table 2(1)* that the point prevalence of psychiatric disorder is somewhere between ninety and 200 per 1,000 at risk, and that the female rates are approximately double the male rates. Estimates based upon clinical assessments of random samples are within or slightly lower than the range predicted by the screening tests, but it will be seen that Brown's surveys are confined to females; and it should also be remembered that a considerable reduction should be made to the one-year period prevalence rates if they are to be compared with the point prevalence rates. If like is compared with like, it can be concluded that there is probably more morbidity in South Manchester than in suburban Perth, in industrial than in rural Wales, and in Ugandan villages than in Camberwell. The factors that produce such differences need not be social or environmental; they could equally be due to genetic factors or to selective migration. Finally, the difference could have been more apparent than real and caused by differential willingness to admit symptoms, or different ways in which the surveys were carried out.

Most of the illnesses reported in these surveys are minor mood disorders taking the form of various combinations of depression and anxiety. The major psychotic syndromes are rare in the community, and even the depressions seen in community surveys have lower average severity than those seen by the psychiatric services.[2]

The single most common psychiatric diagnosis among random samples of the community is depression, and some results of recent estimates are presented in *Table 2(2)*. Once more, rates are higher among females than males, and depressive symptoms as measured by various self-rating scales are more widely distributed in the population than depressive syndromes which meet research criteria for a diagnosis of depression. There is rather more variation between the various rates shown in this table, with the rate for the Hebrides being lower than one might expect (since it is an annual rate) while that for the Ugandan villages is strikingly high. It is probably reasonable to compare these rates since the same method of case identification was used.

Brown and his colleagues speculate that the higher rate for depression encountered in their Camberwell women may be related to the fact that these women encounter more 'inner city stresses' peculiar to working-class women living in a big city, such as rehousing, debt, unemployment, and trouble with the police. Orley and Wing (1979), for their part, consider that possible reasons why their Ugandan villages had so much *more* depression

Table 2(2): *Prevalence rates per 1000 population at risk for random samples of the general population for depressive illness and depressive symptoms*

type of rate	investigators	location	case-finding method	size of sample	depression only: rates per 1000 at risk		
					males	females	total
point prevalence	Weissman and Myers (1979)	Newhaven, USA	SADS-RDC	511	55	79	68
	Hallstrom (1970)	Goteborg, Sweden	Hamilton depression	796	–	80	–
one-month period prevalence	Wing (1979)	Camberwell, London	PSE-ID	800	39	74	57
	Orley and Wing (1979)	Two Ugandan villages, Africa	PSE-ID	191	143	226	183
one-year period prevalence	Brown and Harris (1978)	Camberwell, London	PSE	458	–	148	–
	Brown et al (1977)	North Uist, Outer Hebrides	PSE	154	–	82	–
self-rating depression scales	reviewed by Weissman and Myers (1978)	England and USA 7 studies	various scales	total 9,841	100-160	200-240	160-180

Note: For key to abbreviations see *Table 2(1)*.

than their Camberwell counterparts might be because depressive disorders in rural Africa remain untreated or because of untreated parasitic infestations. As these authors properly point out, the reason for the different rates cannot be determined by a simple cross-sectional survey, and the range of possible explanations is very wide. It is interesting to note that even with these present results, it is no longer possible to invoke urban/rural factors to account for the differences between the three surveys.

PSYCHIATRIC DIAGNOSES IN RANDOM COMMUNITY SAMPLES

The two best known American surveys of the post-war period suggested that psychiatric symptoms were very common in random community samples; thus Srole *et al.*'s (1962) Midtown Manhattan Survey reported that 815 per 1,000 New Yorkers had psychiatric symptoms, while Leighton *et al.*'s (1963) Stirling County Study suggested that 690 per 1,000 of the population of the town of 'Bristol' were 'genuine psychiatric cases'. It should be noted that neither of these surveys used clinicians to examine the community respondents, and it is a relief to report that recent research using clinical criteria report much lower figures that are in better accord with everyday experience.

Thus, Weissman, Myers, and Harding (1978) reported that in their New Haven study 'although psychiatric disorders were common, they were not ubiquitous. Over 80 per cent of the subjects had no psychiatric diagnosis, either probably or definitely, including any type of personality disorder, anxiety reaction or minor depression'. It is, of course, true that psychiatric symptoms are more widely distributed in the population than the 20 per cent who met the RDC criteria for diagnosable illness, and the fact that a large proportion of the population has the occasional symptom of dysphoria, fatigue, or insomnia probably accounts for high rates reported by the earlier surveys.

It is possible to use psychiatric survey methods to arrange a population in a fairly stable rank order ranging from asymptomatic respondents to those incapacitated by many symptoms. The distribution is a reverse J-shape, in that there are many asymptomatic patients and then substantially fewer as the number of symptoms increases. Naturally, with greater numbers of symptoms it becomes more likely that characteristic symptom patterns or syndromes will be found, so that most case finding methods can state the critical number of symptoms at which the probability of being able to assign a syndromal diagnosis will exceed 0.5. The fact that there is no sharp dichotomy between non-cases and cases has meant that researchers have tended to use 'intermediate' classifications: thus the Research Diagnostic Criteria use the concept of 'probable case', while Wing (1976, 1980) has a 'borderline' or 'threshold' category and Brown and Harris (1978) and Goldberg and Blackwell (1970) have a category of 'subclinical disturbance'. It is worth pointing out that there is considerable agreement about the sort of symptoms which are reported by patients who are thought by researchers to be on the hinterland between subclinical disturbance and just clinically significant illness. The symptoms are those of minor mood disorders, and consist of symptoms such as fatigue, irritability, insomnia, fatigue, and dysphoria. Taylor and Chave (1964) estimated that almost a third of their respondents reported 'subclinical' neurotic symptoms of this sort; we have seen from *Table 2(1)* that a rather smaller proportion of the population may be expected to have some diagnosable disorder. At the threshold for diagnosis, the symptoms become more numerous, but they are otherwise similar. The core symptoms are abnormalities of mood, most typically various combinations of symptoms related to depression and anxiety. These minor illnesses can either be grouped together as 'minor affective disorders' or 'dysthymic states'; or they can be classified as either minor depressions or anxiety states depending on which mood predominates, or which mood seemed to develop first.[3]

It follows from what has been said that the more elaborate syndromes with many symptoms will be relatively infrequent in community samples, so that if the size of the sample is small it is not possible to make very accurate assessments of prevalence for them. For this reason, they tend to be gathered together into a 'miscellaneous' category in those community surveys which have given a diagnostic breakdown of the case encountered. If the Present State Examination is used as the case-finding tool, then between 85 per cent and 94 per cent of the diagnoses made will be depression or anxiety states; but this is partly because the PSE does not record alcoholism, organic states or personality disorders as psychiatric illnesses. Weissman, Myers, and Harding's (1978) study in New Haven using Spitzer's SADS-L reports only 63 per cent of the diagnoses as mood disorders, but this is because 25 per cent of the diagnoses were for alcohol or drug abuse; while Dilling's (1979) Bavarian study using the CIS also reports 63 per cent minor affective disorders, but here again 21 per cent of the diagnoses were either alcoholism or organic states. It is usual for the number of cases of 'depression' greatly to exceed the number diagnosed as 'anxiety states', but this is because cases exhibiting both anxiety *and* depression are often diagnosed as depressions (see note 3).

SEVERITY OF ILLNESS AT DIFFERENT LEVELS OF THE MODEL

The demonstration that far more psychiatrically ill patients are cared for by family doctors than by the psychiatric services should not be allowed to obscure the fact that the psychiatric services do tend to see the most severely ill patients; severity of psychopathology is certainly an important factor in determining permeability of the filters. For example, a patient who suddenly develops an acute schizophrenic psychosis associated with grossly disordered behaviour is likely to pass through the filters rapidly, or to bypass the second and third filters altogether and be admitted directly to a psychiatric bed. In contrast, patients with minor mood disorders accompanied by somatic symptoms may either not go and see their doctor at all, or if they do attend, their physician may confine himself to excluding serious organic disease and prescribing symptomatic medication.

There is much convergent evidence for the assertion that severity of illness increases at each succeeding level of the model. Helgason (1964) intensively studied a cohort of 5,395 Icelanders born between 1895 and 1897, and showed that schizophrenics had an 83 per cent chance of being admitted to psychiatric beds, while neurotics had only a 15 per cent chance. Cooper (1966) showed that the percentage of patients with psychotic illnesses increases at successive levels of the model, so that 4 per cent of patients seen by family doctors, 25 per cent of psychiatric outpatients, but 72 per cent of admissions to psychiatric beds are accounted for by those with schizophrenia and affective psychoses. Wing (1976) compared severity of illness using his Index of Definition derived from ratings from the Present State Examination and showed very striking differences between levels 1, 4, and 5 of the present model. If one adds together the two highest levels of his Index of Definition, then such severe illnesses were found in none of his general population sample, 20 per cent of his psychiatric outpatients, but 59.4 per cent of his psychiatric inpatients. Turning specifically to depression, he showed that the patients seen by the psychiatric services are predominantly characterized by depressive delusions and hallucinations or pathological guilt, yet these symptoms are relatively rare in the general population sample. These findings fit with Fahy's (1974) demonstration that depressions seen in a family practice setting are less likely to have psychomotor retardation, less likely to have made a suicide attempt, and have lower psychological distress scores, than those seen in psychiatric outpatient clinics. Finally, Weissman and Myers (1978) showed that the more depressed the individual in their general population sample, the more likely he or she was to have sought medical care.

These findings have been set out in detail to underline the importance of severity of psychopathology in determining whether patients are seen by the psychiatric services. However, it will be noted that most of the surveys were in countries where referral to psychiatric services is by family doctors; it is not known whether patients seen by private office-based psychiatrists in the United States are more severely ill than those seen by primary care physicians in that country.

DEMOGRAPHIC VARIABLES AND MENTAL ILLNESS IN THE COMMUNITY

Psychiatric disorders are more common among women than men; this can be seen in surveys based on random samples and in treated morbidity. Since women consult doctors more than men,[4] and since doctors are more likely to detect psychiatric illnesses in women (see Chapter 4), one might expect an even more marked female preponderance among cases treated by psychiatrists. In fact, the preponderance is no greater at level 4 than among random community samples, probably because women are less likely to be referred than men.[5]

Rates are higher for persons who are separated and divorced, and several recent surveys have shown higher rates for the unemployed, and higher rates for the blacks than whites.[6] Some of the effects previously attributed to urban versus rural differences in previous surveys may be due to the greater availability of services in towns: Helgason (1978) has shown that his earlier demonstration (1964) that rates for neurosis were much lower in rural areas – based on cases of neurosis recognised by Icelandic doctors – no longer holds when prevalence is estimated by sending a psychiatric screening questionnaire to a random sample of all Icelanders.

SOCIAL FACTORS ASSOCIATED WITH DISORDER IN THE COMMUNITY

The measurement of social variables in community surveys has as many inherent difficulties as arriving at a satisfactory definition of a psychiatric 'case'. The first problem is the selection of social variables, since they are numerous and are of many substantially different types, e.g. marital interaction and quality of housing. Second is the difficulty of establishing the validity of judgements about family relationships, or about the quality of life of a subject; and third is the problem of the development of instruments which permit reliable judgements to be made. Finally, for those concerned to examine the associations between social and clinical pathology, the task is made all the more difficult by the lack of agreement upon the classification of social problems. The development of a reliable problem classification would go a long way to help both practitioners and research workers.[7]

In order to illustrate some of the problems of measurement, one need look no further than to social class, perhaps the most widely studied social variable. Social class has been rated using quite different source data.

Hollingshead and Redlich (1953) originally conceived the Index of Social Position as a three-variable composite. The variables were ecological area of residence, occupation, and education. The Registrar General's Classification of Occupations is widely used in the UK in order to determine an individual's social class and socioeconomic group from occupational type. It has fundamental problems in that no results from attempts to validate it have ever been published, and it provides no easy way of classifying the relative positions of certain important groups in the community, such as students, housewives, and the retired. Attempts have been made to remedy the position by basing scales on the relative social standing of certain occupations. The relative position is determined by samples of opinion carefully selected from the community (Goldthorpe and Hope 1974).[8]

The confused picture of the relationship between psychiatric disorder and social variables which emerges from the literature is due to the fact that studies have used different status measures as well as different conceptions of what constitutes a psychiatric case. In some cases the definition of psychiatric disorder has included an assessment of social dysfunction, making it impossible to discuss the resulting associations betweeen social factors and disorder without entering into a circular argument.

An additional factor which contributes to the confusion is the failure to distinguish clearly between the results of studies conducted in very different settings. Findings based upon the study of patients treated in hospital must take account of the selection procedure involved in hospitalization, and the way in which different social circumstances act to encourage hospitalization in some patients, and to prevent it in other patients. Studies of samples from the community are free from this particular disadvantage and may be of more value to the investigator who wishes to make statements about social factors as causal agents in the genesis of psychiatric disorders.

The voluminous Stirling County studies (Leighton *et al.* 1959, 1963) examined the relationship between sociocultural factors and psychiatric disorder.

We have already hinted that there must be doubt about the validity of the estimates of psychiatric morbidity made on these surveys since it is by no means clear that an individual described as 'psychiatrically impaired' would meet clinical criteria for one of the recognised syndromes of psychiatric illness. It is therefore not possible to give much value to the estimates of lifetime prevalence made by the investigators, but some of the overall relationships reported are of interest since there is bound to be some correlation between the measures of 'caseness' used and the numbers of psychological symptoms experienced by their respondents. The study aimed to test several specific hypotheses, each of which examined the relationship betweeen sociocultural disintegration and psychiatric disorder and each specified an intervening variable which mediated the effect. The mediating variables were physical insecurity (mainly poverty); restricted sexual expression, restricted hostile and aggressive expression; limitations on the giving and receiving of love, restriction of the opportunity to achieve socially valued ends by legitimate means, restriction of spontaneity; interference with a person's orientation regarding his place in society, interference with a person's sense of membership in a definite human group, and interference with the individual's sense of membership in a moral order.

The basic proposition was that social disintegration is conducive to psychiatric disorder.

The findings showed that in disintegrated areas there were all types of disorder and that the highest total percentage of symptom patterns existed; in particular there was a high proportion of sociopathic symptoms and the highest percentages for psychoneurosis and mental deficiency. The differences between the integrated and non-integrated areas were greatest with regard to the categories 'psychiatric disorder with significant impairment' and 'probably well' (fewer than 10 per cent obtained the latter rating in the disintegrated areas).

The authors argue that the index of occupational advantage was less important in determining risk of psychiatric disorder than living in a disintegrated community, and that poverty is only associated with disorder by operating in conjunction with other aspects of sociocultural disintegration.

In contrast, they propose that aspects of family life are important discriminators between the integrated and disintegrated communities, and that the higher rates of disorder in the disintegrated communities are in part a product of the relative absence of complete nuclear families in the disintegrated area. They also find evidence to support the view that the sense of membership in a moral order is an important intervening variable. They comment that there is an absence of the sort of moral guidance and support provided in an integrated area which 'prevent the emergence of self-defeating sequences and the ultimate emergence of symptoms' (Vol. III: 389).

The largely inadequate specification of what constitutes 'family life' and 'moral guidance' makes it hard to draw very much from such conclusions. The finding that occupational advantage does not act independently of other social phenomena is not particularly surprising, and the conclusion that occupational advantage is of little consequence is hard to accept given the methodological inadequacies in its conception.[9] It is also difficult to draw meaningful conclusions about the possible relationships between current social standing and circumstances and the 'lifetime' measures of psychiatric impairment used in the enquiry.

Another major enquiry into psychiatric disorder and its social correlates in the community was the Midtown Manhattan Study (Srole *et al.* 1962). This enquiry studied both prevalence and incidence in an urban environment, and related a series of sociocultural factors to these rates in a sample of 1,660 non-institutionalized persons. Much of the criticism of this study related to its use of ratings of psychiatric impairment which do not sufficiently eliminate social factors from the judgements, making the findings with relation to social circumstances ambiguous. The authors were aware of such criticisms and a procedure was devised to take account of them. It was essentially similar to that undertaken in the Stirling County Study and consisted of an exercise to see how much change was produced in psychiatric classification by the introduction of social data. The results led the authors to conclude that no systematic biases were introduced which would skew the morbidity findings. In this study as in the Stirling County Study the authors then perversely chose the data with the social information rather than that without (p.165).

The symptom ratings which formed part of the interview were drawn from two previous instruments which although far less satisfactory than recent case-finding methods, at least resulted in a reasonable rank ordering of their respondents from asymptomatic to those incapacitated by many symptoms. The remainder of the Home Interview Survey (HIS) consisted of demographic, religious, and socioeconomic enquiries. The major findings were that socioeconomic status of origin and current age level are almost equally strong determinants, independent of each other, of adult mental health. The twenty to twenty-nine age group from high socioeconomic status of origin had the highest number of psychiatrically well;

and the fifty to fifty-nine age group with low socioeconomic status of origin, especially those from poverty-level childhoods, had the most impaired. The use of socioeconomic status of origin rules out the possibility that 'drift' to lower status influenced these findings.

A male respondent whose socioeconomic status was higher than his own father's was said to be 'upwardly mobile'. The mental health status of those who remained in the upper level, and of those who rose to that level was good; whereas the less healthy sons tended to be the ones who were downwardly mobile. The authors suggest that pre-adult personality differences may be responsible for the direction of status change in adulthood but also that upward status mobility is rewarding both materially and psychologically, whereas downward status mobility is depriving in both respects.

Among the important influences on mental health from the past were childhood health, parental quarrelling, and childhood economic deprivation. Influences in the present included work worries, the adequacy of affiliations, and socioeconomic worries.

The importance of the role of socioeconomic problems and the inadequacy of affiliations has been stressed in a major community survey conducted in England. Brown and Harris (1978) compared two groups of women between the ages of eighteen and sixty-four who lived in the Camberwell area of London: a group consisting of 114 patients treated by the psychiatric services, and two separate random samples of the general population chosen from Local Authority records totalling 458 women. Clinical assessments were made by a trained research worker using the Present State Examination and a subsample were reinterviewed by a psychiatrist to check the original assessments. Their approach developed from the hypothesis that clinical depression is an understandable response to adversity, and to explain differences in rates between random community samples and patients treated in hospital settings by reference to 'the everyday lives' of depressed individuals.

It is not unreasonable to suppose that in their everyday lives, working-class women are more often faced with social difficulties than their middle-class counterparts. Brown and Harris found however that class differences in the rates of severe life events and of major household difficulties were confined to women with children. Thirty-four per cent of both middle- and working-class women without children at home had at least one severe event as did 34 per cent of working-class women with children at home, whereas in middle-class women with children at home only 27 per cent had at least one severe event. The types of event largely responsible for this class difference were *household events* concerning finance, the home itself, and husband and child; other severe events did not differ by class.

Household difficulties were also more common among women with children at home, and class differences were consistent with those for events: 19 per cent of middle-class women and 34 per cent of working-class women had household difficulties (p <.01).

Brown and Harris point out that the rates of severe events and difficulties are different in patient and community samples. Severe life events occurred in 61 per cent of depressed hospital patients and 68 per cent of 'cases' identified in the community, but in only 20 per cent of the normal women, and major difficulties were three times as common in the patient and community cases as in normal women.

The impact of these severe events and difficulties upon the depressed women was mediated by intervening factors. The risk of depression was only increased in those women who were the subject of what the authors call 'vulnerability factors'. The four factors which mediated the effect of events were the lack of an intimate confiding relationship with a husband or boyfriend; loss of mother before eleven years of age; having three or more children under fourteen at home; and unemployment. The last three factors (when analysed together) had approximately the same effect on the risk of depression as the intimacy factor alone.

The identification of these mediating variables is also important in two other ways. First, the presence of an intimate relationship or the other three vulnerability factors appears to confer a degree of invulnerability to depression to women in the community. Second, the presence of the vulnerability factors, especially having three children under fourteen at home, actually makes women less likely to come into treatment by a psychiatrist, or to attend their GP for their psychological problems. Brown and Harris show that the rates of vulnerability factors in treated samples and in a small sample of GP attenders are significantly lower than the rates in the sample of cases in the community. The vulnerability factors are therefore also important factors in the first filter in our model in that they act to filter out some working-class women from level 1.

Recent Australian research has used random population samples to study the relationship between clinical and social variables. Andrews *et al.* (1977, 1978) showed no association between either physical or psychiatric morbidity and social isolation, but were able to confirm the well known relationship between physical and psychiatric morbidity.[10] Life event stress, adverse childhood experience, and poor social support were found to be related to both physical and psychiatric illness. Two further variables were related to one sort of illness but not to the other: low occupational status was related to physical illness, and a defective coping style to psychiatric illness. The investigators used the concept of 'attributable risk' (McMahon and Pugh 1970) to show that 20 per cent of the variance of physical illness, and 37 per cent of the variance of psychiatric illness can be attributed to the four social variables mentioned. There are two important limitations to this research. The main variables – physical and psychiatric health – were measured by screening questionnaires (the Belloc scale and the GHQ), and the results should therefore be looked upon as preliminary to a definitive study in which second-stage clinical assessments are made. The other point is that the social variables are not necessarily antecedent to the illness measures: it is possible that to some extent the social disruptions are consequences of the illnesses. Now it is theoretically possible that a future study with better measures of the illness variables and the social variables will succeed in accounting for a greater proportion of common variance: but until such studies are available, these results should be looked upon as maximum estimates of the importance of social variables in this particular population.

Interest has recently turned to the size and nature of the social network reported by patients with psychiatric illnesses. Also from Australia, Henderson *et al.* (1978) compared psychiatric patients with matched controls and described features of the 'primary group', defined as 'those with whom one has interaction and commitment'. The patients were found to have a smaller sized primary group, to have less contact with its members, and to have an inferior quality of affective interaction in transactions with the 'primary attachment figure'. In a further study, Henderson and his colleagues (1980) related psychopathology as measured in the Canberrra population by the GHQ – PSE – ID method to social relationships as measured by the 'Interview Schedule for Social Interaction'. Their findings fit well with Brown's and Harris's demonstrations that lack of intimacy is associated with depression, in that a set of variables which the investigators describe as 'attachment' are found to be negatively related to neurosis. The measure of 'attachment' covered the availability and adequacy of loving, intimate relationships; and the investigators also assess 'social integration' in terms of the availability and adequacy of other social ties. Social integration had the same sort of negative correlation with neurosis as attachment, and in each case the relationship is independent of the effects of adversity as measured by a measure of recent experiences. The associations between neurosis and social ties were all stronger for women than they were for men.

Dalgard (1979) has studied the interaction between supportive social network and urban ecology as correlates of psychiatric morbidity in a random sample of the population of Oslo. Five types of urban areas are described, and were arranged in rank order using ratings by neutral observers, assessments by inhabitants and objective data from the point of view of availability of services and the collective resources of each area. In the three most desirable areas there was no relationship between psychiatric morbidity and the quality of the social network of his respondents; but in the two poorest areas there was a strong association in the predicted direction, so that those with the least supportive social networks had significantly higher levels of morbidity.

NOTES

1. The best known studies are the Stirling County studies (Leighton *et al.* 1963). Other studies which use the same methodology include a study in Nigeria (Leighton 1963) and in South Africa by Gillis *et al.* (1968).
2. This point is discussed in more detail later in this chapter: see the section 'Severity of illness at different levels of the model'.
3. If one examines the factor structure of common psychopathological symptoms, based on samples drawn from the community, one finds that items reflecting anxiety, tension, and worry tend to co-vary with items reflecting depression, sadness, and crying spells. For example, Dohrenwend and his colleagues (1979) administered a lengthy structured interview schedule to community respondents based on questionnaires used in the Midtown and Stirling county studies, and administered by fifteen psychiatrists to 127 adults. The investigators were able to produce five scales which were internally consistent and were thought to reflect conceptually similar dimensions by the clinicians engaged on the project. These scales were named anxiety, sadness, enervation, psychophysiological symptoms, and perceived physical health. The investigators note that:
    'the correlations among these five scales are extremely high in the community sample. Sadness and anxiety, for example, are correlated .63 in the samples. Since both scales have alphas of about .7, one would expect their correlation to be about .7 if they were measuring the same thing. The fact of the matter is that all five scales are intercorrelated almost as strongly as their reliabilities permit.'
    In the validity studies of the General Health Questionnaire carried out in Philadelphia, it was observed that the rating for anxiety made at clinical interview correlated +.7 with the rating for depression made at clinical interview; furthermore, the factor structure of the GHQ-30 showed that anxiety and depression came out on the same dimension (Goldberg 1972; Goldberg, Rickels, Downing, and Hesbacher 1976). A more recent study of the factor structure of the GHQ-60 by Goldberg and Hillier (1979) shows that while it is possible to produce separate factors of anxiety and insomnia on the one hand and suicidal depression on the other, the two affects are in fact correlated in that the item

'Have you recently felt unhappy and depressed?' loads equally on the two scales. Different investigators have responded in different ways to this problem. Those who use hierarchical taxonomical models adopt different views depending on the structure of the lower layers of their particular hierarchies. Foulds (1976) did not find it necessary to distinguish between depression and anxiety, since they are both reflections of 'personal distress' that being the lowest level of his hierarchy of classes of personal illnesses. Wing and his colleagues (1974) on the other hand, devote a special page of the Present State Examination, when anxiety and depression are both present, to getting the rater to decide which of them is primary. Subjects whose symptoms are confined to those of subjective anxiety, situational anxiety, or specific anxiety are diagnosed as anxiety states; but if depressed mood is present the subjects are recruited to a higher class, Class N – neurotic depression. If, in addition to the depressed mood, one or more of retardation, guilt, depreciation, or agitation is present, the respondent is recruited to an even higher class, Class R – retarded depression. Finally, if depressive hallucinations or delusions are present in addition to depressed mood, the subject is recruited to another class – D + depressive psychosis. It is common for those using the Clinical Interview Schedule in community settings to find themselves in great difficulty in trying to decide whether depression or anxiety is primary, and therefore to diagnose 'mixed affective disorder' in cases where both abnormal moods are present, and it is not easy to say which one predominates over the other.

4. This has been shown in all British surveys – for example, Shepherd *et al.* (1966), Weissman and Klerman (1977) have reviewed sex differences and the epidemiology of depression, and conclude that 'women cope with problems by visiting doctors, and, by every measure of utilisation of the general health care system, women preponderate. They have increased rates of use of out-patient facilities, of visiting physicians, of prescriptions, of psychotropic drug use.'

5. This is discussed further in Chapter 7: relevant references are Ingham, Rawnsley, and Hughes (1972); Weissman and Klerman (1977); and Helgason (1978).

6. See Weissman and Myers (1978) for data relating to marital status, unemployment status, and race; Goldberg, Kay and Thompson (1974) for data relating to marital status. Henderson and his colleagues (1980) report the effects of sex, age, educational level, marital status, employment status and country of birth on psychopathology measured in a random sample of the Canberra, Australia population, using the GHQ linked to the PSE. (They confirm the findings of others concerning marital status, although there is no significant interaction with sex. This study is odd in showing no significant effect of employment status: this may be because housewives were included together with the unemployed. Furthermore, the investigators note that none of the housing in the area surveyed is substandard and the 'visitor is usually struck by the affluence of the community, the high standard of recreational facilities, and the geographical dispersal of their housing'.) The study of Tischler and his colleagues (1975), to be described in more detail in Chapter 3, also confirms these findings.

7. Sociologists have always seen the measurement of social problems, events, and relationships as problematic. Two views about the nature of the

problem have developed and in simple terms are: first the view that measurement (the assignment of numbers to represent properties) is possible, but that questions of validity and reliability must be resolved before any measuring instrument can be accepted in use (Campbell 1952); the second is that the measurement of social processes cannot be undertaken without first specifying the rules governing the use of language, by both the research worker and the subject of enquiry, on the grounds that if the rules governing the use of language to describe the objects in everyday life and in sociological discourse are unclear then it becomes impossible to assign numbers to properties of these objects and events (Cicourel 1964). For simplicity we refer to the first view as the scientific view and the second as the phenomenological.

To some extent the scientific view, which is our concern here, does rest upon the assumption that the researcher and the subject share a common view of certain social events and experiences. A good example of this assumption is inherent in Brown's and Harris' (1978) method of scaling the severity of life events and difficulties, in which the research team were read out an account of the event and of the surrounding social circumstances of the subject without any details of the subject's reaction to the event. The rating was made independently by members of the team using their judgement of how much an event would involve for *most people* (our italics) in biographical circumstances like those of the respondent. Brown makes the point that the investigator cannot be in the subject's position in the same practical sense, but 'like the ambassador' must understand events by taking account of as much of the surrounding circumstances as possible. Brown and Harris report that there was a good measure of agreement between the 'contextual' or 'ambassadorial' measure and the self-report of threat amongst a general population sample (95 per cent) and a little less in a sample of depressed patients (84 per cent). From the scientific point of view outlined above the high level of agreement suggests that the scales may be useful research tools. Brown and Harris report that the 'rules' which they had developed (anchoring examples, discussions about discrepancies, and the standard ratings for events such as death) did not allow sufficient flexibility to take account of the meaning of some events to particular individuals, e.g. for a patient whose fourteen-year-old dog had died. The 'rules' in this case were specified by the workers on the basis of their assumptions about the everyday world of the subject and were not derived in the way which is specified by the phenomenological view described above. An important point however is that the inability of the 'rules' to encompass events was only slight (in three instances only) and that for the most part the specifications in the rules must have shared a good deal with the subjects' common sense view of the threat of events. The self-report scales (or common sense views) of threat were, however, mediated by the research worker and so it is still the worker's *conception* of threat which is used, although the worker's *rating* of threat is based upon what the subject says about the events during the interview. In these circumstances the proponents of the phenomenological view would argue that it was not surprising that the 'self report' and contextual scales agreed so consistently.

Brown made one of the most important contributions to the debate about the reliability and validity of measuring scales when, in seminal articles with Rutter (Brown and Rutter 1966; Rutter and Brown 1966) he showed that it is possible to reach satisfactory levels of reliability and validity for interview measures of many aspects of family life and relationships. He rightly criticized the use of fixed-response questionnaires to measure aspects of family life, because of the fact that respondents will refer to different and unspecified reference groups when answering the questions, that questionnaires which use agreement/disagreement statements are seriously biased by the educational background and social attitudes of the respondent, and that retrospective questionnaires are unlikely to be accurate.

The findings of Brown and Rutter's enquiry showed that *interviewers* could be trained to agree in their judgements about the feelings expressed by an informant towards his spouse or children, that a joint interview of spouses was extremely effective in picking out those who were most critical when seen alone, and that husbands and wives accounts of family activities do not agree to a great extent when they are interviewed separately.

On the basis of this experiment the authors recommend that questions about family life should concentrate on a specified period of time in the recent past rather than asking about the 'usual' pattern of behaviour; questioning should be about frequencies rather than relying upon answers of 'often' or 'sometimes' and that scores should be based on frequencies rather than on general ratings.

With regard to the measurement of emotions and attitudes Brown suggests that obtaining a high level of inter-rater reliability is the main methodological issue and emphasises that the training of raters is vital. In the subsequent years he and his colleagues have developed a system for training interviewers in the recognition of expressed emotion, based to some extent upon the master tape-recordings which illustrated the phenomena to be rated, discussions, and the use of unipolar rating scales with detailed rules for rating each scale.

This approach, the measurement of facts and feelings separately, is also embodied in the work on the Social Interview Schedule (SIS) (Kedward and Sylph 1974; Clare and Cairns 1978) as is the view that it is necessary to train interviewers in the application of social assessment interviews. In addition the interviewer using the SIS conducts the interview in the presence of an informant, in order to reduce the possibility of interviewee bias. The three major sets of measurements on the SIS concern the subject's material circumstances, his social functioning, and his satisfaction. All three types of measure (on four-point scales) are made in the major areas of social life, housing, occupation, family relationships, etc. Of the three sets of measurements, material circumstances are the easiest to rate reliably because many of the items can be rated against externally validated criteria, such as income level or occupational status. Social functioning, or management presents more difficulty, although an effort was made in the construction of the instrument not to write middle-class definitions of adequate functioning into the rating definitions. Satisfaction measurements rely heavily on the expressions of the subject which may be influenced by illness or by personality and in practice it is difficult to distinguish between the dissatisfied and mildly dissatisfied ratings. Reliability studies on the use of the instrument have demonstrated high levels of overall agreement between interviewers with agreement generally higher on the material circumstances items. The instrument has been used in a study which demonstrated the usefulness of attaching a social worker to a metropolitan practice (Cooper *et al.* 1975). Subjects in the service with a social worker were shown to have improved more than those in the service without a social worker in all three areas of the SIS, social functioning, satisfaction and material conditions. It has also been used in a study which demonstrated that social predictors of outcome in minor psychiatric disorders in particular the material circumstances measures of the SIS are equally good predictors of the course of minor psychiatric disorders as clinical predictors (Huxley *et al.* 1979).

The SIS and major American equivalents have been subjected to principal components analysis in order to reduce complexity due to the number of different items, and to facilitate scoring. Results of the analysis of the SSIAM (Gurland *et al.* 1972) revealed six factors including isolation, work inadequacy, and family friction, and the analysis of the SAIS (Weissman and Paykel 1974) which is derived from the SSIAM, produced five different factors and a similar one related to work. In the analysis of use of the SIS Clare and Cairns (1978) report that on each application of the SIS different factors emerge and none clearly corresponding to the material, management and satisfaction category of the SIS. The same negative result was obtained by ourselves in an analysis of data from the SIS in a pilot study of the prediction of the course of minor psychiatric disorder (Huxley 1973). Clare and Cairns (1978) make the important point that in any particular study many items do not apply to the respondent and are discarded from a principal components analysis, and therefore, rotated solutions are likely to reveal different factors. In addition it is reasonable to suppose that the inter-relationships between individual items on the SIS will vary depending upon the social circumstances of the population from which the sample is taken – a sample of premenstrual women for example, will differ considerably from a sample of chronic neurotic outpatients or a sample of clientele from a social services department.

In this respect it is not surprising that social workers have not used the SIS in 'clinical' work as advocated by Clare and Cairns. Although the instrument contains a comprehensive set of ratings many of these are insufficiently specific for social work purposes – for example the management of children category. The SIS could be used as a screening instrument to identify areas of dysfunction, but because of its emphasis on *dys*function would require the social worker to invert some of the responses to identify positive features of the client's environment.

It has already been argued that the *range* of social problems elicited by the SIS is insufficient for the needs of social work assessment, but it has also been shown that social services departments in the UK do not classify cases on the basis of 'social problems' alone; and that they may also classify cases on the basis of client category, resources provided or legislative grouping, or more frequently, a mixture of all four bases of classification (Fitzgerald 1978). The classification of client problems may be undertaken by different parties within the departments and this fact alone may be responsible for the apparent disappearance of the mentally ill from the area office returns in some departments. The mentally ill client may still present to the department but may not have his or her problem recognized as one of mental illness by the social worker or the receptionist, but rather as one of financial difficulty or as a problem of child care. In a study of the results of one case review system (Goldberg *et al.* 1977) clients whose problems were recorded as financial difficulty or housing problems commonly had emotional or psychiatric problems, and of those recorded as child or family problems a number were referred to psychiatric units or clinics for help. In the same study it was reported that many of the problems classified as mental or emotional disorder were recorded as closed because the problem was not amenable to social work help.

The case review system devised for this study (Goldberg 1976) represents one of the few systematic attempts to record consistently the nature of the problems dealt with by the SS department; even so the results of reliability and validity tests upon the instrument are not reported in detail; there are two references, one to the careful piloting of the form and the other to trial runs in which a high level (unspecified) of agreement between practitioners was reached in the allocation of the social work activities which they undertook with the client. The authors point out themselves that the sub-divisions of the casework category of help overlap, and that there is therefore scope for refinement and further development. In the absence of unambiguous data on the reliability of the problem classification, the changes in the frequency of, for example, the reporting of financial difficulties (which were higher in 1975 than in 1972) may simply be due to the inconsistent use of the scale rather than to any real differences.

There are at least two fundamental tasks which need to be undertaken before a combined 'clinical' and research instrument can be developed. One is that the problem classification needs to be tested against externally validated criteria where this is possible – and this will most easily be done in relation to poverty, occupational status, and norms relating to housing and other items derived from the General Household Survey (OPCS 1973).

The second task is the production of a genuine classification i.e. without overlap, of social and relationship difficulties, which can be used reliably by practitioners.

One way in which social assessment and problem classification might be taken forward is by the analysis of the client's social network (Henderson *et al.* 1978). Descriptions of the quality of network support can be used as baseline measures against which therapeutic manipulations of network support can be judged. Network analysis could also provide a basis upon which to classify the relationship problems of the client. A preliminary classification of the provisions of relationship has been made (Weiss 1974; Huxley 1980) and it may be possible to use this not only to compare the deficiencies of the networks of different client groups but also to indicate how to match the provisions made by the helper with that needed by the client.

8. There is a tendency, on both sides of the Atlantic, to regard the measurement of social class as nonproblematic and to review the findings of research studies without identifying the means used to measure social class, and to compare the results without acknowledging the fact that the studies have used different conceptions of class (Kohn 1968; Liem and Liem 1978; Grad 1976).

In both the UK and the US indicators of socio-economic status are usually based upon classification of occupation. Hollingshead and Redlich (1953) originally used the index of Social Position based on individual's weighted score on three dimensions: ecological area of residence, occupation, and education.

Subsequently, the two-factor index of socioeconomic status was used more frequently; that is, an index based upon occupation and education. The specific nature of the area unit used in the original index does not seem to have been clearly specified.

A good illustration of the use of different measures of social class comes from the Midtown Manhattan study (Srole *et al.* 1962) in which four different measures were used. In their treatment census socio-economic status was not based upon income, or occupation, or education, because the data required were often missing from the patients' notes. Instead, the ratings were based on individual residences – specifically on the ratings of the quality of housing and condition of upkeep made by four volunteer businessmen who were experts in local residential properties, during a housing survey which was part of the study. The ratings were divided into three categories.

In classifying socioeconomic status in the Home Survey, education, occupation, total family income, and rent formed the basis for classification. For parental socioeconomic status the probands were allocated to twenty-seven occupational rubrics which were divided into six grades: skilled, semiskilled, unskilled manual work; professionals and executives; semiprofessionals and intermediate managers; small shopkeepers, sales people, and office staff. The score values of 1 to 6 were allocated to these categories and then added to a six-point scale of father's schooling. These scores were computed for 1,660 individuals and they were then divided into six equally populated groups. The parental strata therefore indicate the relative socioeconomic standing of individuals within the sample, and not the standing of the probands in relation to their communities or origin.

This is an important distinction, because classifications of occupations are usually made on the basis of the social standing of the occupational category in the community. A major criticism of the widely used Registrar General's classification is that the categories do not appear to have been derived from samples of opinion from the community. Bland (1979) has said that: 'It seems possible that the scale represents no more than a series of guesses as to what members of the community would have said if they had been asked.'

Accordingly, there is no guarantee that two basic properties required of a social class scale, that each category should be reasonably homogenous, or that occupations in a higher category should enjoy higher social standing than those in lower categories, are present in the case of the Registrar General's scale. (RG). In contrast Goldthorpe and Hope (1974) did conduct an empirical investigation of the standing in the community of the occupations included in the RG's classification. They used 860 'representative occupational titles' which were ranked by a large national sample. Combinations of the occupational titles were allocated to 124 Hope-Goldthorpe categories which were based upon the authors and experts views of the 'general desirability' of occupations. Their results were consistent with the view that occupational prestige scales do reflect a popular judgement of the general desirability of occupations.

Bland (1979) has shown by cross-tabulating the Hope-Goldthorpe scores (HG) of occupations with their social class values, that the occupations in the RG's social class categories are in fact far from homogeneous in their HG scores. He gives the following illustrations: Social class 2 and 3N both overlap Class 1 at their top ends and Class 5 at their bottom ends. Class 2 contains own account hedgers, ditchers and turf-cutters as well as Cabinet Ministers and airline pilots. If the social class index did not overlap, i.e. it had distinct categories, almost a third of the male population would have to be reclassified. Bland says that the main justification for using the RG's classification is for comparative purposes, and recommends that it should never be used as the sole method for coding new data.

It has always been necessary for workers to devise ways of coping with the RG classification's known inadequacies, such as the difficulty of classifying women at home, the retired, students, etc. In their study of depressed women, for instance, Brown and Harris (1978) took account of education as an index of prosperity. Low status in this scheme (the Bedford measure) consisted of those who were in the semi and unskilled manual categories of the RG's scale, without education after 16+ of husband or wife or possession of a car *and* a telephone. Brown compared the results for the Bedford, RG, and Hope-Goldthorpe measures, and found agreement in 218 out of 274 cases when the Hope-Goldthorpe measure was also divided into two groups of categories (high status 1-22 and low status 23-25).

The proliferation of scales in the UK is in the opinion of some authors (Bland 1979) largely due to the fact that the solution available in the USA is not available here. In the USA Duncan's socioeconomic index (Duncan 1961) is based upon a national census which collects both income and educational data. The Hope-Goldthorpe scale holds out the prospect of a more reliable and valid measure than has been available in the past.

Others have taken the view that the broad measures of occupation or education are insufficiently precise, and have argued for social indices which are composites of several social indicators. It has been suggested (Osborn and Morris 1979) that such indices are likely to be more discriminating than the 'blunderbuss' of the RG's scale.

Osborn and Morris report upon the development of the Social Index Score which includes occupational status and level of education but also includes housing situation, parental level of education, and neighbourhood rating and a measure of overcrowding. They show that the top five Registrar General's classes were all spread over at least five of the Social Index scores; the RG's class 5 was spread over the lowest three points of the Social Index scores (50-52). In an analysis of the development of 978 three-and-a-half-year-old children in England and Wales they show that six out of twenty developmental indices are significantly related to the Social Index score whereas only two are significantly associated with RG's social class. The argument that the Index is more discriminating is hard to sustain, because it almost certainly contains more variance than the RG's classification. In addition, the scale has only been validated for disadvantaged groups, against ratings of housing, social problems, unemployment, and marital relationships made by health visitors. Although the Index does help to cope with inadequacies of the RG's scale with regard to persons with no employment, it does not have the advantages of the Hope-Golthorpe scale which has the best claims to reliability and validity of any measure currently in use.

9. The occupational classification was undertaken on the basis of dividing the three

main types found in the locality, owners, self employed and wage earners, into those whose material style of life was above or below average. An index of occupational advantage – disadvantage resulted:

Group 1   Owner salaried and professional

Group 2   Self-employed: agriculture/fishing
Wage earner: transportation, government service, and construction

Group 3   Self-employed: forestry
Wage-earner: fish processing and wood products

Group 4   Wage-earner agriculture, fishing, forestry

Group 5   Out of labour force five years or more preceding survey

The rates of disorder were highest for both sexes in Group 5, and the introduction this category opens up the possibility of the 'drift' of the severely psychiatrically impaired, who are unable to work, into this group, thus undermining the authors' conclusions that their findings support the argument for a casual relationship between disadvantageous social position and psychiatric impairment.

10. This relationship was conclusively demonstrated in the General Morbidity survey carried out by Shepherd and his colleagues (1966) and has been reviewed at length by Eastwood (1976). We shall return to the problem in later chapters.

CHAPTER 3

The first filter: the decision to consult

It will be recalled that the 'first filter' refers to those factors which determine whether a particular individual with distressing psychological symptoms decides to consult a primary care physician. Although we will be emphasizing variables which relate to the patient in our discussion, it must be recalled that there are also variables which relate to the doctor and to the medical service which he offers. It is likely that those who have to make long and arduous journeys to see their doctor will not see him for trivial symptoms, and it also seems that more patients will use a free service than one in which there is a fee for service. For example, the 1974 Health Interview Survey showed that 57 per cent of the civilian non-institutionalized US population was seen in a physician's office in the course of one year, while the 1972 National Morbidity Survey (RCGP 1979) showed that 62 per cent of men and 70 per cent of women consult their family doctor in the course of one year in the British National Health Service.

The most striking thing about recent survey data is that most patients with marked psychiatric disorders, and the majority of those with mild disorders, do consult their doctors. This is not to deny the existence of an interesting minority who do not, but merely to record the existence of a wood before drawing attention to particular trees.

The most comprehensive data which bear on this point are those derived from Hagnell's (1966) survey of two adjoining parishes near Lund, Sweden. The author of this survey is an experienced psychiatrist who personally examined 3,286 inhabitants who comprised 98.9 per cent of the population of the two parishes. He gathered information from other sources about others, so that he was able to account for 99.3 per cent of the population at risk. The aim of his interview was to gather information about mental illnesses experienced by them in the previous ten years. For our present purposes, we will compare 'Dr Hagnell's diagnosis' – irrespective of whether the individual had consulted a doctor – with 'Dr Hagnell's diagnosis and consulted a doctor'.

Table 3(1): *Estimated cumulated risk for all psychiatric illness assuming survival to age 60*

	men		women	
	Dr Hagnell's diagnosis	*Dr Hagnell's diagnosis and consulted doctor*	*Dr Hagnell's diagnosis*	*Dr Hagnell's diagnosis and consulted doctor*
disorders causing severe impairment only	7.9%	6.7%	16.4%	15.4%
all degrees of impairment	43.0%	36.9%	73.0%	71.6%

Derived from Hagnell 1966: 80-82.

It can be seen from *Table 3(1)* that if a Swedish man survives to the age of sixty, the cumulated risk for him developing a psychiatric illness is 43 per cent, and the risk for an illness with a medical consultation is 36.9 per cent. For women, the cumulated risk is very much higher, and almost all will have consulted a doctor. With assessments of risk as high as this, it is hardly likely that Hagnell has overestimated the proportion seeking medical help by ignoring trivial illnesses for which help was not sought!

Lest these results are dismissed as some sort of Swedish artefact, recent surveys in England and the United States tell much the same story. Of the seventy-six cases of depression reported in Brown and Harris's Camberwell Survey (see Chapter 2) at least 68 per cent had consulted their doctor (the real figure may be substantially higher, since it was not certain whether thirteen had consulted or not – so these have been counted as non-consultations). It is true that only nineteen of the thirty-seven onset cases had received help for their depression – but that concerns the second filter, not the first. Wing's Camberwell Study showed that of twenty-six women with diagnosed depression in the community, only three had not seen their doctors while in a fourth it was not known whether or not she had seen a doctor in the previous year.

Weissman and Myers (1978) showed that although only 18 per cent of their community patients with an RDC diagnosed depression had seen a mental health professional, that 90 per cent had seen a primary care physician for their symptoms. The more severe the depression, the more likely it was that help had been sought.

ILLNESS RECOGNITION

It is well known that both psychological and physical symptoms are widely distributed in community samples, and that there are individuals in the community with symptoms as incapacitating as those receiving medical care.[1] Before considering the factors determining whether medical help will be sought, it is logical to ask what makes an individual consider that his symptoms are worthy of professional attention.

Transient episodes of malaise and dysphoria are widely distributed in the population.[2] It is worth remembering some of the reasons for this: subclinical viral infections, combinations of dietary excess and insufficient exercise, and the dysphoria which naturally follows stressful life events. As Suchman (1965) has pointed out, it is usual for individuals experiencing pains or discomforts first of all to ask themselves why they are having such an experience: this is an interpretation of meaning. Headache and nausea the morning after a drunken party will be interpreted as a hangover, while the same symptoms coming out of the blue may be emotionally disturbing since their meaning is both not apparent and non-lifethreatening. At this stage illness may be denied, and treatment delayed; the individual may not wish to burden others, or he may be unwilling to resolve the disturbing implications of his new symptoms.

The next stage has been called 'provisional validation' of the individual's state of sickness. It is usual for those experiencing disturbing symptoms to describe them to 'significant others' – usually key family members or friends – before making the decision to consult a doctor. This discussion may be for information and advice, and the advice will often include the other person's agreement to the sick individual suspending his normal obligations. The sort of advice given by the other person will often be critical in deciding whether or not the sick role is adopted, and it is at this stage that many of the cultural influences described by Mechanic as 'illness behaviours' may have a decisive effect. Kadushin (1969) has pointed out that the decision to seek psychotherapy is most often made at this stage, during discussions between the dysphoric individual and those in his social network who are favourably disposed towards psychotherapy.

If the sick individual obtains provisional validation of his state of sickness, the next step is to attempt to obtain professional legitimation of the sick-role by consulting a doctor. At this stage, it is often impossible for the doctor to make a diagnosis: in Britain, for example, the Royal College of General Practitioners' Research Committee (1958) estimated that firm diagnosis could only be made in just over half the patients seen. However, it is rather unusual for doctors to refuse to concede that the patient is ill even when no diagnosis can be made: they commonly bestow a temporary status of illness on such patients and predict a return to normal functioning.

With certain well known exceptions – like prison doctors and army doctors – most doctors will agree with their 'sick' patient that he is unable to function, and will provide certification to excuse him from work. The provisions of such certificates reinforces the patient's illness behaviour, and confirms his inner conviction that all is not well. The doctor will typically assume that there is an internal derangement and prescribe something for it rather than, for example, telling the patient that he should modify his environment, or behave differently, if he wishes to be well. The doctor's assumption that there is some internal derangement may also be expected to reinforce illness behaviour and to lead to an increased awareness of bodily sensations and an anxious introspection. To the extent that a sick individual becomes preoccupied with himself there will be fewer opportunities to interact with the environment and therefore fewer reinforcers: this may in time lead to a lowering of self-esteem, and the experience of depressed mood.

It is easy to see why lonely people should consult doctors more readily than others, since they are less likely to have others with whom to discuss their symptoms: their visit to the doctor can be seen both as an attempt to obtain reassurance about the possible meaning of symptoms, and as a form of human contact in response to their loneliness. However, whereas a layman may well not advise a symptomatic individual to see a doctor so that he may never enter the 'sick role', once the doctor has been consulted, the transition to the sick role – at least temporarily – is ensured.

Mechanic (1977) has examined the relative importance of several determinants of perceived health status. He assessed both perceived and 'objective' physical health, psychological distress, and socio-demographic variables. Psychological distress was the only variable other than the measure of physical health status that emerged from the statistical analysis as an important determinant of the individual's view of his own 'health'. In a later paper (1979) he argues that neurosis, which he calls a 'distress syndrome' is in part a learned pattern of illness behaviour involving an intense focus on internal feeling states, careful monitoring of body sensations, and a high level of self-awareness.

SYMPTOM SEVERITY AS A DETERMINANT OF SEEKING HELP

Ingham and Miller (1976a) compared 172 patients attending their doctors with the same number of matched controls who had not seen their doctors for three months: each respondent was asked to provide ratings of nine common symptoms on two kinds of severity scale. The investigators found the level of severity for a particular symptom which could be endorsed by at least 70 per cent of those consulting for that symptom, and then looked to see what proportion of non-consulters experienced the symptom at least as severely as that. For example, if one found the lowest point on the backache scale that would nonetheless account for 70 per cent of those consulting for backache, then 32 per cent of the non-consulters have backache at least as bad as that. It is of interest that the proportion of non-consulters who were as depressed as at least 70 per cent of those consulting for depression is only 9 per cent. Another way of looking at this phenomenon was to find what percentage of each group could be exactly matched for symptom severity by a member of the other group; when this was done the overlap for headache was 62 per cent, for backache was 58 per cent, but for depression was only 28 per cent.

These findings indicate that variables other than severity of an individual symptom determine whether medical help will be sought.

The investigators did not consider the hypothesis that consulters with a given symptom might differ from non-consulters with the same symptom by possessing *other* psychological symptoms, although this is a distinct possibility. The fact that psychiatric screening questionnaires work even as well as they do indicates that one must take account of the *number* of psychological symptoms experienced by respondents in order to get a reasonably valid measure of psychological distress. If we take the GHQ-60 as our example, the threshold for 'caseness' falls between eleven and twelve symptoms. This means that *any* twelve symptoms out of the sixty offered will indicate probable caseness, so that significant psychological distress seems to depend on the possession of a critical number of key symptoms, rather than the possession of any particular symptom.

PSYCHOLOGICAL DISTRESS AS A DETERMINANT OF SEEKING HELP

Tessler and his colleagues (1976) measured the relative contributions of social and clinical variables as determinants of the number of consultations made by patients to their doctors over the period of twelve months. The social variables included demographic characteristics, propensity to seek care, and perceived control over illness, while the clinical variables included the number of chronic problems, perceived health status, and a measure of distress. These were all measured at initial consultation, and the researchers then used multiple regression techniques in an attempt to account for consultations over the following year. Distress, and the measure of chronic illness, both made significant contributions. The only other variable which had a significant correlation was sex, in that women made more visits than men. The investigators conclude that:

> 'the relationship between experienced distress and medical utilisation probably occurs in close proximity in time, and the use of services is a coping device to help to come to terms with the stress of the person's situation or the discomfort he or she is feeling.' (Tessler, Mechanic, and Dimond 1976:363)

Fink, Shapiro, Goldensohn, and Daily (1966) studied what they called the 'filter-down' process to psychotherapy in a pre-paid group practice, using a model essentially similar to that proposed in the present book. By comparing a random sample of the population at risk with a sample of consecutive attenders, they were able to show that respondents saying they were 'bothered a great deal by emotional problems' were 1.44 times more likely than average to attend their doctor, and thereafter passed through each succeeding filter with great ease.

Hood and Farmer (1974) compared frequent attenders with infrequent attenders at a general practice in Birmingham, England. Although there was no difference detected by Eysenck's Personality Inventory between the two samples, the frequent attenders were distinguished by their high scores on the General Health Questionnaire, and by having negative attitudes to the 'self' and more positive attitudes to 'help' on the semantic differential.

Goldberg, Kay, and Thompson (1976) showed that consulters were more psychologically disturbed than a random sample of the same population at risk, and that this finding held even if the analysis was confined to those consulting their doctor for physical presenting symptoms.

SOCIAL FACTORS AS DETERMINANTS OF SEEKING HELP

There is much convergent evidence that women not only report more symptoms than men, but that they are more likely to seek help for minor disorders. In their review of sex differences in the epidemiology of mental disorders, Weissman and Klerman (1977) observe that:

> 'Women come for help for minor complaints, but mortalities show that men die sooner. For depression, women seek treatment more often but men have a higher suicide rate. In our society the public assumption of the sick role is interpreted by men as a sign of weakness. Moreover, the health care system is organised in ways which make it difficult for most men to come for treatment.'

However, in order to show that the first filter is more permeable to women it would be necessary to show that the female/male ratio at level 2 is higher than that at level 1, and the available evidence suggests that this is not so.[3]

A paper by. Horwitz (1977) gives a possible clue to explaining the difference. Women are more likely than men to recognize perceived psychiatric problems, to discuss these problems with other people, and to enter treatment voluntarily. The eighty women in his sample of patients at the Connecticut Mental Health Center had an average of 9.1 people in their social network, compared with 7.0 people for his sample of forty men. If size of network is controlled, women are twice as likely to speak to network members about their problems. Women had spoken to an average of 4.5

people in their social network outside the nuclear family, while men had only spoken to an average of 1.0 person. Eighty-five per cent of network members approached for help are the same sex as the patient. Thus women are more likely to discuss their problems with others, and especially with female friends. Fifty-two per cent of the female patients were labelled as 'psychiatric' by themselves or their friends, in contrast to only 26 per cent of the male patients. The men, on the other hand, are more likely to be labelled as 'psychiatric' by their employers or their spouses (47 per cent of the men, in contrast to 14 per cent of the women). Horwitz observes:

> 'In this way, the collective knowledge of women's networks may be used to resolve (psychological) problems. Men, on the other hand, isolate themselves from receiving information about the existence of professionals and their condition is more likely to deteriorate to the point that their behaviour becomes bizarre enough for others to initiate treatment.' (Horwitz 1977: 173)

Horwitz (1978) divided the marital relationships of 120 patients at Connecticut CMHC into four types: uninvolved, separated, mutually supportive, and conflict. The conflict group sought help with the problem with their spouse, rather than for specific psychiatric symptoms, and the conflict had affected their kin and friends as well as the nuclear family. Kin and friends were active in attempting to resolve the psychiatric symptoms of the separated and the symptoms were commonly seen as the natural result of the separation. The mutually supportive group tended to work on their own problems and not to seek so much help from others. The uninvolved group also seek help less frequently, but this is in part because more male patients, who are less prone to seek help, make up the uninvolved category.

Friends are more likely than kin to suggest that a person visits a professional for assistance and they usually suggest that psychiatric help would be an appropriate resolution for the problem. Horwitz proposes on the one hand that this may be because friends do not want to be bothered with the person's problem, or may be more likely to know about available professional services and on the other hand kin may not seek professional help because they are anxious about the stigma of psychiatric treatment.

It is probable that loneliness makes psychologically distressed people more likely to consult. Goldberg, Kay, and Thompson (1976) found that non-consulters with psychological distress were much more likely to be married and living together with their spouses than were consulters with psychological distress.

In Fink *et al.*'s (1969) study of the 'filter-down' process, both single men and single women were more likely than average to consult their doctors, but there was a strong sex difference for the widowed, divorced, and separated: women were much more likely but men much less likely to attend their doctor. For either sex, married people consulted their doctor at about the average rate. Tischler's research, which will be described in the next section, also supports the view that consultation rates are higher among the lonely.

Ingham and Miller (1976b) carried out a further investigation with a subsample of their group of GP consulters and non-consulters which was described in the section concerned with symptom severity. In seeking variables other than symptom measures in order to explain consultation behaviours, they examined the number of life events in the last three months, the presence or absence of a confiding relationship, and a measure of the extent to which the patients were willing to disclose symptoms. Only the life events measure gave any significant results. The consulters had significantly more threatening events in the three months prior to consultation and there was a significant correlation between the number of psychological symptoms and life events among consulters but not the non-consulters, and in most instances the consulters declared these psychological symptoms to their doctor and did not need to use other physical symptoms as a 'ticket of admission' or 'signal behaviour' (Stewart et al. 1975). There is evidence from two surveys[4] that the presence of small children at home makes it less likely that a psychologically distressed mother will consult her doctor, and Brown and Harris (1978) have stated that women who have lost their mothers before the age of eleven are less likely to consult a doctor when depressed. Other findings are more contentious. Brown and Harris have also stated that working-class women are less likely to consult when depressed than middle-class women: however this finding is not confirmed by Weissman and Myers (1978) and is contradicted by Hurry and her colleagues (1980).

THE AMERICAN BYPASS

The first filter can lead directly to psychiatric care in the United States and Canada, and it is therefore possible to bypass the second and the third filters. In Chapter 1 we gave reasons for supposing that a substantial proportion of patients pass through all the filters even in North America; in this section we review studies which deal with determinants of psychiatric consultation behaviours by community samples.

Mechanic has observed that sociocultural characteristics, attitudes, knowledge, and reference group factors all have independent effects in a student population (Greenley and Mechanic 1976). Those who sought help from psychiatrists were higher status, with few strong religious attachments and a sympathetic orientation to the student counter-culture.

In order to ascertain whether other predictors of utilization are important because they are distress-related or because they have an independent effect, the level of distress must be controlled for.

The most comprehensive and ingenious study of the first filter in the United States was that carried out by Tischler and his colleagues (1975) at the Connecticut Mental Health Center (CMHC) at New Haven. A one-year sample of the CMHC patients (n = 808) was compared with a random sample of 1,095 respondents from the catchment area, using the Gurin Scale to measure psychological impairment, and recording various demographic and social features.

For some groups of respondents their apparent over-utilization of services was actually a reflection of the proportion of that group to be found in the psychologically impaired section of the community population. An example may make this clearer. Thirty-four per cent of those using psychiatric services are non-white, which is substantially more than the proportion of non-whites in the catchment area. However, if the random sample is divided into the psychologically impaired and the unimpaired, then non-whites represent 34 per cent of the former and only 19 per cent of the latter population. The utilization of services for the non-whites is therefore a reflection of the proportion of non-whites in the psychologically impaired population. A similar pattern of use of services in direct relation to the distribution of that characteristic in the impaired population was found for the separated and divorced, the twenty to forty-nine age group, those who did not go to high school, those on Welfare between the ages of thirty and forty-nine, and those in Social Class V.

There were, however, some groups that 'over-used' services compared with what would have been predicted from the distribution in the impaired population. As indicated earlier in the chapter, all these groups tended to be isolated and to lack social support: they comprised the unmarried, the unemployed, those who lived alone, and those with no religion.

Finally, three groups under-utilized services compared with the expected rates: these were middle-aged women, those over the age of thirty, and those earning less than $100 per week. (The finding concerning age fits with Goldberg *et al.*'s finding that those non-consulting for psychological distress were older than those consulting; and also fits with Fink *et al.*'s finding that the young pass relatively easily through the filters, and the old with greater difficulty.)

If citizens are to refer themselves directly to psychiatric services, it is obviously essential that they should know about them. Although the high utilization rate in Jews described by Mechanic may be largely understood in terms of 'learned illness behaviour', it may also be due to the fact that Jewish communities in the USA typically contain psychiatrists, so that potential users of psychiatric services are likely to know to whom they can refer themselves.

As Glasser, Duggan, and Hoffman's (1975) study shows however, some sections of the community lack the necessary information to know what to do if need arises. A random sample of 447 members of the United Auto Workers were approached and asked if they could name a single psychiatrist: 90 per cent could not, and 65 per cent could not name a single mental health treatment facility. The investigators then approached eighty-one referral agencies to whom the workers might have referred themselves – including general practitioners, social workers, clergy, court officials, and police: over a third of these could not name a single psychiatrist to whom they might refer a patient. Although treatment from a psychiatrist, psychological testing, and treatment at a mental health clinic are all available free to UAW members, only one fifth of the workers and less than one third of the referral agencies were aware of these benefits.

It would appear that one explanation for a 'failure to display illness behaviour' is quite simple: ignorance.

NOTES

1. Research in both the USA (Commission on Chronic Illness 1957) and in the UK (Epson 1969) confirm that for every individual undergoing treatment for any given physical condition there is at least one person and in some cases several people in the community with equally serious symptoms. Perceived seriousness of the condition is nevertheless an important determinant of help seeking for physical conditions (Hulka 1972).

Hannay (1979), conducted a survey of 1,344 general practice patients in Glasgow, and found that the number of present illnesses and their perceived seriousness were important influences upon medical help seeking, while the number of previous illnesses and lack of basic amenities (e.g. poor housing conditions) were important determinants of help seeking from social agencies. Failure to consult a doctor over a long period of time may of course be an indication of health. Kessel and Shepherd (1965) investigated the health and social characteristics of 3 per cent of patients continuously registered in one general practice who had not consulted their physician in ten years. They found, broadly speaking, that these individuals appeared to be healthy. The non-consulters did not obtain medical help elsewhere, nor did they use self medication more than recent attenders, and they managed recent trivial ailments without going to the doctor. They rated lower on emotional disturbance than recent attenders and had a more positive and favourable view of their past, present, and future health.

2. Numerous community surveys, such as the Stirling County or Midtown Manhattan studies in the United States, attest to the ubiquity of minor psychophysiological symptoms in random samples of the general population. In Britain, the immediate postwar period saw the Surveys of Sickness of people living in selected areas of Great Britain. Questions were asked about minor complaints, as well as about recent medical treatment received. Psychiatric morbidity emerged as one of the more important causes of disability. The survey showed that only 23 per cent of symptoms reported in one month were taken to a doctor. A fairly similar picture emerged from a survey of a new housing estate carried out some years later. Wadsworth *et al.* (1971) in an epidemiological survey in a London Borough have shown that in a two-week period the majority of people experience at least one painful and distressing symptom. The majority of people take non-medical action but less than one third of those who do, consult a doctor.

3. Most of the community surveys reviewed in the previous chapter suggest that the female rates are approximately double the male rates, and this is confirmed by Weissman and Klerman themselves for depression (1977). However, at level 2, the female:male ratio was 1.28:1 for South Manchester, and 1.21:1 for Greater Manchester (Goldberg 1978); and Chancellor, Mant, and Andrews (1977) report a female:male ratio of only 1.2:1 for high GHQ scores among primary care attenders in Australia. This suggests that the increased consultation rates for females reported by many investigators are simply reflecting the very much higher true prevalence rate in community samples: a symptomatic woman is *less*, not more likely to attend than a symptomatic man.

4. The two surveys showing that women with children at home are less likely to consult are Goldberg, Kay, and Thompson (1976) and Brown and Harris (1978).

CHAPTER 4

Level 2 and the second filter: Psychiatric disorders among primary care attenders

It will be recalled that 'level 2' refers to psychiatric disorders among primary care attenders whether or not such disorders are detected by the doctor. It has been shown in earlier chapters that the majority of those in the community with psychiatric disorders will consult their doctors: we will now study the factors that determine whether or not the psychiatric disorder is detected.

THE PATIENT'S COMPLAINT

In both the United Kingdom and the United States, most patients who are considered psychiatrically disordered by their family doctors have not presented to him with psychological complaints. *Table 4(1)* shows the classification of complaint for two large series of patients seen by their family doctors during the validation studies of the General Health Questionnaire. It can be seen that in London, although almost a quarter of the patients were thought to be psychiatrically ill by their doctor, only 7.8 per cent had presented with symptoms that were entirely psychological: the remainder had some combination of somatic and affective symptoms. In the Philadelphia series, the discrepancy is even more striking: of those thought to have significant psychiatric symptoms, only a tenth do not have somatic symptoms.

Although the patients are aware of their psychological symptoms, they usually interpret them in terms of non-specific illness rather than thinking themselves psychologically ill. They will often volunteer that they are 'out of sorts' or 'under the weather', but will seek medical advice for the accompanying somatic symptoms. There are several reasons for doing this: first, the patient thinks that the doctor expects him or her to produce physical symptoms, and will in any case ferret out the meaning of any puzzling symptoms. Somatic symptoms form part of the recognized

Table 4(1): *Classification of complaint of consecutive primary-care patients in London and Philadelphia*

classification of complaint	United Kingdom London			United States Philadelphia		
	number	%		number	%	
physical symptoms	252	45.6	⎫ 53.9	165	32.1	⎫ 51.6
physical symptoms, neurotic personality	46	8.3	⎭	100	19.5	⎭
physical illness with associated psychiatric symptoms	10	1.8	⎫	71	13.8	⎫
psychiatric illness with somatic symptoms	52	9.4	⎪ 24.4	28	5.4	⎪ 31.3
unrelated physical and psychiatric illness	30	5.4	⎪	19	3.7	⎪
entirely psychiatric symptoms	43	7.8	⎭	15	3.0	⎭
miscellaneous reasons	27	4.9		33	6.4	
parents of sick children	93	16.8		83	16.1	
totals	553	100.0		514	100.0	

Sources: London – Goldberg and Blackwell, 1970; Philadelphia – Goldberg, Rickels, Downing, and Hesbacher, 1976.

symptom clusters of affective disorders (for example, palpitations, tremor, and tension headaches are part of an anxiety state) but the patient will typically choose the somatic symptom to justify a visit to the doctor. This is understandable, since such symptoms may have causes other than mood disorder, and the patient may wish the doctor to be responsible for excluding such causes.

Second, the patient may have had a particular symptom for some time, but now be going through a period of stress or depression, so that the symptom seems worse. Because the symptom seems worse – just as chronic pain gets worse when a patient is depressed – the symptom is presented.

Third, patients who are experiencing mood disorders quite commonly become hypervigilant and examine their bodily sensations more closely than they usually would. Thus, an ache becomes a pain, or an irregularity in the breast, a definite lump.

Fourth, there is the stigma of mental illness: it is considered more respectable to have a physical illness. Many doctors share this view, and may communicate it to the patient.

Finally, there is a small group of patients who have developed some new and alarming symptom, such as a lump in the neck, or rectal bleeding, who become emotionally concerned about the implications of the physical symptom. The presentation of the symptoms rather than the distress is both understandable and appropriate.

We will review evidence at the end of this chapter which indicates that a little over half of the patients with a diagnosable psychiatric disorder seen in a primary care setting in the United States will have significant somatic symptom-formation accompanying their mood disorders. In some cultural settings the tendency for psychiatric disorders to present with non-specific physical symptoms is even more marked than in the English speaking world. Thus Ndetei and Muhangi (1979) report twenty-eight cases (20 per cent) of psychiatric disorder among 140 attenders at a walk-in clinic in a Kenyan suburb, but report that none of the patients complained of anxiety (fear) or depression (sadness) in the history. The commonest symptoms were pain, tiredness, weakness, disturbed sleep, constipation, palpitations, impotence, and diarrhoea. The researchers report no cases of psychotic illness, and observe 'in our culture psychotic features carry a lot of stigma, and are generally regarded as non-medical. Therefore few ordinary people will care to report these to the health authorities.' Giel and Van Luijk (1969) reported a similar situation in their survey of attenders to a health centre in a small Ethiopian town: they found sixty-four psychiatric cases (19 per cent) among attenders, but observed that three-quarters of these were related to physical symptoms. In their discussion of some of the more bizarre physical symptoms, the authors observe:

> 'Most important however is that patients do not just state their complaints but dramatize them supported by a clear interaction with their often many and deeply interested companions. It was interesting in this respect to compare our own reactions to this drama with those of our interpreters. We were mostly inclined to think that the suffering of our patients could not be as bad as they seemed to indicate while the interpreters identified themselves immediately and strongly with the patients.'

Elsewhere in their report, the authors touch upon a management problem which is not unknown in more sophisticated settings:

> 'There certainly is a strong tendency in patients to express themselves in terms of physical illness. However, the language of the clinic is entirely limited to somatic conditions. It was sometimes a surprise to the staff of a clinic to learn that their patients were more concerned about the social problems they had and about the resulting psychological complaints than about the vague physical complaints with which they started the interview. Often, however, the triumph of the psychiatrist is not a lasting one, because many an enlightening discussion concerning psychological problems will in the end be dismissed as irrelevant and the patient will insist on treatment, preferably by means of injections, of symptoms for which no physical basis has been found.'

The intimate relationship between physical symptoms and emotional disorder implies that workers in primary care settings should have two groups of skill: the ability to diagnose physical illness, and the management skills required for those disorders which are not caused by physical disease. In the past there was a tendency to neglect the latter group of disorders, perhaps because they were thought somehow less 'real' than physical disease.

Leighton (1976) has given a vivid description of such disorders:

> 'Whichever way one chooses to look upon the psychological and somatic conditions, they are distinctly miserable for those who experience them, and they are not under voluntary control. They are nonrational, counterproductive, and compound the difficulties both for the sufferer and those around him. Of particular importance is that as the prevalence of people with such difficulties increases in the population, there is a

corresponding further reduction in the coping ability and competence of the community.'

An important group of patients whose psychiatric illness will often be undetected by the family physician are those where the psychiatric illness is unrelated to the physical symptoms for which help is being sought. For example, a chronically depressed patient may go to her doctor because she has developed a sore throat and a fever. The doctor examines her, diagnoses tonsillitis, and prescribes an antibiotic. He has responded appropriately to her complaints, but missed a psychiatric illness. Such patients will typically report their depressive symptoms on a psychiatric screening questionnaire and will describe their symptoms to an observant physician who asks directly about them – perhaps because he has noticed some non-verbal cues which relate to psychiatric illness. It is probable that many of the depressed women found in community surveys who have attended their doctors (for example, Brown and Harris' 'onset cases' – see p.34) have in fact, consulted him for other reasons and will not feel disgruntled because their doctor did not detect symptoms which they had not chosen to describe to him.

THE PHYSICIAN'S BIAS

There have now been a number of surveys of psychiatric illness among patients attending primary care physicians in both England and the United States which have shown very great variation between individual physicians in the rates which they report for psychiatric illness.

Shepherd *et al.* (1966) for example, showed a nine-fold variation between family physicians in London, and surveys in the United States have shown even wider variations. The results of the five recent surveys are summarized in *Table 4(2)*, which shows the percentage of consecutive attenders thought 'psychiatric' by the primary care physician. The mean is the figure which is most usually quoted when reference is made to these surveys, and it is often conveniently forgotten that this mean is arrived at by averaging the pronouncements of very heterogeneous observers.

When psychiatric screening tests are used simultaneously during such surveys, they typically show much less variation between the various practice populations than that suggested by the doctors' own assessments. *Table 4(3)* shows that there is in fact no correlation between the level of disorder reported by the doctors and the level of disorder in the population predicted by a screening questionnaire.

Table 4(2):   *Inter-practice variation in the detection of psychiatric morbidity*

	number of physicians	mean %	range %
Marks, Goldberg, and Hillier (1979)			
Manchester, UK	91	14.2	15-64
Locke *et al.* (1967)			
Prince George's County, Md., USA	79	9.0	0-44
Locke and Gardner (1969)			
Monroe County, NY, USA	58	16.9	0-37
Leopold, Goldberg, and Schein (1971)			
W. Philadelphia, Pa., USA	32	16.3	0-92
Goldberg *et al.* (1979)			
Charleston, SC, USA	45	39.0	0-85

Note: The figures refer to percentages of consecutive attenders.

Table 4(3):   *Relationship between the level of the disorder reported by the doctor and the level assessed by the psychiatric screening test*

Shepherd *et al.* (1966)	
14 general practitioners, London, England	−0.31 (NS)
Marks, Goldberg and Hillier (1979)	
55 general practitioners, Manchester, England	−0.17 (NS)
Goldberg *et al.* (1979)	
29 family practice residents, Charleston, S.C.	+0.08 (NS)

Let us be very clear about the conclusion to be drawn from these data. One cannot conclude that there is no association between an individual physician's assessments and the symptom levels of his patients. The reverse is often true, and we shall be returning to that. But it is reasonable to assume that a doctor who tells you that 80 per cent of his patients are psychiatrically disordered is no more likely to have a greater number of such patients attending his office than a doctor who tells you that only 10 per cent are disordered. The difference between them resides not in their patients, but in their concepts of psychiatric disorder and the threshold that they adopt for case identification.

It is possible to compute the 'bias' of a given physician towards psychiatric assessments by comparing the ratio of observed to expected cases in his practice. If one administers a psychiatric screening questionnaire to a series of his patients then the observed cases are the number identified by him as psychiatrically ill (the 'conspicuous psychiatric morbidity' of the practice), while the expected cases can be calculated from the number of patients with high scores on the screening questionnaire, by using an appropriate conversion formula.[1]

'Bias' therefore allows an investigator to compare a given doctor's tendency to make, or avoid making, assessments that his patients have psychiatric disorders relative to an arbitrary standard. This standard is the concept of a 'just significant psychiatric illness' used by the validators of the psychiatric screening questionnaire. In the case of the GHQ, for example, the concept of psychiatric disorder was one thought appropriate to the setting of general medical practice: case vignettes are given to illustrate such patients in Goldberg (1972), and examples of both a mild and a moderate psychiatric illness are reproduced for interested readers as note 2. If one wished to use a concept of 'caseness' that corresponds to the average patient referred to psychiatrists, one would need to adjust the threshold of the GHQ-60 to 19/20 in order to obtain optimal discrimination for the 'moderate' illnesses. (It is of interest that Finlay-Jones and Murphy (1979) have shown that in order to identify 'cases' that correspond to standards derived from the Present State Examination, it is necessary to raise the threshold score.) Of course, provided that one's purpose in measuring bias is to compare one physician with another, the concept of 'caseness' used is irrelevant: a valid comparison can be made whatever standard is used.

One reason that a patient may fail to have his psychiatric disorder detected is because he happens to consult a physician with a very *low bias* towards making such assessment; but there is another equally important reason. His physician may be an extremely inaccurate detector of illness, and make assessments concerning his patients' state of psychological adjustment that bear no relation to the number of symptoms experienced by his patients. An example may make this clear. A particular doctor could have a value for bias of 1 – so that he picks out exactly the same proportion of his patients as predicted by a screening questionnaire – but he could be picking out completely different patients from those identified by the screening questionnaire.

It must be emphasised that one cannot conclude that a doctor with a bias of less than one has a threshold for what constitutes a case that is too high: all that one can conclude is that he makes such assessments more sparingly than the validators of the screening questionnaire.

THE PHYSICIAN'S ACCURACY

There are two main ways of measuring accuracy. The primary care physician's assessment may be compared with those of an experienced clinician using a standardized research interview on a set of his patients. This is not only an expensive method, but there are usually sampling problems since the researchers are able to interview only a compliant sample of the primary care physician's patients, and the clinical assessments of the researchers are themselves liable to error. Probably because of the expense, there are only two examples of this method. Goldberg and Blackwell (1979) showed that there was a high correlation between the assessments of the primary care physician and the research psychiatrist, but that the former nonetheless was failing to detect one third of the psychiatric illnesses among his patients. Hoeper, Nycz, and Cleary (1979) used a standardized psychiatric assessment – Spitzer's Schedule for Affective Disorders and Schizophrenia, the SADS-L – to measure psychiatric illnesss, and found that 27 per cent of consecutive attenders had a diagnosable illness. This estimate agreed well with the estimate of 30 per cent made by a psychiatric screening questionnaire, the GHQ. However, the primary care physicians were aware of psychiatric symptoms, or had prescribed psychotropic drugs, for only 5 per cent of their patients, and had made a psychiatric diagnosis in only 2 per cent.

It is probably easier to dispense with the research psychiatrist altogether, and to measure the accuracy of an individual physician by comparing his assessments of his patients with the patients' reported symptom levels on a screening questionnaire. There is good evidence that assessments of the severity of psychiatric illness are directly proportional to the number of symptoms reported on the GHQ,[3] so that if an individual doctor is an accurate assessor of psychiatric illness, there should be a strong correlation between his ratings of the degree of disturbance of each patients and the GHQ scores of the same patients.

Spearman's rank-order correlation coefficient ('rho') has been used for this purpose, and has the advantage that it is not affected by the threshold that a physician uses to distinguish between 'cases' and 'non-cases', nor is it affected by the cutting score on the questionnaire used to dichotomize the respondents into 'high scores' and 'low scorers'. The great disadvantage is that rho is a very unstable statistic for short runs of patients: one should really have at least forty pairs of doctor-patient ratings.

It is possible to consider aspects of an individual doctor's performance as a case detector by dichotomizing his patients' replies to the GHQ into high scores and low scores, and his ratings into psychiatric cases and normals. One then obtains the following table:

General Health Questionnaire:

	A	B
high scores (probable cases)	symptomatic 'normals' (disagreement)	symptomatic cases (agreement)
	C	D
low scores (probable normals)	asymptomatic normals (agreement) normals	asymptomatic 'cases' (disagreement) cases
	general practitioner's assessments	

There are various ways of measuring agreement from such a 2x2 table.[4] The simplest is to examine the percentage of agreements: $(B+C)\%$. Since some of these agreements could have been expected by chance, an alternative way is to express accuracy using Cohen's Kappa coefficient (Cohen 1960). Kappa has a value of zero if agreement is no better than chance, a negative value of zero if it is worse than chance, and a value of unity if agreement is perfect.

THE PHYSICIAN AS A CASE DETECTOR

From the point of view of assessing a physician's performance as a case detector, it is necessary to measure his ability to identify symptomatic patients as 'cases' and to ignore his ability to identify asymptomatic patients as 'normals'.

This is measured by the *identification index*, which is the ratio of symptomatic cases (cell B) to expected true positives. Another way of saying this is that the numerator is the number of patients *actually* assigned to cell B, while the denominator is the number of patients the doctor *ought* to have assigned to cell B. It is fairly simple to calculate the 'expected true positives', since one merely multiplies the probable prevalence by the sensitivity of the questionnaire. (At first glance it might have been thought simpler to have used the percentage of high scorers identified by the doctor as cases as the index, but unfortunately such an index would be dependent upon prevalence, because the lower the prevalence the greater the expected proportion of false positives to true positives.) Although the identification index is in some ways the most important measure of all, it is in no sense independent of accuracy and bias. For a given level of accuracy, for example, the identification index will increase as bias increases, and as the threshold on the GHQ for determining a 'high score' decreases; and vice versa. On the other hand, for a fixed threshold on the GHQ, and if bias is standardized to unity, then identification index will be determined by accuracy.

Table 4(4) summarizes the relationship between bias and identification index for the three surveys to be described in more detail in the next section. It will be seen that in those settings where the family doctors have a high bias towards making psychiatric assessments, they are inevitably more successful in identifying the symptomatic patients as cases.

The three most important aspects of a doctor's performance as an assessor of psychiatric disturbance – bias, accuracy, and identification index – are summarized in *Table 4(5)*.

THREE MULTIPRACTICE SURVEYS

Leopold, Goldberg, and Schein (1971) compared assessments of psychiatric disturbance made by thirty-two primary care physicians in West Philadelphia with their patients' responses to the thirty-item General Health Questionnaire. The physicians used a recording form called Locke's A-B form, which had been extensively used in other centrally-funded research designs in the United States, but which may well have been responsible for serious under-reporting of morbidity.[5] In view of the wide variation between physicians in their reported rates for psychiatric disorder the investigators recorded various characteristics of the doctors and their patients to see whether consistent patterns emerged. The *status* of the doctors was examined by three measures: medically trained physicians (MDs) were assumed to have higher status than osteopathic physicians (DOs); members of either the AMA or the AOA were assumed to have higher status than non-members of either association; and those with affiliations to nearby hospitals were assumed to have higher status than those without such affiliations. The *stress* on the physicians was measured by dividing the doctors into those with fewer than twenty-six hours of clinic a week (low stress) and those with more than twenty-six hours (high stress). In addition the variable race was examined by dividing the doctor-patient dyads into those where doctor and patient were the same race and those where a white doctor was seeing a black patient.[6]

Finally, patients with private health insurance were distinguished from those on Medicaid, to see whether this variable influenced the doctors' assessments. The results of this study are reported at length by Schein (1977) from a sociological perspective; the results given here were

Table 4(4): *Mean identification indices for psychiatric disorder for family physicians in three different settings, showing the relationship between identification index and bias*

investigators and location	family doctors' assessment	version of GHQ	mean bias	mean identification index
Goldberg, Steele, Smith, and Spivey (1979) Charleston, USA	45 GPs; 6 point scale	GHQ-28 (predicted true positives)	1.46	.80
Marks, Goldberg, and Hillier (1979) Manchester, England	91 GPs; 6 point scale	GHQ-60 (predicted true positives)	.79	.54
Schein (1977) Philadelphia, USA	32 GPs; Locke's A-B form	GHQ-30 (predicted true positives)	.45	.31

Table 4(5): *Summary of the main aspects of a doctor's performance relating to his ability to assess psychological disorders among his patients (B, C, and D refer to the 2x2 contingency table on p.65)*

aspect of performance	what it measures	methods of measurement
bias	tendency to make, or to avoid making psychiatric assessments (inevitably those with a high bias will have a low threshold for making such assessments, and vice versa)	$\dfrac{\text{observed (B+D)}}{\text{expected (B+D)}} = \dfrac{\text{conspicuous psychiatric morbidity}}{\text{probable prevalence}}$
accuracy	overall ability to make assessments of psychiatric disturbances which are congruent with the patients' symptom levels	Spearman's rank-order correlation coefficient (if 'n' is large); Cohen's Kappa; percentage agreement (B+C)%
identification index	ability to identify symptomatic patients as sick: determined partly by accuracy, and partly by bias	$\dfrac{\text{observed (B)}}{\text{expected (B)}} = \dfrac{\text{symptomatic cases}}{\text{expected true positives}}$

Table 4(6): *A comparison of family doctors' ratings of psychiatric illness and patients' self ratings using General Health Questionnaire (30-item) (recalculated from Schein 1977)*

27 family doctors in West Philadelphia rating 4,086 patients	all doctors %	physician status				physician stress		racial homogamy		type of patient	
		high: MD	low: DO osteopaths	high: hospital affiliations	low: no hospital work	low: −26 hrs clinic per week	high: 26 hrs + clinic per week	same race: wh/wh and bl/bl	different race: black pt. white dr.	private health insurance	medicaid
accuracy (total agreements doctor/GHQ)	60.7	63.1	58.3	59.2	62.3	62.9	59.2	63.7	58.0	62.5	57.8
probable prevalence (derived from GHQ scores)	39.5	33.7	45.2	39.5	39.4	34.2	43.3	32.9	45.2	33.8	75.7
identification index	.31	.16	.43	.21	.40	.13	.42	.17	.40	.18	.55
% psychiatric cases (doctor's ratings)	17.6	7.4	27.5	9.2	24.7	5.9	25.9	7.9	26.2	9.3	44.3
bias	.45	.22	.61	.23	.63	.17	.60	.24	.58	.27	.59

calculated from data in Schein's thesis, using the same measures that have just been described (accuracy, bias, and identification index) in order to permit comparisons with other surveys.

It can be seen from *Table 4(6)* that there are no very striking differences in overall accuracy between any of the groups studied, but that there is a definite tendency for some variables to cause doctors to avoid making psychiatric assessments (i.e. have a low bias). Low bias is associated with high-status doctors, those with more leisurely office hours, racial homogeneity, and patients with private health insurance. High bias is associated with the reverse of these situations – low-status, high-stress doctors, racial heterogeneity, and patients on Medicaid. It can be seen that the probable prevalence of minor psychiatric disorder is greater in all the situations associated with high bias and in particular with patients on Medicaid; however, it should be noted that this cannot account for the high bias, since the method of calculation corrects for differences in prevalence.

Since the situations associated with high bias are not associated with greater accuracy, the higher values for identification index must be due to the high bias: when in doubt, these doctors often guess 'case' and are sometimes right; while doctors in situations associated with low bias will typically guess 'non-case' when in doubt and will often be wrong. Put another way, the typical high bias error is an asymptomatic 'case'; while the typical low bias error is a symptomatic 'normal'.

It seemed likely that the doctor's personality and the way in which he interviews his patients might account for some of the observed variation between doctors. Marks, Goldberg, and Hillier (1979) therefore carried out a survey during which a research psychiatrist made detailed observations on 2,098 interviews carried out by fifty-five general practitioners in the Greater Manchester area, all of whom completed a battery of personality questionnaires.

In this study, the doctors were invited to rate each patient they saw on a six-point scale of psychiatric disturbance, and their ratings were compared with their patients' responses to the sixty-item General Health Questionnaire. The probable prevalence of minor psychiatric disorders as measured by the GHQ-60 was 39.6 per cent, a remarkably similar figure to the 39.5 per cent reported in the Philadelphia Survey in *Table 4(6)*. However, whereas Locke's A-B form is so designed that it is a much greater nuisance to report that a patient is sick, with a six-point scale it is just as easy to score the patient sick or well. The result is dramatic: whereas in Philadelphia only 17.6 per cent of the patients are reported to be cases (bias 0.45), in Manchester 31.1 per cent are so reported (bias 0.79). (See *Table 4(4).*)

The doctors in the Manchester study were found to vary between themselves a great deal in their ability to make accurate assessments of psychiatric disturbance. The mean value for Spearman's rank-order correlation coefficient was +0.39 with a standard deviation of 0.15 and a range of from +0.09 to +0.66. This means that although about a third of the physicians had very respectable coefficients, for the lowest third there was no significant correlation between their ratings and the symptom levels of their patients.

The investigators selected thirty-four variables from the various observations that had been made concerning the doctors' practices, their personalities, and their interview styles which had significant correlations with one of the main variables which have already been described in this chapter.[7] The data were then subjected to a series of rotated principal axes analyses, and three further variables were added in an attempt to obtain an optimal prediction of Spearman's 'rho'. In the interest of simplicity we will show the varimax rotation of the seven-factor solution, which accounted for 58.2 per cent of the total variance.

It can be seen from *Table 4(7)* that this solution accounts for about 67 per cent of the variance in Spearman's 'rho' in terms of four factors: 'interest and concern', 'conservatism', 'psychiatric focus', and 'time pressures'. 'Interest and concern' is a dimension which is concerned with an empathic manner, and asking patients questions about their home and family. Probably because of the way in which such doctors interview their patients, fewer of the patients are rated as 'entirely normal' by the observing

Table 4(7): *Table showing amount of variance accounted for, for the 4 main variables with a 7-factor varimax rotation using a total of 37 variables for the analysis*

variance on each varimax factor (%)	Spearman's rho	identification index	probable prevalence	conspicuous morbidity
interest and concern	40.3	37.3	–	25.0
conservatism	18.5	–	–	–
psychiatric focus	5.0	24.5	–	16.8
probable prevalence	–	–	43.0	–
age and experience	–	8.0	–	11.0
time pressures	3.0	–	6.0	–
evasiveness	–	–	–	–
total	67%	70%	49%	53%

psychiatrist. 'Conservatism' is a dimension compounded of personality variables and interview style: at one end came conservatism on the Wilson-Patterson Social Attitude Inventory, Eysenck's Extraversion and the tendency to prescribe hypnotics; while at the other come tendency to ask questions – both directive and closed – with a psychiatric content, and the possession of higher qualifications. Spearman's 'rho' loads on the non-conservative end of this dimension. 'Psychiatric focus' consists of five variables which relate to the emphasis the doctor gives to psychological aspects of illness: it consists of an attitude scale concerned with the importance of psychological factors in illness, the doctor's interest in psychiatry, his use of two types of psychiatric question, and the finding that many of such doctors' patients are rated as having 'entirely psychiatric disorders' by the psychiatrist. Once more, the latter finding is probably related to the way in which the doctor interviews his patient. Finally, 'time pressures' is a dimension clearly related to the speed of the consultation: at the leisurely end patients tend to be reassured and investigated, while at the hurried end the doctor has an authoritarian manner, issues many prescriptions, and carries out indifferent physical examinations.

It can be seen from *Table 4(7)* that both identification index and conspicuous psychiatric morbidity load on the same three dimensions: 'interest and concern', 'psychiatric focus' and 'age and experience'. Age and experience is a dimension that holds together fairly well: in addition to having a tendency to diagnose more psychiatric disorders than his younger colleague, the older doctor asks about home and family, is more likely to have higher qualifications, and will not omit a physical examination, but has a tendency to make 'contentless statements'. (A 'contentless statement' is one that the observing psychiatrist rates as not helping the interview in terms of diagnosis or management of the patient's complaints.)

This research has now been repeated in the United States with various methodological improvements by Goldberg, Steele, Smith, and Spivey (1980). Detailed ratings were made of videotaped interviews between forty-five family physicians in the residency program of the Department of Family Practice at the Medical University of South Carolina. Each resident rated thirty patients (each of whom completed the twenty-eight item GHQ), using the same six-point scale used in the previous research. The residents had all agreed to have videotaped recordings made of their interviews, but they had no way of knowing when the investigators would make the recordings. In fact, we recorded five interviews for each resident over a six-month period using the built-in Departmental videotape system: this time there was no tendency for the doctors to be on their guard because of the presence of an observer.

Figure 4(1): Correlation coefficient between doctor and GHQ.

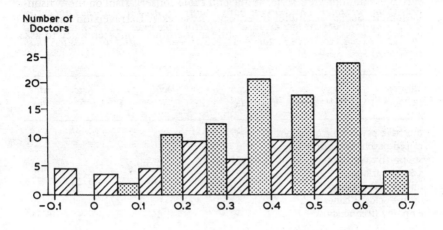

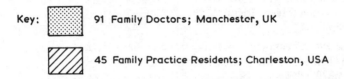

Key: 91 Family Doctors; Manchester, UK

45 Family Practice Residents; Charleston, USA

Once more, there was a very wide variation between the residents in the values obtained for Spearman's rho: *Figure 4(1)* shows that their scores extend over much the same range as their more experienced colleagues in Manchester, although the mean is slightly lower. At least a third of the residents do not have significant correlations between their ratings and the symptom levels of their patients.

It was impossible to replicate the Manchester study by observing exactly the same variables, since on the one hand there were some measures which did not apply to the residents in Charleston, while on the other the Department were able to make available extremely detailed information about the academic and clinical abilities of the residents, as well as far more comprehensive personality information. The sort of measures which we could not repeat included time per patient, physical examination, and age of resident. This was quite simply because all the interviews were leisurely, almost all the patients were adequately examined, and the residents were all the same age. The solution adopted was inevitably a compromise: we included those variables which could be replicated in a satisfactory way

Table 4(8): *Varimax rotation of factor analysis with Kaeser normalization for 45 doctors measured on 30 variables (each one chosen because it relates to a dependent variable). The columns have been rearranged so that they appear in decreasing order of variance explained by factors; the rows have been rearranged so that for each successive factor loads >.5 appear first, and all loads less than 0.25 have been omitted*

variable: (see note 6)	factor 1	factor 2	factor 3	factor 4	factor 5	factor 6
directive psychiatric questions	.87					
closed psychiatric questions	.83					
supportive comments	.71					
asks about home	.64			−.32	.33	.28
misses verbal cues	−.59				−.33	
open-to-closed cones	.54	.45		.27		
empathy (frequency)	.49		.46			−.34
self-actualization (Maslow)		.88				
self-regard (POI)		.84				
needs and feelings (POI)		.69	.32		.29	
introversion (Myers-Briggs)		−.47				
gives advice	−.33	.42			.42	−.28
deals with breaks			.78			
makes eye contact			.74			
buries in notes			−.72			
interest in psychiatry			.65	−.35		
MCQ score				.80		
formal oral-cognitive				.78		
physical oral-cognitive				.72		
management problem: meningitis	.40			.40		−.28
conservatism		−.33		.39		−.26
misses non-verbal cues	−.28				−.72	
accurate concepts of illness					.56	
deals with garrulousness	.37			.30	.55	
clarifies complaint			.36		.53	
directive-physical symptoms		.26	−.42		.51	
past medical history						.82
theoretical (Alport)				−.30		.67
physical symptoms − mental origin			.26	.26		.52
uses technical language		.38				−.39
variance explained	3.8	3.2	3.1	2.8	2.7	2.2

with the new set of doctors, but we added new variables which could be shown to correlate with our main variables.

We also took the opportunity to improve our methods of calculating the results. Instead of carrying out a multivariate analysis which included (and might thus have been distorted by) our dependent variables (Spearman's rho, Cohen's Kappa, identification index, and Bias) we carried out an analysis without them, based only on those variables which had significant correlations to the dependent variables in the raw data. The analysis which gave the clearest results was the six-factor varimax rotation which accounted for 60 per cent of the total variance: this is shown as *Table 4(8)*.

Inevitably, the new variables have meant that somewhat different factors have emerged. There are now three separate dimensions which deal with the doctor's characteristics as an interviewer, one which deals with his academic ability, and two which deal with rather different aspects of the doctor's personality from those included in the previous study. Factor 1 is reminiscent of 'psychiatric focus' in the earlier study: it deals with the use of questions with a psychiatric content, asking about the home, making supportive psychotherapeutic comments, and not missing verbal cues relating to psychological disturbances.

Factor 2 deals with the self-confidence of the doctor, and his ability to handle his own feelings. Conservatism and introversion (as measured by the Myers-Briggs scale) load negatively on this dimension. Factor 3 deals with interview style: such doctors can deal competently with interruptions during their interview, are interested in psychiatry, make eye contact with their patients at outset, and do not bury themselves in the notes while their patients are talking to them. Factor 4 is undoubtedly related to the academic ability of the residents and their skills in internal medicine: it is curious that conservatism should have a significant load on this dimension. Factor 5 is of great interest, since it deals with interviewing skills that can be taught; these residents are sensitive to non-verbal cues relating to psychological disorder, they have an accurate conception[8] of psychiatric illness, they have the skills to direct communication from an overtalkative patient, and they clarify their patients' complaints rather than accept them at face value. Finally, factor 6 faces us with the first real problem of conceptualization. To the extent that one can understand this dimension, it appears to relate to an abstract, woolly quality in a resident: these doctors ask many questions about the past rather than engage with problems in the present, they endorse many physical symptoms as being an indication of psychiatric illness, and they score highly on Alport's 'theoretical' scale of values. These six factors were shown to be orthogonal to one another, in that the inter-

Table 4(9): *Results of separate, stepwise multiple regression analyses to account for 4 dependent variables in terms of residents' scores on 6 independent factors*

six factors derived from rotated factor analysis	accuracy		case detection	
	Spearman's 'rho' (z-transformation)	Cohen's Kappa	bias	identification index
Factor 1: psychiatric emphasis	–	–	16.2%	11.7%
Factor 2: self-assured, extroverted doctor	6.1%	9.9%	–	–
Factor 3: good interview behaviour	11.2%	–	–	10.1%
Factor 4: academic ability	7.1%	12.5%	–	–
Factor 5: directive interviewer with accurate concepts	18.0%	8.2%	–	7.2%
Factor 6: abstractness	7.6%	–	–	–
Multiple R	.71	.55	.40	.54
R^2: variance accounted for	50.1%	30.5%	16.2%	29.0%

correlations between them for the set of forty-five residents were a set of zeros.

The next step was therefore to take the dependent variables one by one (Spearman's rho, Cohen's Kappa, Identification Index, and Bias) and to carry out four separate stepwise multiple regression analyses using the residents' load on each of the six factors instead of their scores on the original thirty variables. The results of this procedure are summarized in *Table 4(9)*.

It can be seen that Bias loads only on factor 1, and that neither of the measures of accuracy have a significant load on this factor. Spearman's rho – in some ways the best measure of overall accuracy – loads on all the remaining factors, which together account for a multiple R of +0.71. Cohen's Kappa, our measure of agreement, loads on factors 2, 4, and 5, which together account for a multiple R of +0.55. As one might expect, the identification index is partly determined by bias (factor 1) and partly by accuracy (factors 3 and 5).

DETERMINANTS OF BIAS

Since there is no correlation between a physician's estimate of conspicuous psychiatric morbidity (CPM) and the probable prevalence of morbidity suggested by a psychiatric screening questionnaire (*Table 4(3)*), it must be concluded that CPM is largely a measure of bias. It is therefore of interest to summarize the findings related to the determinants of CPM.

Shepherd and his group (1966) were able to account for 51 per cent of the non-random variance of the doctor's assessments in terms of two variables: the 'mobility index' was an ecological variable related to the turnover of patients in each practice, and the 'psychosomatic score' was an attitude scale which measures the extent to which the doctor thinks psychogenic factors are important in the aetiology of various illnesses. The more important he thinks they are, the higher will be his estimate of psychiatric morbidity.

The recent study in Manchester by Marks, Goldberg, and Hillier (1979) succeeded in accounting for 53 per cent of the variance of the doctors' assessments of CPM. A dimension called 'interest and concern' accounted for a quarter of the variance while the next dimension, 'psychiatric focus', replicates Shepherd's earlier finding. These doctors score highly on Shepherd's scale concerned with psychogenic factors in illnesses, are once more rated as 'interested in psychiatry', and have a tendency to ask questions of a psychiatric nature during their diagnostic interviews. Finally, older doctors who have spent longer times in the practice being observed are likely to have rather higher rates than younger, newly arrived doctors.

The two American surveys measured bias directly. It will be recalled that the Philadelphia study found that high status doctors, working in more leisurely surroundings, seeing patients with private health insurance who were the same race as themselves, were all factors associated with a bias *against* making assessments. The Charleston study could not remeasure these variables since the doctors being observed were far more homogenous, but the study succeeded in identifying a factor which dealt with the way in which the doctor interviewed his patients which was associated with high bias. As one might have suspected these doctors ask many psychiatric questions and questions about the patient's home; they are empathic and sensitive to verbal cues relating to psychological distress; they are not, however, any more accurate in their assessments than those without these behaviours.

DETERMINANTS OF ACCURACY

The Philadelphia survey found that physicians with special interests were no more accurate than those without such interests, and that those who thought that they needed more training in respect of their psychiatric skills were no less accurate than those who did not consider that they needed such training (calculated from Schein 1977). There was no tendency for older, more experienced physicians to be more accurate than younger colleagues in either the Philadelphia or the Manchester surveys: this observation could not be checked in Charleston since the residents were of fairly similar age. However, it is of interest that those in the third year of training were no more accurate than those in the first year.

The differences between the findings of the Manchester and the Charleston surveys concerning the determinants of accuracy are partly due to the alterations which were made in the measurements made on the participating doctors in the two surveys, and partly due to the fact that the established general practitioners observed in Manchester are in many ways different from the family practice residents observed in Charleston. While the Manchester GPs represented a wide range of relatively unselected physicians of both sexes and all ages working in a wide variety of settings, the Charleston residents were highly selected, all young, mainly male, and working in an identical setting. In both studies it was possible to account for a substantial proportion of the variation between the physicians in accuracy in terms of their personalities and the way in which they interview their patients.

The Charleston study was able to take advantage of valuable information concerning the academic and clinical abilities of the participating doctors, and was able to show that those scoring high on certain clinical examinations are somewhat more accurate in terms of both measures of association ('rho') and measures of agreement ('Kappa'). The discrepancy between the two studies concerning extraversion of the doctor may well be due to the fact that the Eysenck Personality Inventory is an empirically derived scale, while the Myers-Briggs Type Inventory is theoretically derived: they are probably not measuring the same thing. The tendency for conservative doctors to be less accurate assessors of psychiatric disturbance is still seen in the Charleston data but it is now over-shadowed by other personality measures which were not included in the earlier study: the accurate doctor is likely to score highly on scales which deal with positive self-regard and responsiveness to his own needs and feelings. It was notable that long before the results of these personality measures were known in the Charleston Study, the researchers had noted the poor self-image and lack of professional confidence of several of the residents with low values of Cohen's Kappa.[9]

It is worth pointing out that in both the surveys all observations concerning the doctors' interview styles, personality, and academic characteristics had been completed before the values for accuracy, bias, and identification index were computed. There was therefore no chance that the researchers might have been influenced in their observations of the doctors by knowledge that a particular doctor was particularly good or bad in any of these respects.

The findings that the more accurate residents in Charleston tended to score more highly on a factor dealing with their knowledge of clinical medicine fits with the observation that the possession of higher qualifications was related to accuracy in the Manchester study. It will be recalled that accuracy was also related to factor 5 ('directive interviewer with accurate concepts') in the Charleston study: this is a new finding since the variables which load significantly on this factor were not used in the Manchester study.

It is possible that the reason why 'accurate concepts' of psychiatric illness should be positively related to the possession and use of directive techniques as an interviewer is that it is difficult for an interviewer to be directive if he has little idea of a likely goal. Doctors with high scores on this factor were likely to be able to control an overtalkative patient, to clarify their patients' symptoms, and to use directive (rather than closed) questions when probing physical symptomatology. Their engagement with the patient's present symptoms meant that they were alert to both verbal and non-verbal cues relating to psychological disturbance, and they tended to ask about the patient's home but not to spend so much time on the previous medical history.

It is an important factor since it is probably largely responsible for the improvements which can be obtained by offering training sessions to doctors who make inaccurate assessments of their patients' state of psychological adjustment.

The investigators in the Charleston survey identified the twenty-four residents who made the least accurate assessments in terms of Cohen's Kappa coefficient and Spearman's rho, and randomly assigned them to two groups of twelve. The index group received four sessions of teaching based upon videotaped feedback aimed at helping them to modify their interview techniques, while the control group received no extra tuition. Four months later, both groups were assessed once more and it was shown that a significant improvement had occurred in the Kappa coefficients of the index group. The investigators went on to analyse the changes that had occurred in the interview behaviours of the doctors in the index group and were able to identify ten medical behaviours which improved significantly as a result of training, and which were significantly related to the physician's accuracy as measured at the outset of the research (see *Table 4(10)*).

Table 4(10):   *10 aspects of a family doctor's interview style which are related to his accuracy as a case detector and which can be modified by training*

---

outset:
1. Eye contact at outset
2. Clarifies presenting complaint
3. Uses directive questions for physical complaints
4. Uses 'open-to-closed cones'

interview style:
5. Empathic style (frequency)
6. Sensitive to verbal cues
7. Sensitive to non-verbal cues
8. Doesn't read notes during history
9. Can deal with overtalkativeness
10. Asks fewer questions about past history

The first nine of these ten behaviours were all part of the model interview that was taught to the residents during their feedback sessions, and which is described in greater detail elsewhere (Goldberg 1979). The trainee is discouraged from using closed questions – those that can be answered with a simple 'yes' or 'no' – at the beginning of a diagnostic interview, and is encouraged to use open and directive techniques which allow the patient to describe his symptoms in his own words. Ideally, the doctor should start with an open question (How are you? What's been the trouble?), go on to clarify with directive questions, and reserve any closed questions for the end of a sequence of questions. This is called an 'open-to-closed cone', and it refers to the extent to which the doctor controls communication from his patient. Television was particularly effective in drawing the doctor's attention to non-verbal cues relating to psychological disturbance, and in demonstrating to the trainees that they do not actually hear what the patient is saying while they are reading the notes. The tenth behaviour, concerning asking questions about the past medical history, was an unexpected finding, but it was possible to make sense of it in retrospect. The less able doctors often seemed to ask many such questions as a refuge from solving the problem posed by the patient's present symptoms. When they had been given a framework for probing a patient's present state of psychological adjustment, they were found to ask significantly fewer questions about the past.

It is of interest that the behaviours which relate to bias (factor 1 from *Table 4(9)*, behaviours 4,5, and 6 from *Table 4(10)*) are not the same as those which determine accuracy (factors 2,4, and 5 from *Table 4(9)*, behaviours 1,2,3,7,8, and 9 from *Table 4(10)*).

In summary, there is no clear relationship between accuracy and bias: those who make many psychiatric diagnoses are not likely to be more, or less accurate than those who make few such diagnoses. Accuracy as an assessor of psychiatric illness seems to depend on three groups of variables: the way in which the doctor interviews his patients, his personality, and his academic ability.

DETERMINANTS OF IDENTIFICATION INDEX

While accuracy is equally related to the ability to identify asymptomatic patients as 'normal' and the ability to identify symptomatic patients as 'cases', the identification index is solely concerned with the latter characteristic. Thus a doctor with a high bias will inevitably have a high identification index, despite the fact that his success in identifying symptomatic cases is achieved at the expense of falsely identifying asymptomatic patients as sick. From a theoretical viewpoint, it is clear that identification index is bound to be determined by accuracy and bias, and we have already seen from *Table 4(9)* that among the Charleston residents it is determined by a combination of the factors that determine these variables.

These results make good sense. A patient with many symptoms is likely to be identified as a case by his doctor if that doctor scores high on factor 1 ('Psychiatric Emphasis' – a determinant of bias), and factors 3 and 5 which relate to certain interview behaviours and which are determinants of accuracy. The lack of relationship between accuracy and bias, but the positive relationship between each of these and identification index, can be summarized by the following correlations between these variables on the forty-five Charleston residents:

	Spearman's rho (accuracy)	Cohen's Kappa (accuracy)	Bias
Identification Index	.51	.56	.83
Bias	.11	.00	
Cohen's Kappa	.75		

But there is more to the determination of identification index than variables which relate to the doctor: certain sorts of patient are much more likely to have their disturbances detected by their doctors than certain others.

In the Manchester study identification index was likely to be higher for females than males and for the middle-aged rather than the young or old. These findings are confirmed by Chancellor, Mant, and Andrews (1979) in an Australian setting. The Manchester study also showed that identification was more likely among the separated, divorced or widowed; among the unemployed; and among those seen frequently before. It was less likely among students, the unmarried, and among those who had received higher education. It is possible that certain stereotyped notions about 'typical patients' with minor psychiatric disturbance tend to increase the doctor's vigilance and thus increase the likelihood of detection; while certain other 'negative stereotypes' serve to lower the doctor's vigilance: thus a middle-aged woman whose marriage had broken up would be more likely to have her disturbance detected than a young professional man, even if they each had the same number of symptoms. These findings are broadly confirmed in an American setting by Fink and his colleagues (1969), except that in that study the educational status of the patients did not emerge as a significant predictor of case detection.

The finding that identification increases with the number of times a patient has been seen before is both understandable, and helps to explain why it is that assessments of duration of illness are longer at level 3 (psychiatric illnesses detected by the family doctor) than they are at level 2. For example, 31.5 per cent of illnesses at level 3, but 56 per cent of those at level 2 have a duration of less than one year (data derived from surveys carried out in Philadelphia, 1970). Many of the disorders picked up by psychiatric screening questionnaires are transient emotional disorders which are highly related to that day's consultation, but which are likely to remit spontaneously with time. In contrast, the doctor is likely to detect chronic disorders, since he will have had more opportunities to observe his patient.

SYNDROMES OF DISORDER AT LEVEL 2

Minor affective disorders – that is to say, anxiety states, minor depressive illnesses, and states of both anxiety and depression – account for the vast majority of illnesses seen in a primary care setting. Just over half these illnesses were found to be associated with significant somatic symptom formation among one survey of eighty-eight patients diagnosed by one of us (DG) in a primary care setting in Philadelphia. *Table 4(11)* shows the relative frequency of twelve common symptoms among these eighty-eight patients.

It can be seen that although anxiety and worry is the most widely distributed symptom, depression and fatigue follow closely behind. The idea that depression represents a more differentiated form of disorder contained within the population of patients with anxiety states, is not borne out by the data.

SOCIAL CORRELATES OF DISORDER AT LEVEL 2

The female preponderance already described at level 1 is even more marked at level 2, since females have higher consultation rates than men for most groups of disorders. Hesbacher, Rickels, and Goldberg (1975) showed that the tendency for females to have higher scores on a psychiatric screening questionnaire administered in a primary care setting persisted even when the data were controlled for social class and race. In the same study, it has been

Table 4(11): *Relative frequency of 12 common symptoms in 88 patients diagnosed as psychiatrically disordered in primary-care settings in Philadelphia (Goldberg 1979)*

	%
anxiety and worry	82
despondency and sadness	
fatigue }	71
somatic symptoms*	52
sleep disturbance	50
irritability	38
excessive concern with bodily functions	27
depressive thoughts	
inability to concentrate }	21
obsessions and compulsions	19
phobias	11
depersonalization	6

*This rating refers only to somatic symptoms that were precipitated, exacerbated, or maintained by psychological factors. The commonest symptoms encountered were headache, backache, and other regional pains, and dizzy spells.

shown that respondents with lower social class as measured by the Hollingshead and Redlich Social Index had higher scores than those of higher social class, and that this effect persisted when the data were controlled for sex and race. The tendency for blacks to have higher scores than whites, however, which was significant beyond the 0.01 level in the raw data, disappeared when allowance was made for the fact that the black respondents tended to be of lower social class than the whites.[10]

The findings concerning social class appear to hold up in Australia (Finlay-Jones and Burvill 1977), but findings in England using the Registrar General's Classification are not so clear cut – possibly because of difficulties in making accurate classification on this system from a simple reply on a survey form. However, there is good evidence that those with the statutory minimum of education (leaving school at fifteen) have higher levels of disorders than those remaining at school beyond the age of sixteen (Marks *et al.* 1979).

In view of the finding reported in the previous chapter concerning characteristics of those who pass the first filter easily, it is hardly surprising that rates for minor psychiatric disorder are high for the married but living apart who consult their doctor. For this group the probable prevalence is

65.6 per cent, to be compared with 52.2 per cent for the divorced, 40.6 per cent for the widowed, 37 per cent for married living together and 37.2 per cent for the single (data from Goldberg 1978; Greater Manchester Study).

HIDDEN PSYCHIATRIC MORBIDITY: THOSE WHO DO NOT PASS THE SECOND FILTER

The term 'hidden psychiatric morbidity' was introduced by Goldberg and Blackwell (1970) to refer to psychiatric disorders which are unrecognized by family doctors, in contrast to Kessel's 'conspicuous psychiatric morbidity' which refers to those illnesses which they recognize. The original paper showed that for every two patients recognised by the family doctor (Dr Blackwell), a third psychiatric patient could be identified by a research psychiatrist (Dr Goldberg) using a two-stage model for case identification consisting of a screening questionnaire followed by a standardized research interview. Subsequent research has indicated that family doctors vary widely between themselves in their ability to identify psychiatric illness correctly, and therefore in the amount of hidden psychiatric morbidity associated with each practice.

We have reviewed the characteristics of doctors which lead some to have a high bias towards making psychiatric diagnoses, and the characteristics that are associated with accuracy. It is evident that the reverse of these characteristics will be associated with large amounts of hidden psychiatric morbidity. In our original survey, we were able to show that the patients with hidden illnesses had as many symptoms as the conspicuous illnesses, and that they did not have a better prognosis. In a more experimental study, Johnstone and Goldberg (1976) showed that if a family doctor was made aware of these hidden illnesses, then the patients were more likely to get better quickly, and would have fewer symptoms when seen at follow-up a year after their initial consultation.

To the extent that there is anything peculiar about the patients who are unlikely to have their illness detected, it is that they will typically present to their doctor with physical symptoms and will not volunteer their psychological symptoms unless the doctor makes a direct enquiry.

The following patient is a fairly typical example of a 'hidden psychiatric illness', taken from our original survey (Goldberg and Blackwell 1970). She was seen by the psychiatrist because of a high score on the GHQ, having been rated as normal by the family doctor:

'A 50-year old housewife from South Africa came to see her doctor because the chronic breast abscess that she had had for 15 years had begun to discharge pus in the past three days. She was prescribed an antibiotic by the general practitioner, and was asked to see the psychiatrist only because she had a very high score on the screening questionnaire she had completed in the waiting room. At psychiatric interview she described a depressive illness that followed the birth of her first child. She developed ideas of self-blame because the baby seemed so thin and began to hate him. At the same time her breast milk dried and the abscess began. In the recent past she described lassitude, irritability and classic panic attacks with fears of death. She was constantly depressed with ideas of self-blame and hopelessness. The only thing that deterred her from suicide was the thought of her son finding the corpse. Asked why she had not mentioned these symptoms she said: "Why should I tell the doctor such things – how can he treat a profound sense of loneliness and isolation?" Reluctantly, she accepted treatment, and a six month follow-up told the psychiatrist, "I am a completely different person: my life changed the day you told me I had a treatable condition". The sinus from her breast abscess had healed for the first time in 15 years.'

NOTES

1. If a population of 100 respondents contains P cases then there will be $(100-P)$ non-cases. Let us consider the two groups separately. We can estimate the number of cases who will have high scores on a psychiatric screening questionnaire by multiplying P by the sensitivity of the screening questionnaire. Similarly, we can estimate the number of non-cases who will have high scores on a screening questionnaire by multiplying $(100-P)$ by the false positive rate of the screening questionnaire. The false positive rate is $(1-\text{specificity})$ of the questionnaire. We can now write the following equation for the proportion with high scores: % $\quad HS = (100-P)fp + Ps$

   where % $\quad HS =$ proportion of respondents with high scores on psychiatric screening questionnaire

   $P =$ prevalence of psychiatric illness

   $s =$ sensitivity of psychiatric screening questionnaire

   $fp =$ false positive rate of screening questionnaire; i.e. $(1-\text{specificity})$ of the questionnaire expressed as a proportion

   This equation can be rearranged as follows:

   $$P = \frac{HS - fp}{s - fp}$$

An example may make this clearer. If 30 per cent of primary care population are shown to have high scores on the sixty-item GHQ, then:

$$\text{Probable prevalence} = \frac{0.3 - 0.0594}{0.9102 - 0.0594} = \frac{0.2406}{0.8508} = .2828\%$$

Expressed as a percentage, the probable prevalence is therefore 28.28 per cent, since for the sixty item GHQ the specificity was shown to be 94.06 per cent and the sensitivity 91.02 per cent in a London setting (Goldberg 1978). Rogan and Gladen (1978) also discussed this problem, and produced similar equations.

2. The following case vignettes are given to illustrate examples of both the mild and the moderate psychiatric illness and they are taken from the original validation studies of the GHQ. They are reproduced from Goldberg (1972):

VIGNETTE OF CASE NO 21: AN EXAMPLE OF A MILD PSYCHIATRIC CASE (FEMALE)

Presenting complaint:
Miss FF was a twenty-year-old girl who had broken off her engagement two months previously, very much against her parents' wishes. She had felt ill ever since that time, and five days before had developed 'piles and an anal infection'. She had also lost some weight and was having some dysmenorrhoea.

Semistructured interview: RATING

Somatic symptoms:	Bad headache every evening in past week, related to problems	3
Fatigue:	Fatigue every day, having to go to bed early	3
Sleep disturbance:	Lost one night's sleep with headache	2
Irritability:	Snappy with people at work. Unusual for her	2
Lack of concentration:	Cannot concentrate on a book, getting forgetful at home, knocks into things, difficulty in concentration causing difficulties with boss	3
Depression:	Occasional weeping spells in past week related to broken engagement	2
Anxiety and worry:	Worries a little about what others think of her	1
Phobias:	Frightened of dark and going out at night	1
Obsessions, etc:	None	0
Depersonalization:	None	0

Manifest abnormalities at interview:

DEPRESSED	She appears clinically depressed in a mild degree	2

Formulation:
Her headache, malaise, loss of weight, fatigue, and irritability are all part of a minor affective illness that has followed her decision to break off her engagement. She has felt depressed and had periods of weeping during this time.

Psychiatric diagnosis:

Mild depression. Overall severity rating: '2'
(ICD 300.4- depressive neurosis)

Extract from the general practitioner's daybook:

Complaint: Ischiorectal abcess. Recent engyesis
Diagnostic category: Unrelated psychiatric and physical illness.
Psychiatric severity rating: '2' mild psychiatric case

GHQ Score: 26

VIGNETTE OF CASE NO 246. AN EXAMPLE OF A MODERATE PSYCHIATRIC CASE (MALE)

Presenting complaint:

Mr G G was a forty-five-year-old examiner in bankruptcy who had attended his GP because of a sudden feeling that a big cloud had come down on him. This odd and unpleasant feeling was accompanied by a constant headache and a feeling of heaviness in his eyes. He felt constantly on the verge of tears. He depicted himself as a cyclothymic personality who had had no previous attacks of this sort, although after the death of his father when he was a boy of ten he had developed a bad stutter that had persisted for some years.

Semistructured interview: RATING

Somatic symptoms:	Frequent distressing headache came on at the same time as other symptoms, accompanied by stiffness of neck	2
Fatigue:	Occasional feelings of fatigue	2
Sleep disturbance:	Distressing nightmares, antedated symptoms but none in previous week	0
Irritability:	Occasional bursts of irritability at home and in office	0
Lack of concentration:	Has noticed difficulties in concentrating in previous week	2
Depression:	Constant feeling of depression, on verge of tears	3
Anxiety and worry:	Constant worry over his job in previous week	3
Phobias:	Occasionally feels claustrophobia at home, not in past week	1
Obsessions, etc:	None	0
Depersonalization:	None	0

Manifest abnormalities at interview:

DEPRESSED	He has a clinically significant depresssion of mood of moderate degree	3
ANXIOUS, TENSE	He is noticably tense at interview, and his	

headache and stiff neck suggest that this has
lasted for some days 2
DEPRESSIVE   Although he is not suicidal at present he has
THOUGHT CONTENT chosen the gas taps at home that he would use
                           for his suicide 2
EXCESSIVE   Very worried about his smoking, more than
CONCERN WITH   twenty per day – this worry has begun recently
BODILY FUNCTIONS (Non-morbid rating assigned for this) 1

Formulation:

An intelligent man who gives a clear and convincing account of a depressive illness. He describes a cyclothymic personality, and notes that a period of mild elation which had lasted for nearly four months ended seven days ago. He has been under considerable strain at work for some time. The present episode has a number of features that distinguish it from his usual swings of mood. It was ushered in by a number of nightmares of coffins and corpses, and has been accompanied by many somatic symptoms of anxiety. The depressive mood itself is unlike his usual feelings of gloominess to external circumstances, but is a pervasive heavy feeling as described above.

Psychiatric diagnosis:

Affective illness: depression
(ICD diagnosis: 296.2 – manic depressive psychosis, depressed type)
Overall severity rating: '3'

Extract from the general practitioner's day book:

Complaint: Depression: manic personality
Diagnostic category: Entirely psychiatric condition
Psychiatric severity rating: '3' moderate psychiatric illness

GHQ Score: 19

3.   There have now been a large number of validity studies of the GHQ by different psychiatrists in different countries. The lowest correlation so far reported between the GHQ and a standardized psychiatric assessment was by the author in 1974 in Philadelphia, USA: nevertheless this was +.7. Other studies have shown correlations between +.76 and +.88 between GHQ scores and standardized psychiatric assessments using either the Present State Examination or Clinical Interview Schedule. This research is summarized on page 17 of the *Manual of the General Health Questionnaire* (Goldberg 1978). Another way of studying the same problem is to examine the probability of being a case for respondents with ascending GHQ scores: this is to be found on page 92 of *The Detection of Psychiatric Illness by Questionnaire* (Goldberg 1972). This shows a sigmoid curve relating GHQ scores with the probability of being a case, with a sharply ascending probability between 11 and 12 on the GHQ-60. Respondents in the score range 6 to 11, the probability of being a case was +.11; while between 12 and 17, the probability of being found a case was .84.

4. The various ways of measuring agreement from a 2 by 2 contingency table are discussed in a paper by Maxwell (1978). In this paper, Maxwell disapproves of the Kappa coefficient since he questions the procedure whereby a chance agreement is estimated by multiplying the marginals. In its place, he proposes a measure of agreement called 'random error' agreement index, calculated by subtracting the sum of the disagreements from the sum of the agreements. There are certain disadvantages in using the random error agreement index in the present context, since a doctor who does not discriminate in his judgement between high scorers and low scorers (that is to say he judges the same proportion of each to be 'cases') will be rewarded with a random error index of greater than zero providing that his estimate of prevalence is reasonable. This does not happen with Cohen's Kappa and for this reason it is preferred in the present context.

5. Locke's A-B form is a two-sided form in which the front (side A) must be completed for every patient seen on a survey by the receptionist or technician working with the primary care physician, while the obverse (side B) is completed by the primary care physician only for those patients in whom he considers there is a significant psychiatric disturbance. It is necessary for him to answer a number of detailed questions about this disturbance, and in our experience it takes him at least ten minutes to complete the form. The primary care physicians in the West Philadelphia Survey used Locke's A-B form as their method of case identification, and reported very much lower rates than primary care physicians who were members of the Psychopharmacology Research Group in Philadelphia, and who were given a simple six-point scale to report their view concerning the degree of psychiatric disturbance in each patient. (Goldberg, Rickels, Downing, and Hesbacher 1974). Since the GHQ predicted the same probable prevalence in West Philadelphia as in the latter survey, the much lower rates reported by the West Philadelphia physicians are probably an artefact of the 'A-B' form.

6. The thirty-two participating doctors were divided in the following way: eight black physicians, twenty-four white physicians, seventeen MDs (five internists, twelve general practitioners) and fifteen osteopathic physicians (DOs); there were 4,086 patients of whom 66 per cent were female, 80 per cent were black; of the various racial combinations possible there were not enough white patients seeing black doctors (n = 12) to permit data analysis, but there were large numbers of the other three possible combinations.

7. The main variables in the Manchester study were Spearman's rho as a measure of accuracy; identification index as defined earlier in this chapter; conspicuous psychiatric morbidity (this is largely a measure of bias); and probable prevalence as predicted from the GHQ (see note 1). The investigators calculated correlation coefficients between each of the four main variables and the other measures being studied. When this had been done, thirty variables were found which had correlations significant beyond the 0.05 level with one or more of the main variables. These thirty variables were taken together with the four main variables and a principal axes analysis was carried out using the SPSS programme (Nie *et al.* 1975) for the sixty-five doctors on the resulting thirty-four variables. These thirty variables consisted of two demographic characteristics of the doctor: the number of years he had worked in that practice; and whether or

not he had higher qualifications. There then followed eight variables which related to the way in which he interviewed his patients, and were based upon counts of the following behaviours over all interviews observed: the number of greetings; open questions; closed questions relating to physical symptoms; directive questions relating to psychiatric adjustment; closed questions relating to psychiatric adjustment; 'contentless' statements in the sense that they would not assist the interview to reach a satisfactory conclusion regarding diagnosis or management; asking about the patient's family; and asking about the patient's home. Eight further ratings were global ratings made at the end of a period of observation on a particular doctor. They were: his interest in psychiatry; his use of hypnotics; his use of jargon; his authoritarian style as an interviewer; empathy as defined by Truax and Carkhuff; extent to which he buried himself in the notes while the patient was talking or buried himself in the notes while talking to the patient; and his estimate of the number of patients he saw each week. Seven further variables were proportions of all interviews observed in which the following occurred: indifferent physical examination was carried out; the patients were further investigated; patients were given prescriptions; the observing psychiatrist rated the patient as entirely normal; the observing psychiatrist rated the patient as 'entirely psychiatrically ill'. Finally, five variables relating to the personality and attitudes of the doctor: conservatism as measured by the Wilson-Patterson Social Attitude Inventory (WPSAI); extroversion, neuroticism, and lie score from the Eysenck Personality Inventory; and attitude towards the role of psychogenic factors in physical illness, this being the scale devised by Shepherd *et al.* (1966) and called by them the 'Psychosomatic Score'.

Eleven significant factors were found to account for 75 per cent of the total variance. Most of the variance of Spearman's rho was on the first seven factors, which together accounted for 59.3 per cent of the variance. This solution was then subjected to Varimax orthogonal rotation, and the resultant factor structure was carefully examined. The investigators then added additional variables in an attempt to increase the amount of variance of Spearman's rho which could be accounted for. 'No physical examination' was chosen because, although it just fell short of a significant correlation with Spearman's rho, it was an important variable which would relate to the quality of the doctors. Two other variables – the doctor's age, and the mean time spent per patient – were included because of their theoretical importance. The unrotated and Varimax solutions to the analysis were calculated after each variable was added. Addition of the extra-variables increased the amount of variance of the main variables account for (Spearman's rho from 58 per cent to 67 per cent; conspicuous psychiatric morbidity from 52.5 per cent to 53 per cent) and did not significantly alter the main factor structure. The investigators found that the 7-factor solution using thirty-seven variables accounted for 58.2 per cent of the total variance, and seemed to be the best solution in terms of the amount of variance of the four main variables that were accounted for (See *Table 4(7)*).

8. The accuracy of a resident's conception of psychiatric illness in the primary care setting was measured by a specially constructed scale. The residents were presented with a list of thirty-two symptoms or problems, and asked to make a mark against all of those symptoms of psychiatric illness. The thirty-two symptoms or problems consisted of four sets of eight: the first set consisted of

eight symptoms of minor psychiatric disorder which had been shown to be common in a primary care setting during validation studies for the General Health Questionnaire. These were feeling of hopelessness; crying spells; inability to concentrate; losing sleep over worry; feeling constantly under strain; feeling depressed; feeling worthless; and feeling that life is not worth living. The second set of symptoms undoubtedly indicated psychiatric illness although they are all symptoms which are rare in a primary care setting. The consisted of: hearing one's thoughts spoken aloud; a short-term memory disorder; seeing visions; feeling oneself to be a famous person, e.g. Napoleon; hearing mocking laughter; feeling that ones thoughts are being controlled; feeling that one's body gives off a bad smell; and feeling systematically plotted against. The third list consisted of common physical symptoms which, although they may be associated with emotional disorder are not themselves necessarily indicative of it. They consisted of: eczema or dermatitis; unilateral headache; pins and needles in hands and feet; low back pain; tinnitus; vertigo; unsteady gait; hay fever. The fourth list consisted of a set of social problems which were similar to the previous set in that they may be associated with emotional disorder but are not necessarily indicative of it. They were: losing one's job; concern about a child's schooling; having an argument with one's spouse; having nowhere to live; being in debt; failing an examination; having a sick child; and getting divorced. The four lists were arranged in random order and presented to respondents with instructions to check as few or as many as they liked. The idea behind the design of the scale was that the sixteen symptoms in the first two lists are indeed symptoms of psychiatric disorder, while the sixteen symptoms in the last two lists are not. Having completed his or her list, a respondent was asked to re-examine the items they had checked and to draw a circle around those checked items which occur most frequently in a primary care setting. The investigators experimented with a number of scores which could be derived from the responses to these four scales and found that the index which produced the best results against the four dependent variables in the main study was that which measured 'too psychotic a concept' of psychiatric illness. This index was computed by taking as a numerator a number of neurotic symptom items ringed; and as a denominator eight plus the number of psychotic items ticked. Such an index would have a maximum value of 1, if the residents' construct was appropriate, but would have a low index to the extent to which he was unaware of common neurotic symptoms but included psychotic symptoms as part of his concept of illness. The investigators also examined a measure which they called 'too vague a concept': this was an attempt to produce a number which reflected the extent to which the residents distinguished between psychological symptoms on the one hand and social problems and physical symptoms on the other. The sum of social problems and physical symptoms checked was subtracted from the sum of psychotic and neurotic symptoms checked to obtain a number which varied between -16 and $+16$. A high value would reflect to relatively precise concept of psychiatric illness. It is of interest that this measure had to be discarded since it did not correlate with either accuracy or bias on the part of the residents studied. It was found that many residents with relatively accurate powers of rating their patients' degree of psychological degree of maladjustment nevertheless rated many social problems as being indicative of psychiatric illness. As a matter of interest the scale was then administered to faculty members of the Department of Psychiatry and Behavioural Sciences at the Medical University of South Carolina. It was found that many of the psychiatrists on the Faculty were similar to the residents in that they made no distinction between life problems and symptoms while the clinical psychologists as a group tended to have a relatively accurate concept of psychiatric disorder. Whether this was because they are more wary in taking psychological tests, or whether they are more thoughtful as in the matter of distinguishing between illness on the one hand and life problems on the other, is a task best left to future investigators.

9. The Charleston study involved the investigators in giving remedial training sessions to those residents who were found to have low values for Cohen's Kappa and Spearman's rho. The chief investigator (DG) kept detailed notes about these training sessions and recorded at the time that seven of the twelve residents had problems relating to their professional self-image. The following is an example of remarks made by a resident during a teaching session which were thought to relate to such difficulties: 'I have a feeling of frustration with the clinic here – as a matter of fact, I am thinking of leaving family medicine. I feel I do not achieve anything for the patients. I am haunted by thoughts of my crocks: I have a fantasy that one day all my worst ones will come in on the same day and say that they are better.' These problems were dealt with in the supervision sessions. This particular resident said at the completion of his fourth session: 'I feel better about coming to the clinics now. I no longer feel responsible for all diagnoses that the patients have. I just relate to each individual patient, and assess their psychological adjustment. It is a whole lot better for me.' The personality measures mentioned were all collected by the Department of Behavioural Science as a separate exercise before the investigation began and the results were only made known by the investigators at the conclusion of the study.

10. The results reported are those for the Symptom Checklist, a thirty-six item version of the scale now known as the SCL 90. In the same study, a rather smaller subset of patients (569 whites, 339 blacks) completed the General Health Questionnaire. This screening questionnaire showed a tendency for blacks to have slightly higher scores than whites remained significant even after an analysis of variance had been carried out to correct differences between the samples for social class (f = 5.67 on 1; 905 df: p < 0.05).

CHAPTER 5

Level 3: conspicuous psychiatric morbidity in primary care settings

Level 3 refers to psychiatric disorder as it is perceived by primary care physicians: what Kessel (1960) describes as 'conspicuous psychiatric morbidity'. It follows from the previous chapter that the widely varying estimates that have been made of the extent of this morbidity are partly due to differing modes of case identification, and partly due to differences in professional style among the physicians responsible for carrying out the various surveys. Those surveys that require the collaborating physician to fill up a lengthy form in order to indicate that a patient is psychiatrically ill will tend to under-report morbidity but will rarely falsely identify patients as psychiatrically ill (eg Schein 1977); while those that require the physician to make the same amount of effort whether or not he considers that the patient is sick will result in higher rates, but will tend to be less accurate in that errors of each kind will occur (asymptomatic 'cases' *and* symptomatic 'normals').[1]

The importance of such surveys is not that they tell us what we need to know about the distribution of psychiatric morbidity in this setting but that they tell us about morbidity as it appears to those responsible for delivering medical services to a community. The data from such surveys therefore can be used to plan services, as well as to measure relationships between variables within a particular survey.

Hankin and Oktay (1979) have provided an extensive review of the literature concerning psychiatric disorders in primary care settings, and have tabulated the results of seventy different surveys that have been carried out since the early 1960s, mainly in England and the USA. The differences which they report between surveys can plausibly be related to the differences between researchers, in methodology, and in deciding what is to be regarded as a case.

The task of sifting through the conflicting results of the various surveys is considerably simplified if one confines oneself to those studies that express their results per 1,000 population at risk, rather than as a percentage of consecutive attenders. Even with this type of survey, much of the variation may be due to the stigma associated with the classification of a respondent as 'psychiatric' in a particular cultural setting. For example, Glasser and Duggan's (1969) finding that 6.4 per 1,000 per year of members covered by Blue Cross/Blue Shield had 'psychiatric' consultations must be contrasted with Shepherd *et al.*'s (1966) finding that 140 per 1,000 of Londoners are classified by their family doctor as having a 'formal psychiatric' or 'psychiatric-associated' condition, especially in view of the fact that minor morbidity as assessed by the GHQ seems very similar in the two countries (see Chapter 4). Indeed, Shepherd's results are comparable to those obtained more recently by Hankin and Shapiro (1979) in their analysis of data from the Columbia Medical Plan at Baltimore. The latter is a private, prepaid group practice which caters for a predominantly middle-class suburban population and it is therefore unsafe to generalize from it to the wider scene. The advantage of such prepaid schemes is that they provide the aspiring researcher with a denominator, so that for this scheme one can say that 230 per 1,000 per three years seek some form of psychiatric therapy.

Regier and his colleagues (1977) reviewed rates for psychiatric illness in four comprehensive health schemes in the United States which were able to express results in terms of an enrolled population at risk: two of these are 'Health Maintenance Organisations', another is a 'Neighbourhood Health Center' while the fourth is a fee-for-service Group Practice. The rates varied from twenty-seven to 125 per 1,000 per year, and led the researchers to speculate on the possible reasons for some settings reporting rates which were so much lower than those predicted by community surveys in the general population. Perhaps these particular populations really have lower rates than those predicted by the community surveys; or, in terms of the present model, perhaps the patients did not pass the first or the second filter. The scheme with the lowest rate (twenty-seven) was the Marshfield Clinic in Wisconsin, and we saw in the previous chapter from the work of Hoeper, Nycz, and Cleary (1979) that this low rate is largely accounted for by patients failing to pass the second filter.

Interesting confirmation for this viewpoint comes from the work of Goldberg, Babigian, Locke, and Rosen (1978) who have looked to see whether patients known to the Monroe County Psychiatric Case Register are identified as 'psychiatric' by non-psychiatric physicians. The doctors were asked to indicate if each patient they saw 'had a current or past emotional problem', and it was found that private office physicians identified 48 per cent, industrial dispensaries 51 per cent, and general medical clinics 63 per cent of the cases known to the Register.

Despite the differences between surveys produced by varying methods of case identification and different permeabilities of the second filter, if one examines relationships within the various surveys some findings are remarkably consistent over time and between countries. For example, the higher female rates, the increased prevalence in the middle years, and the types of complaint in a primary case survey carried out in seventeenth-century England were very similar to patterns of morbidity reported in the twentieth century (Shepherd 1980); while primary care surveys in both England and the United States show that the predominant disorders are neuroses and psychophysiological disorders, and that rates are highest among the separated and divorced (see note 1).

SYNDROMES OF DISORDER

The great majority of patients with diagnosable psychiatric disorders seen in primary care settings have minor mood disorders, most typically some combination of depression and anxiety. During the validation study of the General Health Questionnaire in Philadelphia, it was possible to compare diagnosis made by the psychiatrist using a standardized research interview and the classification used by the International Classification of Disease (ICD), with diagnostic assessments made by the primary care physicians using a diagnostic classification prepared by the Psychopharmacology Research Unit of the University of Pennsylvania. The latter classification was broadly comparable to the ICD, but it did allow the diagnosis 'mixed anxiety/depression', which is not in the ICD.

The psychiatrist made ninety-seven diagnoses among the 247 patients receiving a full assessment interview, while the five primary care physicians made 262 psychiatric diagnoses among the 1,310 patients completing the General Health Questionnaire. (It was shown afterwards that there had been a tendency to refer selectively those with high scores on the screening questionnaire to the psychiatrist – but at the time neither psychiatrist nor primary care physician were aware of the GHQ scores.)

It can be seen from *Table 5(1)* that the primary care physicians diagnosed 95 per cent of the patients as minor mood disorders or phobias, while the psychiatrist tended to use a wider range of diagnostic categories. Agreement is fairly good for schizophrenia and minor mood disorders, but it was disturbing to find that the primary care physicians never used the categories 'organic mental state' or 'manic depressive illness'. During the period spent observing residents at Charleston (described in Chapter 4), one of us (DG) observed two patients with hypomania, neither of whom were so diagnosed by the resident who had interviewed them.

Table 5(1) *Comparison between psychiatrist's diagnoses and general practitioners' diagnoses among primary care attenders in Philadelphia*

psychiatric diagnoses	*Level 2* *n = 97 psychiatrist's* *diagnoses among 247 attenders*		*Level 3* *n = 262 GP's diagnoses* *among 1310 attenders*	
organic states	3.1%		–	
psychoses – schizophrenia	1.0%		0.8%	
– affective	2.1%		–	
neuroses – depression	36.1%		25.0%	
– depression/anxiety	–	78.4%	31.0%	87.0%
– anxiety	40.2%		31.0%	
– phobias	2.1%		8.0%	
– hypochondriasis	1.0%		–	
miscellaneous	14.4%		4.2%	

There is good reason to believe that there is an association between psychiatric and physical morbidity in a primary care setting. The association was conclusively demonstrated in a general morbidity survey by Shepherd and his colleagues (1966) and the evidence has been well reviewed by Eastwood (1975). Eastwood and Trevelyan (1971) carried out a survey in which psychiatrically ill patients seen on a health screening survey were matched with psychiatrically healthy controls. The members of the ill group were shown to have a significant excess of major physical disease detected by the physical multiphasic screening programme.

Hankin and Shapiro (1978) have recently shown that younger patients who have used psychiatric services at the Columbia Medical Plan have a higher utilization rate for non-psychiatric illnesses than those who have never used psychiatric services. They observe that while authors such as Mechanic and Balint have supposed that patients suffering from psychological symptoms feel uncomfortable presenting these complaints to a physician and instead present a variety of minor physical complaints, an alternative explanation of the observed 'illness behaviour' of utilisers of psychiatric care is that psychiatric symptoms increase the vulnerability to acute physical illnesses and may lower the patient's ability to cope with minor physical illnesses.

This idea is not new. As Eastwood and Trevelyan (1972) observe, the idea that individuals have a generalized psychophysical propensity to disease appears to be a valuable alternative model to that which seeks only a specific single cause-and-effect relationship. Murphy and Brown (1980) have recently explored this notion further, by investigating the relationship between stressful life events and new episodes of physical illness in a random sample of London women. The results of their study suggest that there is indeed an increased likelihood of stressful life events before such episodes, and that the mediating variable appears to be the experience of symptoms of depression and anxiety.

TREATMENT OF PSYCHIATRIC DISORDERS IN PRIMARY CARE SETTINGS

Shepherd and his colleagues (1966) write that 'treatment of minor psychiatric disorders in general practice is often haphazard and inadequate. This state of affairs seemed in many cases to be as unsatisfactory to the doctors concerned as to their patients'. There was a gap between theory and practice. When the general practitioners in the survey were asked to say how they would treat a series of imaginary patients presented to them in a series of brief vignettes, psychotherapy by the GP himself was frequently chosen as the correct management (p.66). However, when the records of their identified psychiatric patients were examined, the three commonest treatments were 'no treatment recorded'; sedatives; and reassurance. Psychotherapy by the GP was recorded in only 1 per cent of the cases (p.153). Type of treatment offered was related to the age and sex of the patient. Thus women were more likely to be given sedatives, tranquillisers, or antidepressants, while men were more likely to be given nothing. The use of tablets of all sorts increased with increasing age of the patient, while advice, reassurance, psychotherapy by GP, or psychiatric referral all became less likely with increasing age. In the United States Rosen and her colleagues (1972) report that in general medical clinics patients identified as psychiatric receive supportive help in 84 per cent of cases, drugs in 60 per cent, and environmental modifications in only 19 per cent; broadly similar figures are reported in three other American surveys.[2]

Although psychological help, drug therapy, and environmental modification represent the three principal modes of treatment open to a primary care physician, it is worth recalling the views of the WHO on this topic:

> 'Transcending in importance these three broad methods of treatment there are certain general needs, such as a tolerant attitude, dependability, continuity, and interest that allows a doctor to take even minor disorders seriously and give attention to the needs of close relatives of the patient.'(WHO 1961)

This description comes very close to a description of 'simple psychotherapy' put forward by a Working Party of the College of General Practitioners under the chairmanship of Watts (1958):

> 'This includes the ability to listen with understanding and consideration to the patient's difficulties, and to dispense sympathetic explanations, reassurance, advice and support in the setting of an intimate doctor-patient relationship. The report admits that this ideal may be hard to realise in large urban practices, but nevertheless insists that "the better the doctor the nearer he approaches it."'

If the doctor-patient encounter is examined from the patient's point of view, results are not as clear as these surveys might lead one to believe.

In their research among depressed women found during a community survey in the London borough of Camberwell, Brown and Ginsberg (1979) report that the majority of such patients attend their doctors hoping that they will have an opportunity to discuss their problems with him. What they typically get is a short interview and a prescription for a psychotropic drug. In Ginsberg's words: 'Women go to the doctor with the hope that they might gain help but usually with low expectations that the kind of help they will receive – that is, a prescription for a psychotropic drug – will be effective.'

Johnson (1973) interviewed seventy-three patients who had recently attended their family doctor with a new episode of psychiatric illness, and compared information derived from the doctors' records with that obtained from the patients themselves by psychiatric interview at home. Only two patients were specifically offered psychotherapy, and neither of these returned to see their doctor. Despite the fact that the patients generally held their doctors in high regard, only 15 per cent of the patients acknowledged any personal help or support in their illness, while a further 12 per cent thought their doctors attitudes had been unhelpful. Despite the fact that stress factors had a highly significant correlation with observed outcome in the patients' clinical condition, no doctor had attempted to modify the precipitating factors in any way, nor had social agencies been involved in the treatment of any of the patients.

The situation was little better where antidepressant medication was concerned: only 72 per cent had been prescribed antidepressants in what are usually regarded as therapeutic dosages, and of these 59 per cent had defaulted within twenty-one days – almost always without the doctor's knowledge. Other surveys have also shown high defaulting rates in primary care settings.[3]

In a further study with a larger sample, Johnson (1974) concluded that even among good family doctors in the Manchester area, knowledge and interest in psychiatry was strictly limited, and that psychotropic drugs were often inappropriately prescribed, or prescribed in inadequate dosage. Another worrying feature was the high proportion of patients on medication for more than three months who were given repeat prescriptions without seeing their doctor.

In a survey carried out for the Medical Research Council, Rawnsley and Loudon (1962) came to broadly similar conclusions with a sample of Welsh country doctors:

'The majority say that they find their psychiatric work irksome by comparison with other aspects of practice, mainly because of the considerable time demanded by psychiatric problems and because of the uncertain and comparatively poor response to their efforts. They are, in the main, apprehensive of any potential increase in the number of chronic psychiatric cases under their care in the community. Drugs form the mainstay of therapy, together with advice and reassurance. Exploratory psychotherapy is rare as a method of treatment; this is not only due to lack of time, but also to serious doubts on the part of the doctors as to the value of such treatment at their hands.'

SOCIAL FACTORS AT LEVEL 3

A limited number of investigations have been made into the social circumstances of identified psychiatric patients in primary care. There are some studies of social work in this context which report the rates of particular social problems in those clients who were referred to the practice social worker. Not only does the referral process select cases who may not be psychiatric patients, but the type of social problem referred is very much dependent upon the setting of the practice and upon the nature of the relationship between the doctors and social workers.

Hesbacher, Rickels, and Goldberg (1975) collected data on 1,310 mainly neurotic patients from seven family practices in Philadelphia and related sex, race, and social class to patient scores on a symptom checklist. Social class was rated on the Hollingshead Two Factor Index. Each variable was related to the patient's symptom scores while controlling for the effects on the others, in order to determine the relative importance of each association with neurotic illness.

Social class was related to symptomatology for males (p<.05) and females (p<.001). In each case, higher class patients (I-III) were less symptomatic than the lower class patients (IV and V). Females presented more extensive symptomatology than males, and this relationship was independent of class and of race. Lower social class patients were 'sicker' than upper-class patients and this relationship was independent of sex and race. The more extensive symptomatology presented by blacks was found to be masking a relationship with social class, since this association with race disappeared when class was controlled.

A comparison of the frequency of life events in new cases of neurotic illness identified in general practice (Cooper and Sylph 1973) has shown that, when compared to a matched control group of consulting patients, the neurotic patients experienced significantly more life events during the three months before the onset of illness. Events particularly associated with neurotic illness were unexpected crises and failure to achieve various life goals. Cooper and his colleagues have also demonstrated differences in the social circumstances of chronic neurotic patients and matched controls. They matched eighty-one chronic patients with controls and conducted semistructured clinical and social interviews with both groups. The social instrument which was used covers material circumstances, including amongst other variables housing and income, social management or functioning, and satisfaction with social circumstances.

The two groups of patients differed significantly on all the social functioning and satisfaction items, the chronic patients functioning less well and being more dissatisfied. Two items on the material circumstances scale produced significant differences, housing, and income; the chronic patients having poorer housing conditions and lower income.

The overall clinical score in this study was not highly correlated with material circumstances, but was with social management ($r = +0.37$) and satisfaction ($r = +0.32$).

The overall score on this social schedule has also shown to be associated with clinical scores (Sylph *et al.* 1969). In a study of an experimental social work service in primary care, Cooper *et al.* (1975) report that changes in the clinical score and overall social score over a one-year period were correlated ($r = +0.36$). There was a general tendency for improvements in social functioning to be accompanied by reductions in psychiatric symptoms over the one-year period. Furthermore, the changes which took place on each of the three dimensions of the social interview were interrelated, and patients who showed the greatest improvement in ratings of material conditions tended to improve most on the social management and role satisfaction ratings. The direction of these relationships is not specified, and it is possible that improved functioning and satisfaction improved the material circumstances of the patients; but it is probably more likely that material changes had more impact and resulted in changes in the other two variables.

Some support for the view that the material circumstances have important consequences for neurotic patients comes from another follow-up study of patients originally observed in the Shepherd *et al.* (1966) enquiry. Kedward (1969) reports upon a three year follow-up study of patients, and comments that:

> 'the patients who got better had, in the main, presented to their doctor at times of social crisis. They were worried about work, about money, housing, or children ... Their recovery took place after the crisis had been resolved (and rehousing particularly often proceded recovery) even in longstanding cases.'

Kedward observed that social problems were apparent in those patients who had failed to recover after three years. Chronic housing problems, bereavement, and chronic illnesses which contributed to financial stringency were characteristics of a large number of cases: 'the reality of their situations had in most cases not changed during the follow-up period.'

THE USE OF THE SOCIAL INTERVIEW SCHEDULE

In the studies reviewed above the most widely used social measure instrument is the SIS (see note 7, Chapter 2). This has been used on at least three different GP samples and on at least two out-patient samples. Clare and Cairns (1978) provide data from a reliability study of the SIS in general practice which was conducted upon patients referred to the study by GPs who had identified that the patient suffered from adverse social circumstances. The two other samples from which they report data are of chronic neurotics and of women who attend their GP with premenstrual complaints. In their comparison of those with high scores on selected SIS items in the three enquiries, they show that both the chronic neurotics and social problem samples score more frequently on all items. Among the interesting features of the comparison is the fact that the neurotics tend to be a little more dissatisfied with their circumstances than those with social problems. For example, 6 per cent of those with premenstrual complaints were dissatisfied with their marital harmony compared with 13 per cent in the social problem group and 54.7 per cent of chronic neurotics. If one examines the six highest percentage items for each group one finds that in the chronic neurotic group most are satisfaction and social management items whereas in the premenstrual and social problem groups objective or marital circumstances, in the form of situational handicaps to child management and opportunities for leisure activities, figure prominently.

Cooper (1972) reported mean scores in the SIS subcategories for a sample of chronic neurotic patients in general practice. The mean score for both men and women were equally high on the material circumstances and satisfaction scores, a finding which has been repeated in one of our out-patient samples (see Huxley 1973). The mean scores in our out-patient sample were very close to those reported by Cooper as significantly different from normal controls. The material circumstances total from the SIS was a predictor of outcome in two enquiries in the out-patient setting, while the other two subtotals of management and satisfaction were not (Huxley 1973, 1978). The out-patient samples were of newly referred cases and only a small proportion of these turned out to be chronic cases, i.e. still unwell at the end of twelve months. In acute cases the material stresses and the illness may remit over time, whereas in some chronic cases social factors, especially marital factors, interact with the disorder, so that both persist indefinitely.

This would explain the lack of correlation between the overall clinical score and material circumstances found by Cooper *et al.* (1972) and the correlation between clinical score and social management and satisfaction in their chronic neurotic sample.

The higher material scores in the general practice sample studied by Clare and Cairns presented a pattern of social difficulty very similar to that seen in the out-patient sample. It was the case that a large proportion of the catchment area of the hospital from which both of the out-patient samples were taken was a social problem area with a substantial amount of deprivation. This may have been reflected in the sample of patients referred to the hospital, although the social class distribution of the sample did not contain a preponderance of patients in the lower classes (44 per cent were in social classes IV and V).

THE OUTCOME OF PSYCHIATRIC DISORDERS SEEN IN PRIMARY CARE SETTINGS

Harvey-Smith and Cooper (1970) report on a comparison between the observed outcome of a cohort of 170 patients identified as 'psychiatric' three years previously by fifteen of the doctors participating in Shepherd's original survey, and a matched group of 170 patients who had attended for other reasons over the same time period. At follow-up three years later, it is of interest that the family doctors now identified 18 per cent of the control group as suffering from chronic neurotic illness. This led the investigators to study the relationships between those with acute and chronic psychiatric illnesses on the one hand, and the healthy population on the other. On the basis of their results it appears that, for a standard population of 10,000, over the course of one year there will be 500-600 new or recent onset cases and about 1,600 chronic cases. The recent onset cases have a turnover of about 70 per cent per year, while the chronic cases have a turnover of only 3 per cent per year. The investigators concluded that 'the psychiatric prevalence rate in a general population is accounted for by a large, slowly-changing group of patients with chronic disorders, and a small, rapidly-changing group of patients with new and recent onset disorders'.

An earlier paper from the same research unit reported broadly similar results: Kedward and Cooper (1966) had shown that only 18.7 per cent of chronic cases were 'recovered or much improved' after three years, as opposed to 60.4 per cent of the new or recent onset cases: this effect was seen for both young and old, and outlook was especially poor for old, chronic patients. The investigators compared their results with the reported outcomes for neurotic patients treated by psychiatrists, and concluded that the outcome for patients seen in the community was no more favourable.

Since the probability of being identified as a psychiatric case increases the more often the doctor has seen a particular patient,[4] it is likely that there will be rather more agreement about the patients with chronic disorders than those with acute disorders. It seems likely that the substantial number of patients with 'hidden psychiatric morbidity' (patients with psychiatric illness not detected by their doctors, see Chapter 4) consist largely of patients with transient illnesses.

Goldberg and Blackwell (1970) compared the outcome of patients with hidden and conspicuous psychiatric morbidity six months after initial consultation, and found that two-thirds of each group were now functioning well. Johnstone and Goldberg (1976) identified patients with hidden psychiatric illness – they had high scores on the GHQ yet had been rated as not psychiatrically disturbed by their family doctor – and randomly assigned to an index condition in which the family doctor was allowed to see the screening questionnaire, and a control condition in which he was not. There was a striking tendency for the index (detected) group to do better than the control group three months after initial consultation (66 per cent recovered versus 42 per cent), but the differences between the groups became progressively less until at one year they were no longer significant. This is because of the tendency of the control group to recover slowly with the passage of time; there is no further improvement in the index group between three and twelve months after detection. Nevertheless, over the whole year the index group experienced significantly fewer illness-months than the control groups.

The tendency for the control group to improve without assistance from their family doctor was especiallly marked for those with fewer than twenty symptoms on the GHQ; when only those with *more* than twenty symptoms were considered, there were still significant differences between index and control groups present at one-year follow-up. Patients in the index (detected) group increased their consultations for emotional complaints over the ensuing year, but they did this at the expense of consultations for physical symptoms, so that their total consultation rate was not increased. Thus while the patients had learned a new pattern of illness behaviour, it might be a more appropriate one.[5]

It would appear that patients often visit their family doctors during times when they are under stress and therefore experiencing non-specific physical symptoms and minor affective symptoms. Such states of dysfunction can be cut short by timely medical intervention which should include the exclusion of organic pathology and a recognition of the patient's state of emotional distress. A study by Thomas (1974) illustrates the transient nature of most of these disorders. This family doctor analysed 3,848 consecutive consultations and found that 29 per cent were for 'services' – innoculations, cervical smears, birth control, etc. – and a further 41 per cent were those for whom he could make a firm organic or psychiatric diagnosis. The remaining 31 per cent were described as 'undiagnosed', and were presenting with a variety of minor physical or emotional symptoms. All these patients were given time to describe their symptoms, physically examined and reassured that they had no serious illness and that soon all would be well, were asked to come back in a week if they felt no better, and were often given an inactive placebo, but were never given any pharmacologically active agent.

Seventy-two per cent did not re-attend, and were declared 'successfully untreated': when these were systematically followed up 82 per cent reported that they had got better, and a further 11 per cent had not sought further treatment despite not getting better. The 'successfully untreated' group were shown not to be different from the 'diagnosed' group in terms of neuroticism, extraversion, intelligence, or demographic factors. The author speculates that 'in response to the ordinary ups and downs of life (these patients) had gone through a state of temporary dependence' on their doctor.

This is true as far as it goes, but there are two other factors which are probably important. When an individual who believes himself to be sick seeks advice from a doctor whom he trusts, then reassurance from that doctor, following proper history taking and physical examination, is a therapeutic factor of the first importance. Secondly, a substantial proportion of Thomas's 'undiagnosed' group did not get better, despite the 'temporary dependence' that was allowed. Presumably some of these later developed 'diagnosable' illnesses: but it seems likely that this group contained many examples of 'hidden psychiatric morbidity', where detection might have favourably influenced outcome.

NOTES

1. The best data for diagnoses made by British General Practitioners is undoubtedly that of Shepherd and his colleagues (1966). The overall annual period

prevalence of 14 per cent was made up of neuroses, 8.9 per cent; psychosomatic and psychosocial problems, 4.9 per cent; psychoses 0.6 per cent; and personality disorders 0.6 per cent. Female rates were very much higher than male rates for neuroses and psychoses. American data reported by Rosen *et al.* (1970; 1972) and Locke *et al.* (1967) report fairly similar data for diagnoses, but they cannot be converted to prevalence rates because of the condition of medical practice in the USA. The finding that rates were higher among the separated and divorced was made by Locke, Krantz, and Kramer (1966) as well as Shepherd and his colleagues; it has been confirmed subsequently by Rosen *et al.* (1970) and Marks, Goldberg, and Hillier (1979).

2. The three American surveys reporting similar data are: Rosen *et al.* (1970), Locke *et al.* (1967), and Leopold, Goldberg, and Schein (1971).

3. Gardiner, Petersen, and Hall (1974) interviewed over 600 referrals to the Ross Clinic, Aberdeen, and found that 45 per cent of the patients had seriously defaulted from the psychotropic drug regime prescribed by their family doctors. Johnson (1974) surveyed 361 patients treated for depression in primary care settings, and found that 65 per cent of them had ceased to take their medication regularly. The three principals reasons for default were: (a) side effects of the drug – which did not appear to have any simple relationship to dosage taken; (b) the patients' attitude to the use of the drugs: here the patients fell into two groups, the first who experienced guilt through relying on drugs, and the second who had the genuine fear of future dependence on medication; and (c) a lack of communication between doctor and patient, so that the patient was unaware of the correct dosage or the need for continuing medication.

4. The evidence for this is briefly discussed in Chapter 4, and is to be found at greater length in Marks, Goldberg, and Hillier (1979).

5. These results are discussed in more detail in Dr Johnstone's MD thesis, *Prescriptive Screening in General Practice*. (Unpublished MD thesis, Victoria University of Manchester.)

CHAPTER 6

The third filter: referral to psychiatric services

The third filter stands between primary care and specialist care, and is the least permeable of the filters separating psychiatrists from the populations that they serve. Filters which hold back many cases are of great potential interest to the epidemiologist, since they have a larger capacity to distort the characteristics of those allowed to pass than those filters which are relatively permeable. The third filter is similar to the second filter in that the general practitioner has a major role to play in deciding who to allow through, although we will show that once more, certain characteristics of the patient will influence him or her in making the decision to refer. A third variable which now makes its appearance is related to the psychiatric services available to a particular community: it can be shown that referral rates are influenced by the numbers of psychiatrists available and the pattern of organization of psychiatric services.

THE GENERAL PRACTITIONER

The London family doctors surveyed by Shepherd et al. (1966) referred only 5.1 per cent of the patients they diagnosed as 'psychiatric' to the psychiatric services; they were less likely to refer acute cases than chronic cases, 3.5 per cent of the acute against 7.5 per cent of the chronic being referred. Put another way, 14 per cent of the population at risk were diagnosed 'psychiatric'; yet only 0.71 per cent were referred. These figures are closely comparable to those reported by Locke, Krantz, and Kramer (1966) for the Washington Group Health Association, where 15 per cent were diagnosed as 'psychiatric' yet only 1 per cent were referred to a psychiatrist.

Those American surveys which have reported lower rates for psychiatric illness at level 3 usually report that a greater proportion were referred for specialist care. Thus Fink and his colleagues (1967) report that 5 per cent of those registered with the Jamaica Medical Group in New York were diagnosed 'psychiatric', and of these 26 per cent were referred: this gives a referral rate of 1.3 per cent to the psychiatric services, which is comparable to the other surveys. In Schein's (1976) West Philadelphia study, only 14 per cent of those identified as 'psychiatric' were referred to the mental health services, which was 1.8 per cent of all patients seen.

Several surveys report that older family doctors refer more patients to psychiatrists than their younger colleagues, and a recent study in Scotland reports that single handed city practices had higher referral rates than group practices.[1] Within a particular survey, there is some tendency for doctors with high rates for conspicuous psychiatric morbidity to have higher referral rates: thus Shepherd reports a correlation of +.38 between these variables. It is of interest that the mean annual referral rates for family doctors in the City of Aberdeen who consider that they use psychotherapy in their management of psychiatric illness is significantly lower than that for colleagues who did not (Robertson 1979).

Many surveys have shown that urban family doctors refer more patients than their rural colleagues.[2] This may partly be due to the fact that the journey to the psychiatrist is likely to be shorter and partly because rural doctors have a lower ascertainment rate for neuroses than urban doctors.[3] Ingham, Rawnsley, and Hughes (1972) showed that referral rates were especially low in a depressed coal mining area of Wales compared with those in a relatively prosperous agricultural area. In the former area one in eighteen of male, and one in thirty-six of female cases were referred; while in the latter one in fourteen of male, and one in twenty of female cases were referred.

One unusual study suggests that the generally low referral rates to psychiatrists would not be affected if the primary care physician was given better information about his patients' psychiatric adjustment. Cummings and Follette (1968) administered a psychiatric screening questionnaire to 10,600 consecutive patients attending multiphasic health screening at the Kaiser Foundation Permanent Medical Group and found that 7.7 per cent suffered from 'psychiatric distress'. Fifty per cent of this group were randomly selected and had 'consider referral to psychiatry for emotional problems' printed by the computer together with the results of other tests. Although 205 were referred to psychiatrists, only five patients actually kept their appointments – and the same number saw psychiatrists in the control group. This finding may be peculiar to this particular setting: the physicians were reluctant to open a 'Pandora's Box' by discussing psychological problems.

There have been many studies of the reasons for referral to psychiatric services, which have inevitably reflected the varying orientations and attitudes of the family doctors whose clinical practice has come under scrutiny.[4] The one common thread which runs through them all is that patients are referred when they fail to respond to treatment from the family doctor. Several surveys have also mentioned severity of the symptoms, although the doctors surveyed by Carey and Kogan (1971) properly pointed out that patients whose illness was highly treatable or untreatable should not be referred.

Perhaps the most important paper concerning the family doctor's role as an initiator of referrals to psychiatrists is that by Fink, Shapiro, and Goldensohn (1970), who studied 697 referrals to psychiatrists under the Health Insurance Plan of Greater New York. These were sub-divided into the self-referred (45 per cent of the sample) and those who reported that referral was mostly the doctor's idea (47 per cent of the sample). The researchers show that the self-referral group are typical of those population groups which tend to seek psychiatric care and are high users of medical care: they are better educated, more likely to be Jewish, are more likely to have used psychiatric services previously and to have positive views about it, and are more likely to have received non-psychiatric counselling for previous emotional problems. They are also younger, and are likely to have known their doctor for a shorter time than those who are referred by their doctor.

The doctor-referred group by contrast, are less well educated and tend not to be psychiatrically orientated. They report less serious and less disabling emotional problems and were taught by the investigators to include those who either fail to recognize or deny their emotional problems. The family doctor has an important role in bringing to treatment those for whom appropriate intervention might either be delayed or not occur at all.

The other side of the coin is to ask why so many emotionally disordered patients are *not* referred to psychiatrists. We have already seen that the third filter is the least permeable of the barriers standing between the psychiatrist and his potential patients. Shepherd and his colleagues (1966) have studied the reasons given for non-referral by general practitioners in England, and report that the two main reasons are the GP's view that the patients would dislike referral, and their view that the care of the emotionally ill is the family doctor's job.

CHARACTERISTICS OF THE PATIENT AS DETERMINANTS OF REFERRAL

In Europe, the third filter is more permeable to men than to women, possibly because a psychological illness in the chief wage earner of a family poses an additional economic threat which may be thought to justify prompt specialist referral. However, the same effect is not seen in the United States, where the economic argument is equally cogent.[5] Where age is concerned, all the surveys show the same finding: younger patients are more likely to be referred than older patients.[6] The tendency for younger patients to be referred is in keeping with principles of secondary prevention; older patients are more likely to be treated by their family doctors with drugs.

The evidence concerning marital status is conflicting, since some investigators have not allowed for the very unequal prevalence rates by marital status at level 3. In order to show that a demographic variable has an effect, it is of course necessary to show that there are relatively more respondents with a given attribute among the referred population than there are among those identified as psychiatrically disordered by the family doctors. The study of the 'filter-down' process by Fink and his colleagues (1969) shows a clear interaction between sex and marital status; among men, the single were more likely to be referred and the widowed, divorced, and separated were less likely to be referred; while among women, both groups were somewhat more likely to be referred. (Married patients of either sex were represented in the referred group in exact proportion to their representation at level 3.) Hopkins and Cooper (1969) confirm the tendency for single patients to be referred, but this study suffers from the disadvantage that it is based upon a single practice.

There is a tendency for those referred to be more severely ill than those seen in primary care. Sims and Salmon (1975) showed that severity as measured by the GHQ was greater among those referred than among a matched control group seen in a primary care setting; while Shepherd (1966) showed that the family doctors studied by his group referred 25 per cent of the psychotics known to them, but only 5 per cent of other diagnoses. Helgason (1978) has shown that psychotics are more likely to be known by the psychiatric services, but showed a disturbing tendency for male alcoholics not to be known.[7]

In the study referred to earlier, Fink, Shapiro and Goldensohn (1970) went on to compare the characteristics of patients referred to psychiatrists with those identified by their doctor as psychiatrically ill but not referred.

The latter group was subdivided into a small group of twenty-three patients who wished they had been referred, and a larger group of 196 patients who were neither referred, nor wished they had been. The group that wished they had been referred was similar to the referred group in terms of their high scores on a psychiatric screening test, the importance to the patient of the emotional problem, and the relatively large number of life activities that were affected. The group who had neither wished to nor had been referred, by contrast, had significantly fewer symptoms, experienced them less frequently, and they affected fewer of their life activities. The evidence available therefore supports the view that more severely disturbed patients are more likely to be referred to psychiatrists. Most surveys that have reported duration of illness have shown that the majority of referrals are for established illnesses rather than new, acute episodes.[8]

Hurry, Tennant, and Bebbington (1980) have studied the selective processes leading to psychiatric referral by comparing the social characteristics of depressed women drawn from random community samples and from a random sample of those attending psychiatric out-patients and known to the Camberwell Register. These investigators do not find the excess of working-class women with depression in their random comunity sample that would have been expected from the work of Brown and Harris: indeed their various samples are fairly similar to one another in terms of social class although there is a significant tendency for the out-patients to be better educated than one of their community samples. The tendency for better educated people to seek help for their depression was also noted by Weissman and Myers (1978). Dohrenwend and Dohrenwend (1969) have argued that the apparent over-utilization of medical services by higher classes is because many of the psychological disorders found in community surveys are transitory reactions to environmental stresses, and that the latter are more common among lower-class subjects. In terms of the present model, the tendency for better educated subjects to be over represented at level three could be due to effects at the first, second, or third filters. The data reported by Fink and his colleagues (1969) strongly supports the hypothesis that the effect occurs at the third filter, and shows that educational status has negligible effects at the first two filters. Certainly, our own data suggests that subjects who have stayed longer in full-time education are somewhat less likely to have their illnesses detected by their family doctor (Marks, Goldberg, and Hillier 1979); and so the evidence suggests that the better educated are more likely to be referred by their doctor for psychiatric treatment, probably because they are more likely to request such referral themselves (Fink *et al.* 1970).

Having described what is, we pass on to what ought to be. Kessel (1963) advised family doctors to be guided by two main considerations – *clinical severity* as judged by degree of distress and associated social disability, and *failure to respond to treatment*. We have seen that both these criteria do appear to influence the decisions that are actually made. Murphy (1976) has taken the matter a step further by comparing sixty patients referred to psychiatrists with a matched group of patients treated by family doctors, and following up both groups for one year. As one might have expected, there was a substantial improvement in both groups, with the patients referred for specialist care being only slightly superior to those remaining in primary care. The investigators then examined the patients' replies to the various questionnaires that had been administered at the outset of the research in an attempt to identify a group that improved with specialist care but did not do so without it. It emerged that introverts (as judged by the reply to a single question: 'Avez-vous toujours été une personne ouverte ou renfermée?') who replied to other questions that they were able to voice anger at their frustrations, found life difficult but manageable, and had not taken psychotropics or taken time off work formed a group who did well with specialist care but improved hardly at all without it. With these patients removed, the outcome of the remaining patients was unaffected by referral to a specialist. It would be unwise to generalize from this study since the argument is *post hoc* and the numbers are small: but it is to be hoped that the study will be repeated, and that eventually it may prove possible to describe types of problem which will respond better to specialist treatment than to the remedies that are easily available to the family doctor.

THE PSYCHIATRIC SERVICE

The nature of the service to which referral must be made appears to be the least important of the triad, but it does seem to exert some effect. In Shepherd's survey of general practitioners in England, for example, only 29.5 per cent gave the delay between asking for an appointment and the patient being seen as a reason for not referring patients, and only 18 per cent expressed dissatisfaction with the way patients were dealt with in the psychiatric clinic.

Grad and Sainsbury (1966) showed that a community-oriented psychiatric service in Chichester, England attracted a higher referral rate than a traditional hospital-based service in Salisbury (6.7 per 1,000 as opposed to 5.4 per 1,000); but the difference was entirely due to higher referral rates for organic and functional psychoses, the rate for neurosis being the same in the two cities. It is noteworthy that the effect of the community-based service was not to attract additonal numbers of mild cases, but rather to bring services to more severely ill patients.

Fink and his colleagues (1969) describe a rather different effect when a free psychiatric service was included as a benefit in the Health Insurance Plan of Greater New York. The referral rate increased from 6.6 per 1,000 to 11 per 1,000, but the extra cases were less severely ill than those who had been referred previously.

It should be noted that the reported rates of referrals from primary care to the psychiatric services in the USA are at least as high as those reported in the European surveys, so that to the extent that private, office-based psychiatrists in the USA see different patients than their European colleagues, it is by the addition of direct referrals from the community, as described in Chapter 3.

NOTES

1. Four different surveys studied the age of family doctors as a determinant of referral to psychiatrists: all of them report that older doctors have higher referral rates. The surveys are: Shepherd *et al.* (1966), Gardiner, Peterson, and Hall (1974), Shortell and Daniels (1974), and Robertson (1979). The last-named survey by Robertson in Aberdeen showed that the tendency for older doctors and for single-handed doctors to refer more patients was confined to those practices in the city; the same relationships were not found for doctors practicing in the surrounding countryside.
2. Studies which have shown higher referrals to psychiatric services from urban and rural areas include Bahn *et al.* (1961); Innes and Sharp (1962); Gardiner *et al.* (1963); Grad and Sainsbury (1966); Robertson (1971); Bain (1974); and Robertson (1979).
3. Thus Helgason (1978) shows that there are no rural/urban differences for the prevalence of psychiatric disorder as detected by a psychiatric screening questionnaire (The Cornell Medical Inventory) administered to a random community sample of Icelanders, but that there is a marked difference both for lifetime expectancy of neurosis and for whether respondents are known to the Psychiatric Case Register. Thus for the point prevalence of disorder as measured by the CMI, there are 1.16 cases in the Capital for every one case in the country; for the lifetime expectancy of neurosis there are 1.8 cases in the Capital for every one case in the country; while for the Psychiatric Case Register there are 1.84 cases in the Capital for each case in the country.
4. Rawnsley, Loudon, and Miles (1962) showed a referral rate for Welsh general practitioners of 1.7 male and 1.9 female per 1,000 population at risk. The major reason given by the physicians making such referrals was that the patients had failed to respond to their own treatment. Fink and Shapiro (1966) studied patients in the Health Insurance Plan of Greater New York. 8 per cent of

patients were found to have emotional problems, and 25 per cent were referred to psychiatrists. The reasons given for such referrals were (1) interference with life activity; (2) stems from life stress; and (3) that discussions between the doctor and the patient were not thought 'very helpful'. May and Gregory (1968) studied seventy-five GPs in a London Borough and found that the referral rates to psychiatric services of 5.2 per 1,000 population at risk. The range varied between 6 and 13.6. Reasons given for referral were (1) failure of response to GP's treatment; (2) symptom severity; (3) lack of time; (4) confirmation of diagnosis; and finally pressure for a second opinion from the patient or his relatives. Goldensohn, Fink, and Shapiro (1969) showed that the referral rate was 11 per 1,000 enrollees for the Health Insurance Plan of Greater New York. The family doctors had been asked to refer those they believed to be in need of psychotherapy for the purposes of this study. Kaeser and Cooper (1971) found that the principal reason for referrals of patients to the Maudsley Hospital in London was that the GPs wished the hospital to take over clinical responsibility for their patients. Carey and Kogan (1971) studied seventy-eight GPs in the Group Health Cooperative of Puget Sound. Reasons given for referral were: first, acuteness of the problem; second, the patient recognized the emotional nature of the problem; third, the doctor felt incapable of treating it himself; and finally, cases that were highly treatable or untreatable were not to be referred. Hopkins and Cooper (1969) studied referrals from a group practice in Northwest London and found a rate of referral of 11.8 per 1,000 at risk. The majority of patients referred were suffering from chronic rather than acute illnesses. The same tendency for chronic rather than acute patients to be referred is reported by Goldensohn, Fink, Shapiro and Daily (1969). This is in contrast to the findings of Carey and Kogan; the doctors at Puget Sound looked upon acuteness as an indication for referral. Another point which emerges from the references summarized in this note is that not only is there great variability between practitioners in their referral rates within a particular survey, but there is also great variability between surveys. Thus, the rates reported for Welsh general practitioners in the countryside are very much lower than those reported for London practitioners.

5. There are three British surveys all showing that men are more likely to be referred than women: Hopkins and Cooper (1969) showed that males were more likely to be referred than females, as did Ingham, Rawnsley, and Hughes (1972) in South Wales. Gardiner, Peterson, and Hall (1974) showed that male patients were referred earlier than females. In Iceland, Helgason (1978) showed that for neuroses, males were more likely to be referred than females. However, the opposite effect was seen for functional psychoses and alcoholism. In the United States, Fink, Shapiro, Goldensohn, and Daily (1969) showed that for each step in their 'filter-down' process, the female:male ratio tipped more and more in favour of females. Using a nomenclature of the present model, for level three the female:male ratio was 2.17:1 ; of those referred to psychiatrists it was 2.25: 1; while for those actually successfully obtaining psychiatric treatment it was 2.42:1 (p.258, authors' recalculations).

6. There are five studies which show this effect, and the results vary only depending on how age has been classified. Those studies that have looked at the 'under 40' as a single age group have shown that this group has a very much

higher referral rate than either the 40-60 or 60+ age groups; while those that have coded age in deciles have shown that referral rates tend to rise to a maximum in the 25-35 age group, and to decline thereafter. The studies referred to are: Shepherd *et al*, (1966); Locke, Krantz, and Kramer (1966); Hopkins and Cooper (1969); Fink, Shapiro, Goldensohn, and Daily (1969); Robertson (1979).

7. Helgason (1978) compares the expectancy of consulting a psychiatrist with disease expectancy by age and diagnosis for his birth cohort of all Icelanders studied intensively in 1964. In this study, the 'disease expectancy' is based on whether the illness has ever been diagnosed by a doctor: in terms of the present model therefore, it is a total of level 3 plus level 4 plus level 5. The 'expectancy of consulting a psychiatrist' (level 4 plus level 5) is based on whether the proband is known to the Icelandic Psychiatric Case Register. The results are as follows (the higher the index the more likely it is that the patient be known by the psychiatric services) functional psychoses: male .48, female .65; neuroses: male .41, female .39; alcohol and drug abuse: male .25, female .66

8. The duration of illnesses referred for specialist psychiatric care clearly depends on both the clinical practices of primary care physicians concerned, and the type of service offered by the local psychiatric services. Hopkins and Cooper (1969) report that 19 per cent of their referrals were new illnesses while a further 21 per cent were 'acute or chronic' cases; the remainder – 60 per cent – were unchanged cases. Fink and his colleagues (1969) report that 38 per cent were acute; 28 per cent acute or chronic; and the remaining 34 per cent were chronic. These figures had remained broadly similar between 1965 and 1967. Grad and Sainsbury (1975) report that 44.5 per cent of referrals to a traditional psychiatric service at Salisbury, England had duration of episode of less than six months; but reported that newer, community care services at Chichester had 57.3 per cent of patients with illnesses with duration of less than six months. Carey and Kogan (1971) report that primary care physicians at Puget Sound tended to refer acute cases.

CHAPTER 7

Levels 4 and 5: psychiatric morbidity treated by psychiatrists

Psychiatric case registers provide us with our most accurate information about the extent and distribution of mental illness as defined by psychiatrists. They are more accurate than nationally collected statistics concerning mental illness, since it is possible to make unduplicated counts of cases and it is usually possible to have some control of the quality of the data on which the register depends. In recent years it has been possible to compare estimates of morbidity between the various registers so that comparisons can be made both within and between countries. For example, Wing and her colleagues (1967) compared rates for mental illness in Aberdeen, Baltimore, Camberwell, Nottingham, and Salford and showed that the point prevalence of psychiatric illness in all of them was approximately 1 per cent (range 0.82 − 1.16), while the one-year period prevalence was approximately 2 per cent (range 1.8 − 2.1) − so that the annual inception rate for new episodes of illness is approximately 1 per cent. These figures have the great merit of being easy to remember (for brief review, see note 1).

LEVEL 4: PSYCHIATRIC ILLNESS AMONG OUT-PATIENTS SEEN BY PSYCHIATRISTS

Under conditions of the British National Health Service, the great majority of those seen in psychiatric out-patient clinics will have been referred by their family doctor, and therefore have had to have passed through the first three filters. Mezey and Evans (1971) report on a psychiatric service in the London Borough of Edmonton and show that about 70 per cent of out-patients were referred directly by their GP, while a further 25 per cent came from other hospital doctors; only 5 per cent were self-referred or came from the Courts. It is still true to say that direct access to psychiatrists at 'walk-in' clinics is unusual: a notable exception is the Maudsley Emergency Clinic – although even there a substantial proportion of the patients have referral letters from their family doctors (Birley and Hailey 1972).

A recent case register comparison by Wing and Fryers (1977) shows that while there are 22.7 psychiatric outpatients contacts per 1,000 population at Salford, there are 71.0 such contacts per 1,000 at Camberwell. These figures may be compared with national figures for the twelve health regions of England (DHSS 1977: 19), from which one can calculate that over the whole country the average number of such contacts per year is 33.8 per 1,000 at risk, with a standard deviation of 7.6. It can be seen that while the out-patient services at Salford are about one standard deviation below the national average, those at Camberwell are almost five standard deviations above![2] The comparison between the services is therefore of great interest, since it allows us to compare a service whose resources are somewhat below the national average with one whose resources are very much greater than those available nationally.

It can be seen from *Table 7(1)* that the Salford service is seeing more schizophrenics in its out-patient clinic despite the fact that the Camberwell clinics are providing service to more than twice as many people when all diagnoses are taken together. This is not likely to be due to diagnostic idiosyncracy in Salford, since elsewhere in the report we see that the annual inceptions for schizophrenia are very similar in the two areas (0.4 per 1,000 Camberwell; 0.44 per 1,000 Salford).[3]

The striking difference between the services is that Camberwell is able to care for a substantially larger load of depressions than Salford – the rate is nearly four times as high for both sexes taken together, with an especially marked difference for male depressives between the two services. Male patients with alcohol and drug dependence problems also have much higher rates for treatment in the more liberally staffed service. With the exception of schizophrenia, there is a general tendency for the Camberwell rates to be higher than the Salford rates: an effect which is especially noticeable for those miscellaneous states reported as 'All other conditions' (forty-six compared with ten), which contain psychosomatic and psychophysiological disorders. In summary, if Salford, with out-patient services somewhat below the national average, is looking after at least as many schizophrenic patients as Camberwell, it seems likely that over the nation the existing out-patient services are not prevented from seeing their schizophrenic patients by shortage of resources. However, it seems likely that additional resources would allow psychiatric services to meet the needs of patients with depression and with psychological problems related to physical disease.

Table 7(1): *One-day prevalence (31.12.74) for psychiatric out-patients in Camberwell and Salford (sex-specific rates/100,000 population at risk: attending before or after census day without more than three months between attendances)*

diagnosis	Camberwell			Salford		
	male	female	total	male	female	total
schizophrenia	52	60	56	92	106	99
all depressives	128	318	228	29	87	59
alcohol and drug dependence	25	4	14	7	3	5
total psychiatric morbidity	320	548	440	168	249	209

In the United States, the total number of office visits to psychiatrists has been estimated as seventy-three visits per 1,000 population (this is not an unduplicated count, in that the same individual maybe counted more than once; but it can be compared with the figure of thirty-four per 1,000 already given for the British NHS. (Sources: Advancedata 1978; DHSS 1977.) Part of the reason for the higher American rate is undoubtedly that American psychiatrists see their patients more frequently than their British counterparts; thus for each new visit reported by the National Ambulatory Medical Care Survey to a psychiatrist there were 8.6 'old visits'; this can be compared with Camberwell where there was an average of 4.5 visits per patient, and to Salford where there are 2.3.

Tantam and Burns (1979) have compared community services offered in the USA and Britain by contrasting services available at Bunker Hill Center, Boston with those available in Camberwell. Despite the fact that neither of these services is typical of those found elsewhere in their respective countries, it is worth noting two points: the proportion of the population at risk seeing a psychiatrist is the same in the two areas, and patients with more severe disorders are not likely to see a psychiatrist in Boston, but to see other mental health professionals such as psychologists and social workers.

Since one of us (DG) is a frequent visitor to the United States and has worked in various American Departments of Psychiatry for over two years, it is perhaps permissable to step aside from tabulated data, and to give an admittedly anecdotal verbal description of the two systems of out-patient care. The typical patient who was seen for an office visit in a teaching hospital in the USA is more likely to be self-referred or brought up by a family member, very much less likely to be psychotic but more likely to have mild personality disorder with or without some 'problem in living'. He will wait for his interview in a comfortably furnished waiting area usually complete with armchairs, fitted carpets, and luxurious potted plants. He will be interviewed by an unhurried psychiatrist who will be sitting in an office which looks as little like a hospital clinic as he can make it, and which will often not be equipped with a couch and diagnostic equipment to enable him to carry out a physicial examination. Treatment will most usually be by some form of psychotherapy, the duration of which is often limited by the patient's ability to pay, or the length of cover provided by his health insurance plan.

In Britain, a patient referred to a psychiatrist will first of all give a good deal of information to the hospital record clerks so that his visit will eventually be noted in the hospital's next statistical return, and he will then be referred to a relatively spartan waiting room, usually presided over by a harassed out-patient nurse. After a variable waiting time he will be interviewed by a psychiatrist in an office which makes few concessions to comfort, and which typically looks most decidedly like a hospital clinic. He is relatively more likely to be physically examined and then to have blood tests and X-rays, despite the fact that he will spend less time with the psychiatrist. He is much more likely to be treated by drugs, and very much less likely to be offered psychotherapy on a regular basis. His duration of treatment at the hospital is more likely to be limited by the work pressures impinging on the staff of the follow-up clinic than by his own disinclination to come for further sessions.

It is not possible to substantiate all of these assertions, since fortunately we do not yet have to provide routine statistical information concerning the distribution of potted plants or the ubiquity of a drab, institutionalized atmosphere. However, the information available fits quite well with what has been said. In the USA, psychotherapy will be given in 86 per cent of office visits to a psychiatrist, and drugs will be prescribed in only 25 per cent (Advancedata 1978). In Britain, Johnson's survey (1973) of three very different psychiatric out-patient clinics in the Manchester area – a University clinic, a District General Hospital, and a psychiatric hospital – showed that the patients attending each sort of clinic were very similar to one another in terms of diagnoses made and treatment prescribed. About 70 per cent of the patients received drug treatment – sometimes in combination with help from a social worker – and only 14 per cent were offered psychotherapy by either the psychiatrist or the social worker. Only 9 per cent of the patients were rated as having no diagnosable psychiatric disorder, and only 15 per cent as needing no formal psychiatric treatment. A survey of sixty consecutive new referrals to the Manchester University Psychiatric Out-patients by Skuse (1975) showed that 49 per cent of the patients were distressed to learn that they were being sent to see a psychiatrist, while 38 per cent said that their doctor had never mentioned the word 'psychiatrist' but had told them they would be seeing a 'specialist' or a 'nerve specialist'. Only 20 per cent mentioned talking to a psychiatrist as a form of treatment, and 44 per cent did not know that psychiatrists were medically qualified. Despite the fact that three-quarters had no clear idea what help might be offered them, it is perhaps a tribute to the stolid optimism of these Lancastrian patients that two-thirds thought that the psychiatrist would be able to help them with their problem.

SOCIAL FACTORS AND THE COURSE OF PSYCHIATRIC DISORDERS

The role of social factors once an illness has begun, whether or not it is diagnosed or treated, falls broadly into three related categories. Social factors can be seen to be important predictors of the course or outcome of disorder, and it can be demonstrated, as it has been for hospitalized samples, that social dysfunction appears to impede symptomatic as well as social recovery.

Social dysfunction can also be seen to be related to chronic disorder in the sense that both have been found to coexist in a variety of samples. One cannot escape the question of the direction of the relationship between the presence of dysfunction and the presence of chronic symptomatology but in contrast to aetiological enquiries the answer to the questions which came first is not so pressing. It is likely that chronic social difficulties lead to the persistence of symptoms and that the persistence of symptoms incapacitates an individual to such a degree that he exhibits features of social dysfunction.

Social factors also play an important role in the relapse of psychiatric patients. It has been observed that unhelpful social attitudes on the part of the family may lead to relapse and that the existence of psychotic symptomatology constitutes a burden for the relatives of the psychiatric patient (Vaughn and Leff 1976; Hughes 1978). In order to relieve the distress due to the primary handicap of disorder and the secondary handicap of unhelpful attitudes, we need to know which social factors predict poor outcome, relapse, or the development of chronicity, and to experiment by attempting to control these factors.

SOCIAL FACTORS AS PREDICTORS OF OUTCOME

Only a limited number of enquiries have attempted the hazardous exercise of the prospective prediction of the outcome of psychiatric or of physical disorders. The classic study of the relative importance of clinical and psychosocial factors in the prediction of the course of physical disease was made by Querido (1959), who undertook an assessment of the mental and social stresses acting upon 1,630 physically ill, hospitalized patients. This assessment was then related to the patients' medical condition at a follow-up investigation conducted on average seven months later. Two separate forms of assessment were made while the patient was in hospital: the first was called the 'integrated assessment', and was made by a team consisting of a general physician, a social worker and a psychiatrist; while the second was a clinical assessment made by a general physician. The integrated assessment was made using Weijel's psychological case history and indicated whether or not the patient was suffering from stress or tension which impeded his well-being. It comprised a survey of the patient's life history including major traumatic life events. The clinician who made the clinical assessment was asked to give a favourable or unfavourable prognosis for each patient.

The follow-up investigation showed a significant difference in the frequency of recovery between distressed patients, 32 per cent of whom were in a 'satisfactory' condition at follow-up, and patients without distress, 68 per cent of whom were in a 'satisfactory' condition at follow-up. This result obtained irrespective of diagnosis or of the nature of the tensions from which the patient was suffering. The mental attitude of 'distress' reduced the efficiency of the hospital by half, since only 660 of the 1,128 patients with a favourable prognosis did in fact have a satisfactory outcome.

Not only does this study suggest that psycho-social distress impedes recovery, but it also demonstrates the difficulty of making accurate prognostic judgements about the outcome or the course of disorder. Taking into account false positives and negatives, Querido found that the clinical forecasts were correct in 62 per cent of cases, but the psycho-social assessment was correct in 76 per cent. Querido shows that the increased accuracy of the team over the clinician is due largely to the availability of additional information with regard to the presence or absence of psychological distress: if distress is found then an unfavourable forecast by the team usually approximates more closely to outcome than the clinician's forecast, and distress appeared to give more weight to the forecast than clinical phenomena alone seem to do. Querido concludes that the increase in accuracy which results from taking account of psychological distress makes evaluation of psychic and social factors indispensable in estimating the patients' chances of recovery.

This proposition has been applied to the study of minor psychiatric disorders in an unhospitalized sample of new psychiatric out-patients. In a pilot study (Huxley and Goldberg 1975) fifty new patients suffering from non-psychotic and non-organic psychiatric disorders were assessed using standardized social and clinical interview schedules. Forty-six were successfully followed up six months later and their condition was reassessed using a specially constructed rating scale which took account of the frequency of symptoms and the distress they engendered. The single most important predictive variable was the patients' material social circumstances. Clinical predictions of outcome were closely related to the proportion of time the patient had been ill over the five years prior to inception. The major weakness of this enquiry, the use of a specially constructed outcome measure, was remedied in a subsequent enquiry in which a similar patient group was followed up over a twelve-month period, and who were then reassessed using the same standardized clinical instrument used at inception (Huxley *et al.* 1979). The use of the clinical instrument on the second occasion enabled the authors to calculate a change score representing the percentage loss of symptoms over the course of the year; in addition they also assessed at the follow-up interview the number of months during the survey in which the patient was unwell.

These two outcome measures were successfully predicted by the same social variables; and the social variables were very much the same as those which had had most predictive potency in the pilot study – material shortcomings in the patient's social environment including financial inadequacies, and objective restrictions on social contacts and leisure opportunities. To some extent these variables reflected social class differences and social class was itself a predictor of outcome. The results of the more straightforward correlation analyses were confirmed by a principal components analysis. The first seven components in the principal components analysis accounted for 70 per cent of the variance, and the first component, a social one, accounted for 24 per cent; the second, a clinical one, for 15 per cent and the third, another social component, for 8 per cent. The three-factor rotated solution confirmed the importance of social variables as predictors of outcome because both the outcome measures were heavily loaded on the same factor as social variables. The authors conclude that the outcome of minor psychiatric disorder is predicted best by three discrete types of data which are, in order of importance: the patient's social circumstances – in particular his material circumstances – clinical factors, and constitutional factors.

Social factors have been studied in relation to the prediction of the course of the major psychiatric syndromes and a large amount of data related to the prediction of the course of schizophrenia is provided by the International Pilot Study of Schizophrenia (IPSS) (Strauss and Carpenter 1972; 1974a; 1974b; Sartorius *et al.* 1977; 1979 Hawk *et al.* 1975).

The IPSS is a long-term prospective study of schizophrenia using reliable diagnostic and evaluative criteria. Although the data relates to originally hospitalized patients, large numbers of them have been in the community for long periods since initial admission. To date, two-year and five-year follow-up investigations have been conducted. Sixty-one out of an original cohort of 131 patients were followed up and outcome assessed in terms of duration of hospitalization, social contacts, symptomatology, employment, plus global measures of outcome, fullness of life, and overall level of function. All outcome items were scored to cover the year prior to follow-up interview except the symptom score which was evaluated for the few weeks prior to interview.

The best predictors of five-year outcome were hospitalization, social contacts, employment, and treatment facilities used. Social contacts prior to the first evaluation was the only predictor of social contacts at follow-up and had predictive value for nearly all outcome measures. At both the two and five-year follow-up investigations, the most powerful predictors were the specific functions that correspond to each outcome function, in other words the same picture held for unemployment and symptoms as for social contacts. They were each the best predictor of outcome assessed in the same way. Although a multiple regression analysis was computed at the two and five-year follow-up, it was observed that simply adding the scores on the three main predictors (previous hospitalization, previous social contact, and previous employment) gave equivalent results in the prediction of all outcome variables. Strauss and Carpenter suggest that in any study of treatment intervention these variables should be evaluated and treatment groups matched accordingly.

Sartorius and his colleagues (1977) report essentially similar findings. They identify three sociodemographic factors as important predictors of outcome: social isolation associated with a poor outcome; marital status – widowed, divorced or separated, associated with a poor outcome; and marital status – married associated with a good outcome. Both diagnostic categories and symptomatological criteria were far less effective predictors of the two-year course than length of initial illness episode, degree of social impairment, or the proportion of the follow-up during which the patient had psychotic episodes.

The usefulness of social predictors in the forecast of the course of schizophrenia is supported by Wittenborn and others (1977) who completed a social interview with seventy-five schizophrenic males following hospitalization. The nine factors derived from the social interview were found to predict symptom ratings at two years' follow-up. Of particular importance were an 'interpersonally uncomfortable childhood home' and 'low premorbid self-esteem', which both predicted a poor symptomatic outcome at two years.

Premorbid social indicators such as those enumerated above and measures of current social circumstances contribute in no small way to the prediction of outcome of major and minor disorders (Huxley 1978). In contributing to the prediction of symptomatic rather than simply social outcome, such factors are obviously of importance in the identification of symptomatic states, which are likely to persist.

COEXISTENCE AND COVARIATION OF CLINICAL AND SOCIAL IMPAIRMENT

We have already suggested that chronic social difficulties may be thought of as either the cause or the result of chronic impairment, and several investigators have reported upon the coexistence of chronic social and psychiatric problems. In Goldberg and Blackwell's sample of primary care attenders those patients who were still ill at six months tended to have insoluble life-problems.

Brown and others (1975) confirmed this association among depressed women in the community. Twelve out of twenty-two cases with housing problems had chronic disorders. The author also observed that the more severe problems in the group of middle-class women tended to be of shorter duration than in the group of working-class women, and that four times as many middle-class women had problems which cleared up during their enquiry. Brown points out that the persistence of problems in the case of working-class women did not seem to reflect a personal inability on the women's part to cope with her difficulties.

In the acute stages of illness the relationship between social and clinical impairment has been shown to change over a short period of time. Weissman and Paykel (1974) studied 150 moderately depressed female out-patients who were treated using antidepressants; in addition, half of the sample were randomly allocated to a high contact psychotherapy treatment. In a comparison study of the first forty depressed women and a matched control sample (Tanner *et al.* 1975) they found that depressed women were considerably more socially impaired than normals at the height of their illness and that the remission of social impairments was considerably slower than that of symptoms. The most rapid decrease of social impairments occurred in the first two months, there was slower improvement in the next two months, following which, to a total of eight months, the average course was relatively static. At the end of eight months these relatively symptom-free patients, who had not relapsed during the eight months were still more socially impaired than normal controls.

Weissman and Paykel noted that clinical and social scores were not associated at the height of the illness but that at eight months follow-up social and clinical measures were highly correlated. (This phenomenon has also been observed by Huxley (1978).)

Weissman's and Paykel's explanation for this phenomenon is that the correlation coefficient between clinical and social impairment at the follow-up interview is higher because it is a reflection of the contrast between the majority of patients who have had a considerable symptomatic remission and who in most instances are no longer socially maladjusted, and the minority of patients who continue to be symptomatically impaired and who exhibit considerable social maladjustment.

RELAPSE AND THE BURDEN ON THE FAMILY

Social factors are implicated in the retention of the psychiatric patient in the community (Gillis and Keet 1965) and the important variable in such instances, the attitude of the family and their desire or ability to care for the patient, has been examined in a number of studies; these have attempted to measure the effect of the patient upon the family and have usually described this effect as 'burden'. Numerous definitions of 'burden' exist in the literature, but irrespective of the terminology chosen, burden studies clearly point to the existence of serious social handicaps which befall the relatives of psychiatric patients, and that, in the words of Clausen and Yarrow (1955) 'living in the community is not synonymous with a patient having recovered'.

The type of family group to which the patient returned following discharge from hospital was found to be associated with differential relapse rates (Brown 1959; Brown, Carstairs, and Topping 1959; Freeman and Simmons 1958; Dinitz *et al.* 1961; Goldberg 1966). The original conception that the type of family group was important was later refined so that the quality of the emotional interaction between the patient and members of his household became the focus for attention (Michaux *et al.* 1969; Brown *et al.* 1962; 1970). Brown and his colleagues (1970) interviewed 101 schizophrenic patients and their relatives before and after discharge from hospital. A joint interview was used to observe the interaction and a rating of 'expressed emotion' of the relative towards the patient was devised, based upon observed hostility, over-involvement, dissatisfaction, warmth, and most importantly, the number of critical comments. The data indicated that the degree of expressed emotion was directly related to relapse, measured according to status at clinical interview and not based solely on readmission to hospital. It was noted however that the effect of high expressed emotion was to some extent mitigated by a low level of face-to-face contact between relative and patient. Vaughn and Leff (1976) have since repeated this work with samples of schizophrenic and depressed patients. Combining their results with those of Brown, they had a total of 128 patients, and found in this group a significant correlation between high expressed emotion and rate of relapse. They confirmed that to some extent patients could be protected from relapse by low face-to-face contact with their relatives. Both studies identified unmarried men as the most vulnerable (and married woman as the least vulnerable) to relapse. Unmarried men from high expressed emotion homes were significantly less likely to be protected from relapse by low face-to-face contact and maintenance drug therapy.

Exner and Murillo (1975) in a study of 143 patients (including seventy-one schizophrenics) discharged from Stoney Lodge Hospital, New York, confirm that limited contact between the patient and 'significant others' appeared to protect the patient from relapse. They suggest that a measure of the discrepancy between the patient and significant other on two scales of the Katz Adjustment Scales (Katz and Lyerly 1963) – socially-expected behaviour and free time activities – is highly related to post-hospitalization relapse.

The last two studies would appear to report somewhat contradictory findings since the latter suggest that the effects they observed held for schizophrenic and non-schizophrenic patients while Vaughn and Leff highlight differences between schizophrenic and depressed patients in their response to the emotional atmosphere and in the factors which protect them from relapse. Vaughn and Leff suggest that maintenance drug therapy and reduced contact with relatives do not protect depressed patients from relapse. There is evidence elsewhere that maintenance drug therapy with psychological support can be protective in depression (Weissman and Paykel 1974) and one might expect reduced contact to be more effective as a protective factor in schizophrenia given the control importance of arousal (Venables 1960) and overstimulation (Wing and Brown 1970) in the production of florid symptomatology.

Studies of the nature of the burden imposed by psychiatric patients upon their families have focussed entirely upon schizophrenic patients (Wing *et al.* 1964; Hughes 1978) or schizophrenic patients have comprised a large proportion of the sample (Grad and Sainsbury 1968; Hoenig and Hamilton 1969).

Brown and his colleagues (1958) studied the post-hospital adjustment of 229 chronic patients and attempted to assess the consequences for other persons of the patients' return to living in the community. Seventeen per cent caused 'severe liability' to their relatives or caretakers, 28 per cent caused 'moderate liability', and 55 per cent had no or only limited adverse effect. They report that some relatives 'found even slight psychotic symptoms very disconcerting, whereas others (especially certain mothers) showed extreme indulgence' in the face of what appeared to be very difficult behaviour from the patient. It seems likely that this is the same group identified by Gillis and Keet in their study of schizophrenics who would otherwise have been hospitalized.

More recently Stevens (1972) enquired about the adverse effects of schizophrenic patients on their elderly relatives and found that, in her sample of twenty-nine families, twenty-two families had experienced at least some financial effects, ten had experienced restricted leisure activities, and sixteen had felt that their own health had suffered. She argues that 'the most significant area of burden was on the mental health of the relative where approximately two-thirds felt strain in the form of anxiety or depression'. Grad and Sainsbury (1968) in a much larger enquiry which included 45 per cent functional psychotics, also reported that the mental health of over half of the relatives was adversely affected: one third had leisure activities restricted, 29 per cent had their domestic routine disturbed and 25 per cent had their income cut by at least one tenth.

Hoenig and Hamilton (1969) observed the same tendency as Brown *et al.* (1958) and Gillis and Keet (1965) in that a large number of the 179 families who had lived with a psychiatric patient for four years prior to their enquiry, did not report that they felt 'subjectively burdened'. Sixty per cent however, did so, a figure similar to that reported by Wing (1964) for strained relations in the families of schizophrenic patients. Hoenig and Hamilton assessed the objective burden which befell their families – this comprised the adverse effects caused by disturbed or unacceptable behaviour on finance, health, children, routine; and the frequency of the particular disturbing behaviours – and they found that there was a discrepancy between burden rated in this way and 'subjective burden'. In respect of the schizophrenics' families for instance, of those experiencing some objective burden, 29 per cent reported no subjective burden at all. The authors call this discrepancy 'tolerance', but the factors which contribute to tolerance in this and other studies have not really been clarified.

Hughes (1978) investigated the nature of burden in the families of sixty-four first admission schizophrenic patients four years after discharge, and also examined the social and clinical correlates of burden in this sample. Two methods of measuring burden were employed: the more traditional forms used in previous enquiries, including a global rating of subjective strain, and a second method based upon a principal components analysis of the items which comprised the 'burden schedule'. Four major factors emerged which accounted for 47 per cent of the total variance: these were interpreted as 'impaired interpersonal relationships', 'effects on informant and household', 'florid psychotic symptoms', and 'self-neglect'. Among the interesting findings in this enquiry was the fact that the subjective strain rating was not heavily loaded on any of these independent factors, and did not emerge as a separate component, indicating that subjective burden is hard to disentangle from those behaviours which cause it and that there is some doubt as to the value of traditional burden measures as used by Hoenig and Hamilton which were shown to be highly intercorrelated in Hughes' study.

Hughes also examined social and clinical correlates of burden and found that a hostile relative, younger male patients, unemployment and a poor employment record were all related to greater burden as measured by the factor scores. The clinical variables which were related to burden were a higher symptom score by the patient when interviewed by the research psychiatrist, more admissions during the four-year follow-up, and a greater number of days in hospital when admitted. In addition, Hughes confirmed early suggestions that the health of the relatives was impaired, because a relatives' GHQ score was related to burden. The author suggests, in a more detailed analysis of these results, that it was unlikely that the higher score of some relatives on the GHQ actually influenced the reporting of burden, and so it would appear to be a consequence of living with a more burdensome patient.

Hughes' study, and all those referred to earlier, lack adequate 'before' and 'after' comparisons so that it is impossible to describe the 'changes' which have taken place in these families because adequate baseline measurements do not exist. Hughes argues that burden should be considered: 'as a long-term phenomenon, involving a measurement of the degree of adjustment from onset of the illness to follow-up, and the overall changes in family life required, rather than just the incidence of specific problems recalled at a particular time.'

Only in prospective studies is it possible to identify and predict who will become burdened. It is as interesting to identify those who do not become burdened and to consider whether those who appear to cope with the problem of mental disorder do in fact exhibit a healthy 'tolerance' or whether their apparently successful management of the patient results in undue effects upon themselves, and the patient.

It is only when questions about the needs of the patient and the needs of others in his environment are taken together that the appropriateness of any service can be assessed; only when hospital and community care cease to be seen as alternatives will patients and their families begin to receive care more realistically based on their needs, and upon the respective strengths of the institution and community-based services.

THE FOURTH FILTER: ADMISSION TO PSYCHIATRIC BEDS

We saw that at level 4 the psychiatrist exercises his skill in assessing and devising management plans for the patients referred to him: most of those referred will receive some descriptive diagnostic label, so that he cannot be said to be defining psychiatric illnesses. Given the large pool of psychologically disturbed patients that exists in the community, and the undoubted tendency for the more severely disturbed to be preferentially referred, the psychiatrist's ability to label such patients becomes understandable. The psychiatrist has a major role to play as the main gatekeeper to in-patient care; although even here, his powers are not absolute – in the case of severe disorders, his role as gatekeeper is merely to vet lay decisions. Indeed, if a patient is to be admitted compulsorily, it is essential that the actual application for admission is made by a layman – either a member of the patient's family or a social worker. The psychiatrist's role is to support such applications with his medical opinion. Lawson (1972) studied emergency admissions to a mental hospital in London, and showed that non-medical factors – such as the delay between a request for a visit by a social worker and the arrival of the social worker to see the patient – were powerful determinants of whether or not the psychiatrist was approached with requests for a compulsory admission. Where voluntary admissions are concerned (these comprise 88 per cent of admissions to psychiatric beds in England: DHSS 1979) both psychiatrist and patient will have a part to play in deciding on admission, although once more the psychiatrist is the final arbiter of whether the admission is justified by the nature of the patient's illness.

There is very much less variation between parts of the country for admissions to psychiatric beds. The average annual first admission rate per 1,000 population at risk in the fourteen health regions of England is 1.2, with a standard deviation of 0.17 (to be compared with figures already given for out-patient services, where the average was 33.8 per 1,000 with a standard deviation of 7.6). The female:male ratio is 1.35:1, to be compared with readmissions, where the average is 2.62 per 1,000 per year, with a female:male ratio of 1.42:1.

It would appear that women are less likely to pass the fourth filter than men, but it is not clear that this effect is due to the peculiarities of psychiatrists as gatekeepers to in-patient care. Cooper (1966) pointed out that the female preponderance seen in general practice surveys is not seen among first admissions to psychiatric beds, and suggests that there is some selective process whereby male patients are more readily admitted to psychiatric beds than females. If the female: male ratios for out-patients are compared using data derived from the Camberwell and Salford Case Registers (see *Table 7(2)*) it can be seen that there is a greater female preponderance among out-patients than among in-patients for both areas. It can be seen that although a female is less likely to be admitted to the ward, she is more likely to be offered a day place than a male patient.

Table 7(2): *Female:male sex ratios in the fourth filter*

	out-patients	day-patients	in-patients
Camberwell	1.07 : 1	2.05 : 1	1.35 : 1
Salford	1.48 : 1	1.06 : 1	1.02 : 1

Data derived from one-day prevalence on 31.12.74, from Wing and Fryers 1976: 77-78

The problem about using these data to draw conclusions about the fourth filter is that one cannot assume that patients are admitted to the wards from out-patients, since what evidence we have suggests that only a minority can come by this route. Mezey and Evans (1971) showed that only 30 per cent of a group of 200 in-patients came from out-patients: 47 per cent were referred directly by their family doctor, and the remainder came from other hospital doctors or the courts. Interestingly enough, among the group of sixty individuals who were admitted to the wards from the out-patient clinic, females were more likely to be admitted than males.[4] This may reflect the fact that admission to the wards via the out-patient clinic is the principal way for less severely ill patients to gain admission to a hospital bed. We saw from the work of Horwitz (1977:43) that there is some evidence that men delay seeking help relative to women, so that by the time their psychiatric illness becomes manifest to others they may have become more severely ill. Mezey and Evans (1977) note that among those admitted there were proportionately more schizophrenics and organic disorders, and fewer personality disorders, than in the out-patient population as a whole. There was a tendency for in-patients to have a greater proportion of those in social classes IV and V than out-patients (37.5 per cent versus 32.5 per cent), but it should be recalled that 70 per cent of the in-patients in their study had not been admitted via out-patients. Cooper (1966) has also commented upon the greater prevalence of social class V among admissions to hospital than among samples of psychiatrically disordered patients identified by their general practitioners. This may be partly explained by supposing that a proportion of social class V patients admitted to hospital are either not registered with or do not consult a general practitioner; and it is also partly due to the fact that those who have no home to go to are more likely to be offered admission to hospital.

Cooper (1966) has also drawn attention to the fact that the over-representation of single men and women in hospitalized populations described by workers in several countries does not find a parallel in general practice studies, when single women have somewhat lower rates than married women. Earlier workers had supposed that there was an increased risk of psychiatric disorder among the unmarried, but it is more parsimonious to suppose that there is an increased likelihood of being admitted to hospital – probably because the unmarried are less likely to ·have someone to look after them.

In summary, there is no good evidence that the psychiatrist is introducing very much distortion at the only filter that he has much to do with. As with earlier filters, the more severely disturbed are more likely to be allowed through, and men seem to be allowed through rather more easily than women. There are several possible explanations for the latter finding, but no very good reason for preferring one over the others.

LEVEL 5: ADMISSION TO HOSPITAL

For twenty-five years after the Second World War radical changes in the mental health services have been reflected in changes in national statistics. Thus first admission rates climbed steadily between 1945 and 1970 as the public began to lose their fear of the mental hospital and admission procedures became more informal; while the policy of discharging chronic patients to the community has meant that readmission rates are still rising today while mean duration of stay in hospital has become shorter. In the early post-war years the first of these effects was more powerful, so that in absolute numbers the number of occupied psychiatric beds in England increased to a maximum in 1954; but it has been falling since that time. Since 1970 these changes have been less dramatic: first admissions are now fairly static, while readmissions increase slightly and the numbers of occupied beds decrease slightly each year – meaning that mean duration of stay in hospital is still becoming shorter (sources: DHSS 1977, 1979; Wing and Hailey 1972).

If first admission rates to English psychiatric hospitals are broken down by age and sex then both male and female rates are fairly constant between the ages of twenty to sixty (male about 1.4, female about 1.8 per 1,000 per year) but that rates then rise very sharply in old age, to approximately 4.3 per 1,000 per year in the seventy to eighty-year age group. Wing and Hailey (1972) have shown that as services expanded between 1965 and 1970 the inception rate for schizophrenia remained constant but there was an increase in those treated for personality disorders, alcoholism, and marital problems. Looking at trends with time for the whole country, first admissions for schizophrenia fell between 1970 and 1973, but have remained remarkably constant since then, and all other diagnoses have remained constant between 1970 and 1976 with the exception of alcoholic psychosis, which has shown a recent increase in both sexes (DHSS 1979). Where age is concerned, there has been a steady decrease in the first admission rates for the over seventy-fives between 1970 and 1972 and rates have remained constant since then, but readmission rates for this age group have been rising steadily. These changes presumably reflect new policies with regard to psychogeriatric care.

NOTES

1. Bahn *et al.* (1966) produced figures for case registers based in Rochester, New York, North Carolina, and Hawaii and show results which are comparable to those reported by Wing *et al.* (1967) for Aberdeen, Baltimore, Camberwell, Nottingham, and Salford. Wing *et al.* (1972) show that the rates reported by the Camberwell and Nottingham case registers are closely comparable to one another and go on to compare Camberwell with national statistics from Government sources (Department of Health and Social Security Statistical Report Series 1-12. London: HMSO). Wing and Fryers (1976) compare statistics from the Camberwell and Salford Psychiatric Registers in some detail, from which it emerges that (as one might suspect) facilities are more extensive in London. Hafner and Klug (1979) compare statistics provided by Wing and Fryers for the Camberwell/Salford Registers with a new Register in Mannheim and existing psychiatric Register in Samsø, Denmark. The facilities for in-patients are fairly comparable between Mannheim, Camberwell, and Salford, while the out-patient facilities appear to be more extensive in Mannheim and Camberwell than they are in Salford. Figures given for Samsø are rather different than those provided by the other three registers but this is probably attributed to peculiarities of the psychiatric service at Samsø. This is described further by Neilson (1976) 'The Samsø project from 1957-1974'. *Acta Psychiatric Scandinavica* 54: 198-222.

2. All these calculations were carried out by the authors on data from page 67 of Wing and Fryer's Salford/Camberwell comparison, and pages 18 and 19 of the DHSS report, *The Facilities and Services of Mental Illness and Mental Handicap in England* (1975: Statistical and research report series No. 19). The total number of out-patient contacts per year is not, perhaps, the most illuminating comparison to make: but unfortunately it is the only one possible. Although Wing and Fryers provide information about the number of persons as opposed to the number of contacts per 1,000 per year in their report, this cannot be compared with the DHSS figures which give the number of *new* patients per 1,000 population at risk per year (as a matter of interest, this turns out to be 4.1 per 1,000 per year, SD = .85. Number of persons (new plus old) at Salford is 9.7 per 1,000 per year, to be compared with 15.9 per 1,000 per year at Camberwell).

3. The finding for schizophrenia probably reflects that fact that the total for one-day prevalence for schizophrenia (that is to say, in-patient + day patients + out-patients) is substantially higher in Salford than in Camberwell: 277 per 100,000 in Salford; 198 per 100,000 in Camberwell. If we look to see what proportion of the total schizophrenics looked after by the service are actually cared for in out-patients then we find that the percentage being cared for in out-patients is 28 per cent at Camberwell, and 35 per cent at Salford. The Salford Service therefore appears to be coping with its rather larger load of chronic schizophrenics by caring for a somewhat larger proportion of them in an out-patient setting. Indeed, elsewhere in the report one can see that there is a special 'injections only' clinic which is caring for 285 patients (opposite page 69).

4. Mezcy and Evans compared the sixty patients admitted to the wards from the out-patients clinic with the 258 out-patients from whom they had been drawn. They were able to show that while one in ten of the male out-patients was offered an in-patient bed, no fewer than one in four of the female out-patients subsequently became in-patients. The findings is of interest since it might be thought that in this setting the psychiatrist has most choice about who he should offer a place to, so that it is of interest that the filter is more permeable to females in this setting. On the other hand, it should be recalled that patients admitted directly from the community as emergencies who have to bypass the out-patient clinic are likely to be more severely ill than those admitted through the out-patient clinic. Thus the greater permeability to females in this portion of the fourth filter may simply reflect a tendency for severely ill female patients to enter hospital via this route.

CHAPTER 8

Interview techniques in primary care settings

Research described in previous chapters has demonstrated that psychiatric disorder is often missed in primary care settings, and experience teaching those in training to become family doctors in South Carolina (Goldberg 1979b) has shown that trainees often do not have a simple scheme to enable them to assess the psychiatric disorders which are so common in this setting. Unfortunately the various schemes for mental status examination taught to medical students in departments of psychiatry are ill-suited for routine use since they tend to be focussed on conditions which are relatively rare in primary care settings, such as psychotic illnesses and organic mental states. Furthermore, they tend to outlast the time available and to alienate the patient.

The simple scheme for making such assessments given in this chapter derives from two sources. Extensive research in the General Practice Research Unit, London had indicated the common symptoms that are indicative of disorder in this setting; and experience watching forty-five family practice residents on close-circuit television over the course of one year at Charleston, South Carolina indicated the common faults which lead doctors to miss psychiatric disorders in the course of their diagnostic interviews (Goldberg, Cooper, Eastwood, Kedward, and Shepherd 1970; Goldberg, Steele, Smith, and Spivey 1980).

STARTING THE INTERVIEW

The first few minutes are critically important in the diagnostic interview: when things go wrong, they usually do so from the beginning. Yet if the opening is well handled, it is usual for psychologically disordered patients to give cues about the nature of their disturbances from the outset. The commonest mistake is for the doctor not to allow the patient an opportunity to express the nature of his disorder in his own way. This may be because the doctor preempts free communication by starting with a closed question – 'How is the diabetes getting on?'; 'What's happened with those backaches of yours?' – or because although the interview starts with an open question, the question is asked before any rapport has built up. For example, if the doctor asks 'How are you today?' as the patient walks through the door, the question will often be responded to as a social pleasantry ('Fine, thanks'); whereas if the patient has sat down, and eye contact has been established, the same question may produce a very different response. Another common mistake is for the doctor to bury himself in the clinical notes: at first perhaps to read details of recent investigations and past history, later writing notes about the present consultation. Doctors who do this commonly miss verbal and nonverbal cues which relate to psychological disorder. Furthermore, it is often forgotten that the presence of other people – nurses, students, and relatives – can often inhibit communication.

The positive rules for beginning an interview are easily stated. The interview proper does not begin until doctor and patient are both sitting comfortably, and should be started with an open inquiry such as 'What brings you to see me today?' or 'What have you noticed wrong?'. The doctor should use such facilitations as are necessary to enable the patient to make a complete opening statement, and should use these early minutes to observe the patient closely. The patient's posture and mannerisms may suggest tension or depression, and the patient may say things in his opening statement which require clarification later: for example, 'I was feeling rather low last week, and the headache started on Saturday'. The doctor allows the patient to complete the history of the headache, but later on should say, 'You said you were feeling low last week?'.

CLARIFICATION OF THE COMPLAINT

It is common for doctors to assume they have understood the nature of the patient's complaint before it has been communicated properly. Patients often encourage doctors to do this, and use vague impersonal phrases about themselves like 'these headaches of mine', 'suffering with my nerves'. The patient is relieved when the doctor appears to have understood the nature of their complaint, and continues with a disembodied analysis of the symptoms: 'What makes *them* worse?'; 'When did *they* begin?'.

The remedy for this problem is to encourage the patient to describe his experiences in his own words, using directive questions aimed at helping him to communicate the nature of pains, abnormal experience, or behaviour. For example, 'Describe the pain to me' rather than 'Is the pain sharp or dull?'; or, 'When you say "nerves", what exactly is it that you mean?'.

Once the patient has been encouraged to clarify the nature of his complaint, the doctor can elicit information regarding time of onset of the symptom, when and in what situations it occurs, and also the consequences of the symptom for the patient and his family. In the case of children, it is important to obtain an exact description of the behaviours that are causing concern.

If it becomes necessary to look something up in the notes during the early minutes of the interview, it is important that the patient should not go on giving the history while the doctor is reading, since although the doctor will think that he is listening, he will in fact fail to hear much of what is said. A simple request like 'Hang on a moment, I need to look something up in your notes' will suffice to make the patient pause; so that the doctor can divert his whole attention to the notes, and then return to the patient when he has found what he wants.

CONTROL OF THE INTERVIEW

Although the doctor should start off as a passive facilitator of communication, it is essential that he assumes more responsibility for controlling the interview as time goes on. Once directive questions have succeeded in clarifying the complaint, it is appropriate for the doctor to fill any gaps in his knowledge by asking closed questions. These are highly focused questions which can be answered by a 'yes' or 'no'; such as 'Does the headache make you feel sick?' or 'Have you lost any weight?'. If a patient introduces a completely new symptom during the course of an interview, it is advisable for the clinician to revert to directive questions aimed at clarifying the symptom before asking closed questions.

The clinician also needs to be able to control the quantity of communication. The liberal use of facilitations and reflections can increase communication with shy, defensive patients and this can be helped further by the simple expedient of moving one's chair nearer the patient and looking expectantly at him: 'The headaches got really bad when you lost your job?'

Garrulous, circumstantial patients typically cause more difficulty than shy ones. Often the patient pours forth a flood of life-problems and day-to-day events before the nature of any health problems has been established, and the beginner may be reluctant to interrupt in case some relevant social factor is missed. He may not appreciate that very talkative patients often count on the doctor to somehow pick out the relevant facts from the flood of communication: tactful attempts to focus communication are almost never resented. Luckily even the most garrulous patients must breathe, and the doctor can slip in a directive question aimed at their recent health when they do so: 'How did all this affect your health?' or 'You mentioned a pain: what was it like?'

The skills described so far will ensure that most psychologically disordered patients will give at least preliminary evidence of such disorder in the first few minutes; the interviewer will then need to follow through and ask questions which will assess the nature and severity of the common psychological disorders.

A SIMPLE MODEL FOR ASSESSMENT OF CURRENT PSYCHOLOGICAL ADJUSTMENT

There are no hard-and-fast rules for conducting such assessments: different patients need to be interviewed in different ways, and each individual doctor will inevitably develop his own style for asking questions in particular areas.

The rationale for the simple scheme described below is really quite simple: most of those with more complex psychiatric illnesses – for example, obsessional states, hypochondriacal states, and acute psychotic states – will also experience the non-specific psychological symptoms described below.

The interview is divided into roughly three areas. It is assumed that the interview will have started with a discussion of any somatic symptoms which may be troubling the patient. It makes good sense to go from these to a more general discussion of those areas of healthy functioning which are commonly affected by psychological disorder, and only then to go on to a direct discussion of anxiety and anxiety-related phenomena. Well delineated depressive syndromes are more unusual than less specific mood disorders, so it makes sense to ask about them at the end.

If a depressive mood disorder is elicited the patient should always be asked about symptoms in two related areas: the 'biological' symptoms of depression, and certain disturbances of thinking which occur in severe depression, and which are quite common in a primary care setting.

1. General psychological adjustment

It is helpful to ask whether the patient's presenting somatic symptom seems worse when the patient is upset, or whether it is brought on by stress. Headache is such a common symptom of affective disorder that it is useful to inquire directly about it in addition to a general inquiry about other symptoms. The interview should now pass on to the areas of appetite, weight, and sleep, and should include fatigue and irritability, inability to concentrate, and loss of libido. Most patients with significant mood disorders will report symptoms in several of these areas.

2. Anxiety and worries

It is now natural to ask about tension and worry. Worry is not of much significance in its own right, but the patient should be asked if they worry at night when they should be sleeping, and whether worry makes their body tense, so that they just cannot relax. Always ask whether the patient has any worries about their health at present, and if they are afraid that their present symptoms are related to serious disease. If the patient reports symptoms of tension and anxiety, remember to ask about panic attacks at this stage: it is often very helpful to the patient to discuss hypochondriacal and irrational fears with the doctor.

3. Depression

It is quite common for clinicians to diagnose depression merely because the patient mentions depressed mood during an assessment interview, or perhaps sheds some tears while describing some painful event. Depression is a syndromal diagnosis, and should imply a persistent depression of mood accompanied by several other characteristic phenomena. It is helpful to make sure that these areas are covered: the intensity of the mood disorder; the presence of 'biological' features of depression; and phenomena which relate to an altered self-concept.

The intensity of the mood disorder is assessed by asking how frequently the patient feels depressed, and asking them to describe how bad they feel. It is tactful to ask them if they have 'felt like' crying, and to ask those that have been crying whether it brings relief, and whether they can stop if need arises. As depression increases, the answer to both these questions is likely to be 'no'. One then ascends a hierarchy of questions, each succeeding question connoting a greater intensity of depressed mood. A positive answer means that the next question should be asked. Thus the questioning proceeds from hopelessness to life not being worth living; to ways in which it might be ended; to suicidal plans; and finally to what has prevented them from putting such plans into effect.

The 'biological' features of depression are well-known and include early waking, diurnal variation in mood, loss of libido, and slowing down of thoughts and actions in addition to the areas which should already have been covered relating to anorexia and weight loss.

Many clinicians never ask about depressive thoughts and altered self-concept, yet the patient's replies to questions in this area are as important in deciding the need for anti-depressants as are the presence of 'biological' features. The topic is best approached by asking what the patient thinks about when he is feeling depressed. Are there some thoughts which he keeps coming back to, or which he cannot get out of his head? Does the patient ever blame himself for being like this? If so, why? Does he ever feel that he is not so good as other people? Does he ever feel a failure, or that he has done wrong? Once more, the questions are roughly hierarchical: questions relating to ideas of worthlessness and wickedness may be followed by those relating to nihilistic ideas. It is also helpful to ask about sensitive ideas such as thoughts that people are laughing at the patient or talking about him behind his back – since such experiences are not uncommon in depressive illness, and it is often therapeutic to confide in another person.

For convenience, the salient features of this brief model interview are tersely expressed in *Table 8(1)*.

It must be stressed that although such questions will give primary care clinicians a simple framework for the routine assessment of the vast majority of their psychiatrically ill patients, additional areas need to be covered for adequate assessment of major disorders such as organic brain syndromes, schizophrenia, mania, and anorexia nervosa.

ASSESSMENT OF THE PSYCHOSOCIAL CONTEXT

Once the clinician has decided that a patient has a significant mood disorder, the next step is to move outwards into the interpersonal and social field in which the disorder is occurring. The patient will typically have given many details in the course of describing his symptoms. Depressed patients commonly consider draconian solutions to their problems such as leaving their spouse or resigning their jobs; the clinician will firmly discourage such actions – at least until the patient is well. Now is the time to allow the patient to discuss reasonable modifications which may need to be made to assist positive adjustment, and to assess the possibilities of working with other family members.

Table 8(1): *A brief model for the assessment of current psychological functions*

general:		somatic symptoms appetite, weight, sleep, libido, tiredness and irritability, lack of concentration
anxiety:		worry causing tension and insomnia, panic attacks, health worries, hypochondriacal fears
depression:	mood	depressed mood, crying, hopelessness, suicidal thoughts
	biological features	diurnal variation, anorexia, weight loss, early waking, loss of libido, retardation, slowing of thoughts
	depressive thoughts	depressive ruminations, ideas of self blame, worthlessness, and inferiority, sensitive ideas of reference

FORMING AND EXPLAINING A PLAN OF MANAGEMENT: THE THERAPEUTIC CONTRACT

It is quite common for markedly depressed patients seen in primary care settings to resist strongly the idea that they have anything the matter with them psychologically. The clinician's first job with such patients is to interpret their complaints to them in such a way that they attribute a different meaning to their somatic complaints. A carefully taken history which covers the ground described in *Table 8(1)* will be a great help to the clinician, who will typically remind the patient of the set of symptoms that have been described, and explain how the somatic presenting symptom forms part of this larger set.

The clinician will have his own views on the relative contributions which can be made by discussion of the patient's problems, by work with other family members and by drug therapy. It is important that the clinician does not crudely attempt to impose his solutions on the patient, since this is likely to lead to low compliance. However, it is helpful for the clinician to be clear and forthright in explaining to the patient how he sees the problem that has been described, and to invite the patient to discuss his feelings about the component parts of a possible solution. Where drug therapy is concerned, an explanation which includes the likely duration of treatment and the side effects which may be experienced is likely to result in much greater compliance. If an antidepressant is prescribed and the patient has described suicidal ideas, it is helpful to ask the patient to pledge not to take an overdose of the medicine. It is also generally unwise to start patients on medication which produces dependence if there is no hope of withdrawing it at a later stage.

It will frequently be the case that the clinician has identified areas of psychological conflict during the first session which require more prolonged discussion. The essence of the therapeutic contract is that the clinician and the patient should agree with one another about these problem areas, and that the clinician should suggest a plan of management which will often involve arrangements to meet on a regular basis for a certain length of time. Ideally, the objective of such therapy – which should be quite clearly stated at the outset – is that the patient should become autonomous and independent as a result of the sessions, and such a model should be used for disorders of relatively short duration. It should be agreed that if the patient does not improve as a result of the limited number of sessions offered, then the clinician will consider referral elsewhere. The covert message is given to the patient that if he wishes to continue his relationship with the primary care clinician, he should therefore get well rather than stay sick.

When the clinician is confronted with disorders of long duration, serious consideration should be given to possible amelioration of long-standing disabilities (perhaps by referral to a social worker), and the clinician should avoid entering a relationship which is intensive and interminable. The pace can be more leisurely, and the clinician should set up limited objectives with the patient. In this way both parties can be satisfied with modest gains, and neither will feel that they have failed if the relationship cannot be terminated.

Having apprehended the mood disorder, the family physician needs to be able to assess the severity of the patient's depression, and to form a management plan which takes account of the patient's state of interpersonal and social adjustment. To do this every family physician needs to be proficient in the simpler forms of psychotherapy. The more recondite forms of psychotherapy may be looked upon as optional extras. They can be incorporated in a family physician's repertoire if he has a personal interest in them – just as some have a special interest in anaesthetics, while others prefer sailing or golf – but the fact is that a family doctor can get along very well without them. The forms of psychotherapy that cannot be dispensed with include reassurance allowing ventilation, and the many subvarieties of supportive psychotherapy.

CHAPTER 9

Non-medical models of care

If Engel's (1977) propositions are correct, a wide range of skills are necessary in order adequately to assist patients:

> 'A biopsychosocial model would include the patient as well as the illness. The doctor's task is to account for the dysphoria and the dysfunction which lead individuals to seek medical help, adopt the sick role, and accept the status of patienthood. He must weigh the relative contributions of social and psychological as well as of biological factors implicated in the patient's dysphoria and dysfunction.'

Given that these skills are not the sole province of the medical profession, the question of co-operation between professional groups becomes a key issue. To date, it is not clear what arrangements are the most successful but there is interesting experimental evidence about a range of approaches which include attachment schemes between general practitioners and nurses, social workers, and psychologists. Unfortunately, each of these disciplines belongs to separate organizational structures, and this can produce obstacles to effective co-ordination. In Britain, a parallel development in nursing, social work, and psychology has been the establishment within each professional group of a career structure, which in each case means that movement upwards in the hierarchy and bureaucracy reduces face-to-face contact between the worker and patient, and, equally important, reduces the contact with those professionals who *do* retain contact with the patient. The reorganization of the services has resulted in services in which the staff who are best able to work with patients have been promoted to senior 'non-contact' positions.

In the hospital, until recently at any rate, multidisciplinary working arrangements have been well developed; to develop a similar level of contact and co-operation in the community requires the active participation and encouragement of the administrators of the separate bodies, the general practitioners, the nursing administrators, the local authority social services administrators, and the soon-to-be-constituted area psychology services. This 'splitting' of responsibility for the patient and his family has become the norm, and comprehensive care very much the exception.

It is probably true to say that the service which a patient currently receives from the embryonic teams in the community depends more upon the composition of the team than upon the needs of the patient. It has also been argued that the work of non-physician health workers is determined more by the organization of the practice than by any formal definition of working role (Stoeckle and Twaddle 1974). The structure of the services offered by nurses, psychologists, and social workers in the community is obviously of prime importance in determining the nature of service experienced by the client.

THE ROLE OF OTHER PROFESSIONALS: SOCIAL WORK

Experiments in co-operation between social workers and doctors have a long history – the importance of such collaboration was recorded in 1922 by Marie Jahoda in *The Kingdom of Evils*. Adolf Meyer, who was initially responsible for encouraging the community psychiatric model, was married to a social worker who provided him with details of the patients' social background. Work since then on the role of the social worker in primary care has developed on an empirical rather than a theoretical basis. With one or two notable exceptions (e.g. Parsons, Mechanic, Brown), sociology has not made a substantial contribution to the development of our theoretical understanding, largely because of its anti-psychiatric posturing.

As might be expected on the basis of surveys of psychiatric problems in general practice (see chapter 5) studies of the social work contribution in the primary care setting show that large numbers of the clients referred to the social worker have formal psychiatric disorder or emotional disturbances. A number of the clients originally present to the GP with vague psychosomatic difficulties (Goldberg and Neil 1972) and many clients who eventually reach social services departments from other referral sources initially discuss their presenting 'social' problem with their GP (Rickards *et al.* 1976).

The primary care level would appear to be an advantageous setting for social work to identify clients and to offer them services.

The nature of the service offered by social workers to clients in this setting may well vary from that offered in a local authority area team. Corney and Briscoe (1977a) compared the clients of a primary health care team social worker and those of local authority intake team. The two groups

groups of clients were similar in age and sex and in poor health; but the clients of the attached social worker were more likely to need psychological help than practical measures. There were seven times as many referrals for emotional or mental illness among the attached social workers clients, and the difference in psychiatric morbidity shown by clients in the two settings was statistically significant (p.>.01). Those suffering from major psychiatric disorder tended to be the elderly and they showed relatively less improvement in response to social work help than the younger clients with more minor psychiatric disorder, usually depression.

Corney and Briscoe (1977b) also compared attachment schemes in general practice with 'liaison' schemes. The attachment scheme covered three pratices in a health centre, where there was a room available for social workers who attended four mornings a week who were members of an Area team for the remainder of the time. A liaison scheme covered two single handed practices and three group practices. Most of the referrals in this scheme were made by telephone and social workers visited fornightly to discuss patients, and no general facilities were made available in the practice. One third of the attachment scheme referrals were made by health visitors, but only 5 per cent of referrals to the liaison scheme were made by health visitors. There was a high rate of psychiatric problems referred in each scheme, but in the attachment scheme more practical and relationship problems were referred, and many of these came from health visitors. Discussions about patients were more informal and highly flexible in the attachment scheme, and discussions with health visitors quite frequent. Corney and Briscoe note that:

> 'it was through these frequent meetings that the different professions operating in the health centre learned about each other's work and roles. The social workers felt that this resulted in increasingly appropriate referrals as the scheme progressed, and preconceptions as to what type of cases were appropriate for referral were often changed and extended.'

Unfortunately, the economic circumstances in the UK have meant that expenditure on these valuable services is unlikely to continue at the same rate, and some services may even contract. One interesting development is that other services may be created which perform many tasks which can be performed by a social worker but with additional as well as useful competence in certain areas. The way in which the role of the Community Psychiatric Nurse has developed is perhaps one example. Another example of this sort of development is the creation of the post of Regional Coordinator for haemophilia, in the North East Thames Regional Health

Authority, funded by the Haemophilia Society for fourteen months on an experimental basis (Colvin *et al.* 1977). Among the functions performed by this trained nursing sister were home visits, home assessments, including looking for an adequate home environment and assessing patients motivations, visiting schools to discuss children's problems with teachers, and contributing towards the judgement regarding suitable schools for the child to attend. Child guidance social workers may find this description very familiar.

One might argue that the creation of this kind of post is due to the reluctance of the new Social Service Department administrators to see Social Work in health care as a priority and their insistence upon fostering those areas of social work which remain largely the province of area-based social workers, namely work with children, most of it statutory. The neglect of health service work and work with the elderly in most authorities has produced interesting and innovative interventions outside local authority social work, many of which might have been developed within health service social work had the pre-1974 organizational arrangements remained in existence.

The social work role in relation to the mentally ill client has in most local authorities become stagnant, and the emphasis has remained upon out-dated methods of intervention which has led to the atrophy of skill development. Social workers are preoccupied with either very short-term practical matters or with long-term statutory responsibilities, and neither of these interventions have been shown to be effective. One of the only significant developments has been in the field of welfare rights which in some ways is a genuine application of client advocacy. Only a few centres have engaged in the management of clients problems by goal-directed or task-oriented work, despite evidence of its value in many cases (Reid and Shyne 1969; Gibbons *et al.* 1978). The social work role in relation to the chronic patient is virtually non-existent and one writer has argued that the mentally ill client group, many of whom have chronic conditions, are a 'lost group' as far as social services are concerned (Howe 1979).

Among the areas which British social work has failed to develop to any great extent are those of co-ordination of services, and of consultancy. The only genuine attempts to develop a co-ordinated approach to social problems has been in the field of child abuse. The setting up of at risk registers has, however, owed more to outside pressures than to a belief in the usefulness of such a register. Registration in some areas is now said to mean absolutely nothing. The belief that a co-ordinated Health Welfare and Children's Department would reduce the number of agencies involved in cases was always a forlorn hope, and to some extent the fact that there are just as many workers involved in any one case as in the past is in part due to the narrow interpretation of the department's responsibilities taken by social services managers, leaving the way open to others to adopt different approaches to the client.

Another potential area for development has seen at least one ambitious attempt to make use of social workers as co-ordinators or supervisors of volunteers or other professionals in work with clients (Challis 1978), but on the whole the sort of scheme described by some American authors in which social workers organize caring agents in the community to take responsibility for aspects of client care are entirely undeveloped.

A final area which has been sadly neglected and which has more serious implications is the failure to give evaluation and research anything other than a minimal role in the operation of the social worker and the social work departments. This failure is obviously related to the other matters discussed already, in particular the reliance upon limited and largely unevaluated methods of intervention.

An evaluative experiment of some importance has been described by Cooper and his colleagues (1975) who compared the psychiatric and social status of a group of patients before treatment and after one year, with the status of a control group treated more conventionally over the same period. The social scores of the experimental group dropped appreciably over the twelve months in all the main areas of social functioning – material conditions, social management, and role-satisfaction. Even patients who were referred back to the GP after one or two contacts fared better on the whole than patients in the control group. The authors say that this suggests:

> 'that the therapeutic effect of the experimental service was not confined to the work of any single member of the team but was to some extent the result of a group interaction.'

In order to examine more closely the precise nature of the social work contribution, and to identify those patients who responded best to the social work intervention, Shepherd and his colleagues undertook further enquiry into the role of an attached social worker. Separate clinical and social assessments were conducted by psychiatrists and social research workers for ninety-two chronic neurotic patients, sixty-one of whom were referred for social work help. The group referred to the social worker for help differed from the group of patients who were not referred on only two variables. Fifty-three per cent of the social workers' clients were married compared with ninety per cent of patients not referred and fifty-two per cent of them were rated as severely psychiatrically disturbed compared with only twenty-six per cent of the patients not referred.

In spite of the large number of social variables rated by the Social Interview Schedule (SIS: Clare and Cairns 1978) the two groups differed significantly on only one item: there were relatively more mild marital difficulties among the social workers' clients. It is evident that the referral procedure in the practice studied did not result in those with the highest degree of social disability as measured by the SIS being seen by the attached social worker.

The assessments were repeated at follow-up twelve months later and the patients' clinical outcome was rated on a four-point scale. Outcome was unrelated to the social worker's activities, the number of contacts with patients, or the patients' attitude to intervention. The changes in overall social score was not related to the action taken by the social worker or the nature of her contact with the clients.

The form of intervention and outcome were found to be significantly related, in that short-term intervention was associated with improvement. This finding is in keeping with the popular view already mentioned above that short-term, goal-directed, or task-centred social work is likely to prove more effective.

Sixty-three per cent of the social workers' time was devoted to practical helping activities and twenty-three per cent to 'casework' alone and thirteen per cent to a combination of both forms of help. Casework alone was used in less than half of the cases with whom continuous contact was maintained during the follow up period, which suggests that this group had intractable practical problems of the sort described in Chapter 7 which are characteristic of chronic neurotic patients. Interestingly, the social workers' 'casework' clients said that they were more satisfied with the help they received; this replicates a finding of a previous enquiry which categorized psychiatric social work help in a similar way (Allen 1972).

The effectiveness of psychiatric social work has been suggested by DiMascio *et al.* (1979) who randomly assigned eighty-one predominantly young female depressed patients to a controlled treatment trial. They compared the combination of amitriptyline and short-term interpersonal psychotherapy (IPT) with either treatment alone and with a non-schedule control group. Their results showed the effectiveness of the combined treatment in symptom reduction and the authors conclude that the addictive effect of combined treatment was largely due to their different effect, amitriptyline on the symptoms such as sleep and appetite disturbance and IPT upon the patient's mood, work, and interests.

In an earlier paper (Weissman *et al.* 1974) IPT on a weekly basis was compared to a low contact treatment of brief monthly visits for assessment. The two treatments had a similar impact on the prevention of relapse and the return of symptoms, but IPT significantly enhanced 'social and interpersonal functioning' for patients who did not relapse. These findings are similar to results of psychiatric social work intervention in cases of deliberate self-poisoning. Studies have shown that social work intervention does not prevent the repetition of self-poisoning, but that it does enhance patients' social functioning (McCulloch and Philip 1970; Gibbons *et al.* 1978).

Mental health services in the USA are sometimes incorporated in the primary care delivery system which may be organized around small teams of physicians, nurses, social workers, psychologists, and others. This form of organization recognises that large numbers of people in need of mental health care never reach psychiatric services, and also that the care necessary for such patients can only be provided by many different professional groups (Coleman and Patrick 1976). In addition, Coleman (1979) has suggested that in the Community Health Care Center Plan of Greater New Haven (CHCP), where such working arrangements exist, that 'professional differences (in role) become less important than the functional similarities shaped by similar job demands' and it has been suggested that non-physicians may be the most appropriate providers for 'the less differentiated states of mental morbidity' (Institute of Medicine 1979).

The value and effectiveness of psychiatric social work has been suggested elsewhere in the literature (Grad and Sainsbury 1966) as has the important role that social factors play in the course of both major (Wittenborn *et al.* 1977) and minor psychiatric disorders (Huxley *et al.* 1979).

Unless the social work contribution is available in health settings, then the treatment of patients may well be more prolonged and this will be to the detriment of the service as well as the patient. Social work involvement will not be effective if it is isolated and organized separately from other professional disciplines.

COMMUNITY PSYCHOLOGY

It is generally accepted that the field of community psychology involves more than simply the application of traditional psychological approaches in a community setting. Among the additional functions of community psychology are crisis intervention services, the transmission of therapeutic skills to other helping agents, prevention through education, mental health consultancy, and political and community action.

The extension of community psychology is due in part to general dissatisfaction with the way psychology has been applied and organized in the UK. Following the report of the Trethowan Subcommittee the setting up of Area Psychological Services is anticipated. These recommendations will result in administrative detachment from the psychologists' traditional hospital setting, just as social workers were detached by the administrative changes following the Seebohm report and the reorganization of the NHS.

Area services may result in an extension of political activity among psychologists and in an increase in the psychologists' involvement in community work projects such as those at Beckton, Islington, Hackney, and Battersea (Bender 1976). In many of these schemes, e.g. Beckton, the only factor which distinguishes the role of the psychologist from that of a social worker or community worker seems to be that the former is more inclined to approach clients' problems using a behavioural perspective.

A more traditional approach has been used by psychologists working in Newham, and an attempt has been made in Birmingham to apply behavioural methods in local authority children's homes. The latter was an example of the psychologist as consultant for mediators (residential child care workers) who implemented programmes in relation to the target group, children in care.

Morrison (1976) described a community psychology programme that was based in paediatrician's office in a rural community. Emotional disorder constituted one of the major areas where work with children who had developmental delay and work with parents whose child management procedures were ineffective.

Very few investigations have been conducted into the effectiveness of the treatment offered by psychologists in primary care contexts. Rosen and Wiens (1979) report one such investigation in which they explored the effect of psychological intervention on the health history of medical patients and on their use of medical services. Use of services, medical problems, and patient diagnosis were studied over a two-year period, the first year without the presence of psychological services. Four groups of patients were compared, those who were evaluated and treated (Group 1), those who were evaluated only (Group 2), those who were referred but not seen by the psychologist (Group 3), and those who were not referred and had no contact with the psychologists (a matched, randomly selected group (Group 4)).

Considerable reductions in the number of presenting medical problems occurred in the Group 1 and Group 2. There was an increase in the number of out-patient visits in Group 1, but a significant decrease in Group 2 ($p<.01$), and both Groups 1 and 2 presented fewer medical problems by the end of the investigation. Group 1 showed a reduction in presenting medical problems of forty-seven per cent and Group 2 of fifty-three per cent.

The comparison with the control group showed that the rates of presenting medical problems remained very much the same over the two years. It would appear therefore that the use of psychologist to both evaluate and treat patients was very effective in the reduction of these problems.

The psychologists were least successful with certain categories of psychiatric patients who were high users of medical services. They reduced the overall use of services in psychotics by thirty-one per cent and in depressive neurotics by twenty-six per cent. These are not diagnostic categories which occur most frequently in the type of patients dealt with by psychologists; the most frequent types of patients are those with phobias, general anxiety, sexual dysfunction, and marital discord (Broadhurst 1977; Davidson 1977). Although psychologists' techniques have more to offer some of these patients, the fact that they had some impact on psychotic and depressive neurotics demonstrates the value of the psychologist to the health care team.

In his arguments for close liaison with general practice Kincey (1974) enumerated the contributions of clinical psychology to clinical problems facing the GP. He categorizes the problems into problems of anxiety and stress, habit disorders, educational-occupational difficulties or decisions, interpersonal-social-marital problems, and psychological adjustments to problems stemming from physical illness or other significant life events involving medical care. The functions of the psychologist would include assessment, biofeedback, behaviour therapy, teaching social skills, Masters and Johnson approaches, and counselling at times of crisis. Enumeration of these functions serves further to confirm the overlap in function between the psychologist, the nurse, the social worker, the GP himself, and the psychiatrist, in the community setting. Psychologists have been able to demonstrate that many of their techniques are of proven value, it seems that they have made more progress in this respect than social workers because, as discussed earlier, the latter lack a sufficiently coherent theoretical underpinning. Psychologists on the other hand have developed many techniques on the basis of more adequate theory, and have applied a more rigorous scientific framework which involves evaluation of their techniques. The emphasis placed on the relevance and importance of research into the results of intervention has meant that psychologists have been able to develop their approach to the care of the psychiatric patient in the community more systematically than other professional groups which eschew the need for systematic research.

At the present time the three roles of psychologist, social worker, and

CPN are well developed in primary care in only a handful of centres and there is no way in which they could be said to have a co-ordinated alternative approach to care for the psychiatric patient in the community. It may be that as and when alternative schemes do develop it will be the paramedical professionals who organize and implement them. To date it is psychiatrists themselves who have been instrumental in widening their clinical approach to include alternative proposals and this tendency has been more marked in the USA than in the UK.

Clinical psychologists are so few in number in Britain that it is impossible for them to exert an influence upon the services for the psychiatric patient simply by their 'presence'. They may come to exert a greater influence by teaching other professionals or non-professionals to use the treatment techniques which psychologists have so effectively developed in the hospital setting.

PSYCHIATRIC NURSING IN THE COMMUNITY

We have already suggested that the community psychiatric nurse shares many skills with the social worker, and has additional and useful attributes, such as a familiarity with clinical phenomena and medical treatments. The void left by social workers' withdrawal into a generic form of service has been increasingly filled by the community psychiatric nurse although the development of CPN services has been sporadic, and their bases, modes of referral, and ways of working have varied tremendously (Queen's Nursing Institute 1974).

The development of community psychiatric nursing services has been handicapped by the fact that it has not been easy to transfer the hospital-based model into the community. There is greater freedom and responsibility for the nurse in the community, and an absence of coherent community-based psychiatric 'teams' as in the hospital setting. Additional growing pains have arisen out of the desire of the CPN to avoid becoming trapped in the 'medicine-dispenser' role. In order to avoid this trap the CPNs and their training course organisers have emphasised aspects of the CPN's role other than that of medicine dispenser or supervisor. In effect this meant that the CPN training courses set up in the late 1970s had content very similar to that of specialized psychiatric social worker training courses, the only major difference being that the latter did not entail any training about drug administration.

Harries (1976) emphasized the nurse's contribution to the functioning of the psychiatric team, behavioural and psychotherapeutic techniques, and the use of therapeutic groups. Harris and Solomon (1977) include drug administration as only one of several other roles of the CPN, included in which are a reassessment of individual and family needs and the patient's 'emotional and social context'; knowledge of existing *social service* and mental health systems well enough to use them effectively as resources on the client's behalf; and ability to respond to psychiatric emergencies in the community. Mental Welfare Officers would find these roles indistinguishable from their own, particularly in the pre-Seebohm mental health departments of the local authority. It is not surprising therefore to find that demarcation disputes between social workers and CPNs is a widely discussed topic. Harries (1976) for example proposes a division of labour between psychiatric nurses and social workers which distinguishes the respective roles.

Harries suggests that in terms of the immediacy of service provision the psychiatric nurse in hospital has an advantage over the social worker in that the nurse provides continuous care, but the social worker only intermittent care. In the community this distinction is lost, although the CPN still seems able to retain two particular facets of care which are absent from social worker-client relationships. Social work responses to crises may be made by different individuals who are members of an emergency, duty or intake system, but the nurse retains control over his own caseload and responds to patients known personally to him. The CPN often responds more quickly and from some points of view more appropriately than the social services social worker in the comunity. Landladies who care for the mentally ill in Manchester for example, are much more satisfied with the service given to them by CPNs than by social workers because the CPN responds quickly to an emergency call, and directs his attention to the patient's disturbed behaviour, which he may ameliorate with medication. In contrast social workers are often impotent in the face of disturbed behaviour and respond with less urgency, and it is not always the social worker who placed the client with the landlady who makes the house visit. However, despite the frequency of contact of CPNs with patients, their families still turn most often to the GP when experiencing problems with their schizophrenic relatives (Hunter 1978).

Harries also distinguishes between the psychiatric nurse in hospital and the social worker in terms of focus of care and he argues that the social worker primarily concerns himself with the family. In contrast to the hospital-based nurse, the CPN may equally be concerned with family circumstances which contribute to the production or maintenance of problem behaviours in the client. He may because of his extensive knowledge of the patient's circumstances become involved in meeting long-term needs; for example, supporting applications for housing transfers. This form of help is subsumed by Harris and Solomon's aims of psychiatric nursing in the community 'to make clients more independent of psychiatric facilities and improve social functioning'.

Hunter (1978) has described a study in which two matched groups of chronic schizophrenic patients, one in receipt of CPN services and the other not, were compared five years after their discharge from hospital. The CPN group spent more time in hospital and were readmitted more often. Only 27 per cent of the CPN group were not readmitted whereas 43 per cent of the comparison group were not readmitted. A larger proportion of the CPN group had had day care at some time, fifty-two per cent compared with thirty-seven per cent. The CPN group were more socially isolated even though slightly more of them lived with relatives – seventy per cent compared with sixty-two per cent of the comparison group.

The findings with regard to hospitalization are perhaps not surprising, considering the chronicity of the patients and the fact that nurses may have identified circumstances which necessitated intervention, circumstances which in comparison group did not receive such attention. In spite of the provision of the service, thirty-four per cent of patients still failed to take medication, although the failure rate in the comparative group was higher (fifty per cent). A smaller number of the comparative group were found to be extremely disturbed but were still living at home in spite of this fact. The level of social work involvement in the groups was nil in the CPN group and 'significant' in the comparative group. Social work intervention cannot therefore be held to account for the higher levels of social contact in the comparative group or their lower readmission rates. The differences between the two groups may be due to the selection process; those cases in most need of help having been referred to the CPN service.

The training of CPNs may not fit them to assume the various roles envisaged for them. It could be argued that in attempting to cover too many roles the nurse becomes less effective clinically or psychotherapeutically.

The feasibility of training nurses as clinical specialists to administer specific psychological treatment for adult neurotics has been examined by Marks and his colleagues (1977). Among the arguments for promoting this training is that it is cheaper than training physicians. The authors summarize the quality of the relationships which exist between the nurse-therapist and other professionals as satisfactory on the whole, but their summary also serves to illustrate the substantial degree of overlap in the roles of family doctors, psychologists, nurse therapists, social workers, and community psychiatric nurses who are working with adult neurotics in the community setting.

CONCLUDING COMMENT

One of the major differences between the USA and the UK in the provision of mental health care at levels 2 and 3 is that the team approach to such care is developing rapidly in the USA (Institute of Medicine 1979). Similar developments in the UK are at present handicapped by the problems outlined in this chapter and Chapter 4. Each professional group is unable by itself to provide for the social, physical, and psychological needs of the psychiatric patient in the community but there are few signs of the organization and integration which will be required if Engel's (1977) proposition is to become a practical reality. Attempts have been made in the UK fairly successfully to integrate the various professional groups (e.g. Cooper 1971) but these efforts have been isolated. At the primary care level services for the psychiatric patient can best be described as disorganized and unintegrated. It would make good sense both economically and practically to base the necessary disciplines in the community, preferably in one building. The practice of multidisciplinary teamwork necessary for the care of the patients and their families and which has been at all levels in the USA, and developing at levels 4 and 5 in the UK, might then be more easily transposed to the community.

CHAPTER 10

Overview

'It is a common state of reflective and inquiring minds to be somewhere between untrammelled guesswork and certainty. It would be discreditable if psychiatrists were huddled at either extreme, wholly engaged in guessing or ignorantly certain.'

Aubrey Lewis, 1957

There are still large areas of doubt and uncertainty in social psychiatry, but it is our contention that a consistent picture is beginning to emerge from the research of the last decade, made possible by the union of epidemiological method with operational criteria for defining the various syndromes of psychiatric disorder. It is now generally conceded that psychopathological symptoms are continuously distributed in populations, so that to ask 'what percentage of a population is mentally ill?' is to pose a question which can only be answered by making arbitrary assumptions. Fortunately, several quite similar questions can be readily answered: 'Is there more psychological impairment in population A than in population B?', or, 'If we wish to say that x per cent of the members of population A are mentally ill, then what percentage of population B would be thought mentally ill if we used the same criteria?' This problem is not peculiar to psychiatry; we need to say that an individual is, or is not, hypertensive or anaemic for the same reasons: health planners have to count people in need of care, epidemiologists like to compare rates, and clinicians need to treat patients.

The concept of prevalence therefore obstinately lives on, since it is convenient as an abstraction and has practical value. However, one cannot escape certain difficulties. The severity of the syndromes of disorder gets progressively less at each lower level of the present model although there is considerable overlap between each level. Wing's PSE-ID-CATEGO system is a way of finding what percentage of the general population would be thought psychiatrically disordered using criteria which reflect current practices among psychiatrists in the British National Health Service. If one ignores 'Threshold Disorders' and only considers 'Definite Disorders' then 79 per cent of a group of psychiatric in-patients, 66 per cent of a group of psychiatric out-patients, but only 3.2 per cent of a large random community sample, are as severely sick as this (Wing 1980). (This is clearly a fairly restrictive definition, since one fifth of the hospitalized sample and one third of the ambulant psychiatric patients do not satisfy it; yet we note that as the one day prevalence of psychiatric illnesses known to the Camberwell Psychiatric Case Register is only 0.76 per cent, that the majority of definite cases of psychiatric illnesses in the community are not being treated by the specialist services.)

If one considers 'threshold disorders', then one accounts for all the in-patients, for 88 per cent of the out-patients, and no fewer than 9 per cent of the random community sample (see *Table2(1)* – a point prevalence of 90 per 1,000 at risk). This figure is very similar to that obtained by Henderson and his colleagues (1980) in Canberra using the GHQ linked to the PSE-ID System, but it is somewhat lower than that obtained in random samples of the population using the GHQ on its own (Goldberg 1978). While this could of course reflect a true difference in prevalence between the various populations, it might equally indicate a different set of decision rules to decide what constitutes a case. The concept of a 'just significant' psychiatric illness used to validate the GHQ was one which was thought to have meaning in a primary care setting, and was strikingly similar to the case examples reported by Brown and Harris (1978) in their research on depression in Camberwell. Tennant and Bebbington (1978) have criticized such criteria because they do not distinguish between transient disorders and 'autonomous' disorders, but they do not make clear how – or why – such a distinction should be made.

It is therefore clear that although most of those with 'definite' disorders are not being treated by psychiatrists, the disorders seen in community settings are on average less severe and they are certainly of shorter duration than those referred to psychiatrists. We have thought it more prudent to present the main research findings concerning the relationship between psychiatric disorder and social variables separately for the various levels of our model since it seemed possible that there might be different relation-ships demonstrable for established severe syndromes on the one hand, and transient milder syndromes on the other. We do not think it useful to describe those with dysphoric symptoms in the community as 'demoral-ized' (Dohrenwend *et al.* 1978) as distinct from those at levels 4 and 5, who are presumably allowed to be psychiatrically ill. The distinction between the two groups is quantitative rather than qualitative; and it seems more useful to study the factors which determine why some will develop chronic dis-orders, and how others are selected for passage through the filters, and therefore metamorphosis into 'psychiatric cases'.

THE PATHWAY TO PSYCHIATRIC CARE

We have argued that psychiatrists base their concepts of mental illness on the highly selected sample of patients who are referred to them, and that this selection process is therefore important both in determining who will receive help and in determining what will be thought of as a psychiatric case. The various factors relating to the patients that influence the permeabilities of the first three filters have been gathered together as *Table 10(1)*.

It must be stressed that this table is produced by gathering together heterogeneous data which relate to rather different health care delivery systems: it is presented mainly as a brief resumé of earlier chapters, and it is not intended to suggest that these relationships will necessarily hold good in other cultural settings. Some findings are, however, remarkably consistent.

More severe disorders pass each filter more easily than less severe disorders, and there seems to be a similar tendency for those who are separated or divorced to pass all the filters more easily. Other variables, such as sex, seem to have complex effects on the different filters. Although women consult doctors more than men, and women with psychiatric symptoms are more numerous than men with psychiatric symptoms among primary care attenders, one cannot conclude from this that the first filter is more permeable to women. If anything, the reverse seems to be true, since the female rates are almost double the male rates in various community samples; the female preponderance is less striking among primary care attenders (see note 3 to Chapter 3). Having arrived at the doctor's office, females are more likely to have their illnesses identified than males (and this is true for doctors of either sex: Marks, Goldberg, and Hillier 1979). This results in a substantial female preponderance among those identified by doctors as psychiatrically ill (female: male ratio = 1.78:1; Shepherd *et al.* 1966). In England, females are less likely to be referred to psychiatrists, and are thereafter less likely to be admitted to hospital as in-patients. The small female excess among in-patients is therefore a reflection of a very much larger female excess in the community. It seems likely that the magnitude and direction of these effects depends upon the setting: in New York females were more likely to be referred to psychiatrists than males, while the reverse was true for South Wales.

The doctor himself is a very important variable in deciding on passage through the second and third filter, and these results have been summarized as *Table 10(2)*. It is quite likely that the doctor is fairly important at the first filter as well, in that some are likely to be perceived by their patients as being more approachable – but there is no research which bears directly on

Table 10(1): *Summary of variables relating to characteristics of the patient determining passage through first 3 filters*

	pass less easily	pass more easily
first filter: decision to consult	trivial disorders married women with children married men old and poor (USA)	severe disorders, many symptoms stressful life events lonely people divorced and separated women unmarried people unemployed
second filter: recognition by the doctor	physical presenting symptoms men below 25; over 65 unmarried people better educated, students (UK)	severe disorders women middle aged people separated, divorced, widowed people seen frequently before
third filter: referred to psychiatrists	mild illness new, acute, and transient women (UK)	severe disorders; psychoses more chronic illnesses young people separated, divorced, widowed women unmarried people men (UK) better educated

this point. Further research will undoubtedly modify the findings we have presented in matters of detail, but we believe that the available evidence amply confirms that powerful selective pressures decide who shall be treated by the psychiatric services.

It would be theoretically desirable, but impracticable, for all studies of the relationships between social factors and psychiatric disorders to be based on random community samples, so that one could then escape the effects of selective factors which determine passage to higher levels of the model. In practice relatively common disorders (such as minor mood disorders) are best studied at level 1, while rarer disorders (such as schizophrenia) are usually studied by taking cases known to the psychiatric services. There are two reasons for this: in order to get a reasonable sized group of schizophrenics from a random community sample one would need to screen very large numbers of patients; and most cases of schizophrenia are in any case known to the psychiatric services, so that possible effects of bias are less serious for schizophrenia than, for example, depression.

In this book we have given an account of recent research concerning social factors for each level of the model, but the selection processes have meant that the studies have inevitably related to different groups of patients.

At level 5 a substantial amount of work has been conducted upon the relationship between social variables and psychiatric illnesses, particularly schizophrenia. Workers have examined the influence of the patient on the family as well as the effects upon relatives of having a mentally ill patient at home. The family reaction to coping with the debilitating end-state of many schizophrenic illnesses has been studied and the role of high expressed emotion in the relapse of schizophrenic patients has been identified.

Social variables have also been identified which predict the course of minor and major psychiatric disorders at level 5, but on the whole the majority of studies have focussed upon factors leading to relapse or upon social consequences of the patient's disorder for the family.

Social influences upon the outcome of disorder have not been investigated to the same extent at level 3, and not at all at level 1 (see *Table 10(3)*). There is no reason to suppose that social factors influencing outcome could not be identified at level 3, although at level 1 the same exercise would involve the task of dating the beginning and the end of illness episodes in untreated subjects.

At level 3 research has tended to concentrate upon the large group of chronic neurotic patients who have intractable difficulties, that is to say, both chronic symptomatology and chronic social dysfunction. At this level the focus of attention is not the burden imposed by these patients upon their

Table 10(2): *Summary of variables relating to characteristics of the doctors which determine passage through the second and third filters*

---

second filter   doctors with a high bias towards making psychiatric diagnoses:

       high turnover of patients (entering and leaving practice)[1]

       busy surgeries ('high physician stress')[2]

       low status doctors (professional and hospital affiliations)[2]

       many patients in Medicaid[2]

       'psychiatric emphasis'[1,3]

       uses many 'psychiatric questions'[3,4]

       empathic[3,4]

       sensitive to verbal cues relating to psychiatric distress[4]

       doctors who make accurate psychiatric assessments:

       interest and concern[3]

       confident; responsive to own needs and feelings[4]

       scores low on 'conservatism'[3,4]

       higher qualifications;[3] good knowledge of clinical medicine[4]

       starts interview well[4]

       directive interview techniques[4]

       sensitive to verbal and non-verbal cues relating to psychiatric disorder[4]

third filter   doctors who refer many patients to psychiatrists:

       high bias towards psychiatric assessments[1]

       single handed; urban; older doctors

---

1 = Shepherd's London study
2 = Philadelphia study
3 = Greater Manchester study
4 = Charleston study

Table 10(3): *A summary of social factors at different levels of the model*

	vulnerability factors	precipitating stressors	influences upon outcome	social correlates
level 5	–	life events[2] expressed emotion[3] modified by degree of face-to-face contact	from the past: unsatisfactory childhood home from the present: type of living group[6] social class[7] material circumstances[8] restricted opportunities[7] financial inadequacy[9] social contact/isolation[9] low premorbid self-esteem[5] unemployment	social class[12]
level 3	–	life events	material circumstances:[11] marital disharmony[11] chronic illness in spouse[11]	material circumstances:[13] housing[13] income[13] social functioning[13] social satisfaction[13] marital problems[14] social class[15]
level 1	lack of intimacy[1] mother died before 11[1] unemployment[1] three children under 14 at home[14]	life events and major social difficulties[1,18]	–	social class[1] socioeconomic status of origin mediated by: childhood health childhood socioeconomic deprivation social disintegration[17] mediated by: restricted opportunities poverty defective coping style[18] inadequate social support[19]

Key:

1 = Brown and Harris (1978)
2 = Brown and Birley (1970)
3 = Vaughan and Leff (1976)
4 = Cooper and Sylph (1973)
5 = Wittenborn et al (1977)

6 = Goldberg (1966)
7 = Huxley (1978)
8 = Huxley (1973)
9 = Sartorius et al (1977)
10 = Strauss and Carpenter (1977)

11 = Kedward (1969)
12 = Dohrenwend and Dohrenwend (1974)
13 = Cooper et al. (1970)
14 = Clare and Cairns (1978)

15 = Hesbacher et al. (1970)
16 = Srole et al (1962)
17 = Leighton et al (1963)
18 = Andrew et al. (1977; 1978)
19 = Henderson et al. (1978); Dalgad (1979)

families but rather the extent and nature of the social deprivation which goes hand in hand with long lasting disorder. Chronic housing problems and inadequate finances figure prominently in the lives of these patients and marital difficulties seem to be an enduring characteristic.

The study of the social correlates of psychopathology (at all levels of the model) has preoccupied researchers in this field for many years and they have produced a large amount of information (see *Table 10(3)*). Most of these studies have contributed little to our understanding of the nature of the relationship between psychopathology and social factors and have resulted in the sound but rather sterile conclusion that social factors are indeed correlates of psychopathology.

In community samples, that is at level 1, disorders which have been studied are, in the main, not intractable chronic neurotic conditions or psychoses, but mood disorders. Many of these mood disorders are transient and many occur in response to stressful life events. By comparing treated cases, untreated cases, and normals, Brown and Harris (1978) have been able to identify another important set of social factors which on the one hand may protect some women from the effects of stressful life events, and on the other hand may act to prevent them from coming into treatment. Brown (1976) has suggested that future research should concentrate upon the identification of vulnerability factors. We have seen that much of the literature at level 1 does in fact conceive of a causal model which includes the concept of vulnerability, but so far it has only been systematically studied in relation to depressed women.

As far as we are aware no enquiries have isolated vulnerability factors oeprating at levels 3 and 5 (*Table 10(3)*); one explanation may be that the factors which contribute to vulnerability and those which influence selection into care are highly correlated.

Although many social variables such as life events, social class, poverty, and inadequate social affiliations exert an influence at each level of our model it is still possible to assert that different social factors are important in different diseases – the vulnerability factors in depressive disorder are quite different from the correlates of chronic neurotic disorder or the precipitants of schizophrenic relapse. It is also possible to demonstrate that the *same* social factor may operate differently in different diseases; so, for instance, reduced face-to-face contact with relatives is a protective factor in schizophrenics, but not in depressives.

It is to be hoped that future studies will separate the effects of social factors upon the onset of disorders from their effects upon selection into treatment. Studies based on random community samples are inevitably very much more costly than those based upon those attending primary care physicians and we have seen that the majority of psychiatrically ill individuals are likely to attend their doctor. The family doctor's consulting rooms therefore continue to be a suitable venue for research studies into common disorders, and such research can usually be organized on a much smaller budget. Most of those with long-standing mood disorders ('chronic neuroses') are known to their family doctor, and most of those whose mood disorders have associated somatic symptoms will attend their family doctor, even though the mood disorder may not be detected. Finally, it is likely that studies of social factors related to major psychiatric disorders (such as organic mental states, schizophrenia, and manic-depressive illnesses) will continue to be based on samples known to the psychiatric services.

IMPLICATIONS FOR TRAINING

The available data leave little room to doubt the size of the problem confronting primary care medical services, and it therefore remains to ask what training should be available to equip the family doctor and the various professionals who assist him to deal with such major demands. It is convenient to distinguish between training intended to sharpen skills in the detection and assessment of disorder and training aimed at providing therapeutic skills.

The research reported in Chapter 4 of this book has been largely concerned with the ability of family doctors as case detectors. Although we were able to show that many doctors have satisfactory skills, overall the results provide little reason for complacency. In both Manchester and Charleston, about one-third of the primary care physicians had correlation coefficients between their ratings and their patients' symptoms that did not reach statistical significance; and it will be recalled that in Philadelphia those family doctors who thought that they needed further training in psychological skills were not less accurate than those who did not – so one probably cannot identify doctors who need special training by asking them. Nor can one conclude that accuracy will increase with experience: there was no tendency for older doctors to be more accurate than their younger colleagues.

The demonstration that accuracy as a rater of psychiatric disturbance is related to certain interview behaviours of the doctor which are potentially modifiable by training, led to the experimental part of the Charleston Study, in which a group of twelve family doctors with poor skills were offered videotaped feedback of their interviews with patients, and their behaviour was modified by a combination of microteaching and role-rehearsal (Goldberg, Steele, Smith, and Spivey 1980). In addition, the residents were provided with the simple model for making assessments of psychiatric disturbance already described in Chapter 8. The residents were assessed once more after receiving four teaching sessions lasting approximately three-quarters of an hour each, and were shown to have become more accurate than a matched control group of residents who had not received such training.

The experiment confirmed our view that videotaped feedback of interview behaviour is perhaps the most powerful available teaching method for modifying interview behaviour. Earlier research at Manchester by Maguire and his colleagues (1978) had demonstrated that this was so for teaching interview skills to medical students, and the Charleston study represented an adaptation of these teaching methods to the special conditions of family practice. There have been several other published attempts to modify the psychological skills of family doctors by providing either audiotaped or videotaped feedback: thus Byrne and Long (1976) reported some success in modifying interview behaviours based on small group experiences during which doctors listened to their own audiotapes; while Verby, Holden and Davis (1979) used peer review of two thirty-minute videotapes as a training method for family doctors, and showed that there was a significant improvement in the interview behaviours of an index group of doctors who had had such an experience, when compared with a control group who had not.

There is clearly much still to be learned about the best deployment of feedback of interviews with patients, but it is to be hoped that those responsible for training schemes for family doctors will become more adventurous in their use of such educational techniques. The necessary skills will not be acquired by reading books or listening to lectures, and in-service training is as likely to encourage undesirable behaviours as desirable ones. To say this is not to detract from the value of any of these traditional methods: we intend only to assert that they will not be sufficient on their own.

In the typical primary care setting where triage is carried out by the family doctor it is clearly most important that he should have these detection skills, but they can just as readily be acquired by other professionals working in a primary care setting.

Where management skills are concerned, all of those working in primary care settings need to be proficient in counselling skills, yet only social workers can really claim that their basic training contains systematic instruction in these skills; the provision of such skills to the other three professional groups – at least in Britain – is haphazard and inadequate at present. To the extent that counselling skills are taught, it is typically by a combination of formal instruction, modelling, and in-service training with supervision sessions. Once more, audiotaped or videotaped feedback offers considerable advantages over these traditional methods.

The suggested format for such sessions is that the teacher will view such tapes either with individual trainees or in small groups.

As the recording is played, anyone can ask for the tape to be stopped. Each time the tape is stopped, the trainee is asked to comment on his own performance. The fundamental aspect of this teaching is that a trainee is relating to his own performance and is therefore, in a sense, having a dialogue with himself. The teacher may invite the trainees to make alternative suggestions as to how the situation could have been handled, and he will always be ready to role-play the patient, so that by repeating the patient's last sentence he gives the trainee an opportunity, a new way of dealing with such a moment in a clinical interview. For such sessions to be found useful by the trainees, it is necessary for the teacher to use them not only as opportunities for proving diagnostic interviewing skills, but also to assist trainees to form management plans for their patients. Such sessions are excellent vehicles for teaching principles of therapeutic contracting, the proper use of psychotropic drugs, as well as giving advice on the management of long-term, intractable problems.

Dr A.T. Lesser of MacMaster University has introduced two additional features to such training sessions (1975, 1976). The first is that the trainee is responsible for choosing which extracts of the recording are to be played to the teacher and his colleagues. He must always play the first few minutes, but is then responsible for choosing the sections further on in the interview about which he wishes to have some feedback. As he spins the recording on to such moments, it is usual for him to say a few words about what happened in the interim. Trainees have no difficulty in choosing such extracts, and the teacher is spared the very time-consuming chore of viewing all the trainees' recordings in their entirety before the teaching session. As each trainee completes his presentation, Dr Lesser uses a dictaphone to record his own views as to what happened between the trainee and the patient, and what management procedures are called for next.

The advantages of this are two-fold. First, the trainees are left in no doubt whatever as to what their teacher thinks is going on and what should happen next. Second, within a few days a typewritten report is incorporated into the patient's notes, showing that the patient has been discussed with the attending psychiatrist and recording his opinion.

The essential feature of such teaching sessions is that teachers' views are not just of the residents' highly selective account of what has been happening with the patient, but can be based on a record of exactly what has been said – and perhaps just as important – how it was said.

What role should psychiatrists and clinical psychologists have in the primary care services? Although there have been several experiments in which each have functioned seeing patients in primary care settings, it seems to us that there are logistic reasons for supposing that they should mainly contribute by influencing the training of those responsible for providing services to patients. Thus psychiatrists have a role to play in teaching the recognition and management of major psychiatric disorders; the use (and non-use!) of psychotropic drugs; the indications for specialist referral; and they can assist other clinical teachers in the assessment of pains and other somatic symptoms which may be psychologically determined. Clinical psychologists need to train others to carry out simple behavioural treatments, and to teach the indications for referral to themselves for certain assessment procedures and more specialized treatments. Both psychiatrists and clinical psychologists may contribute to the teaching of interviewing and counselling skills, but it is likely that general practitioners themselves and social workers will also be responsible for such teaching.

A recent development which is of great interest is the advent of the nurse therapist, a specialized nurse trained to carry out various behavioural therapies (Marks *et al.* 1977). Bird, Marks, and Lindley (1979) have proposed that these nurses should have 'unusual autonomy' and should function as case managers, with one nurse therapist 'servicing' ten to fifteen GPs; more mundane tasks presumably being left to less specialized nurses and social workers attached to each practice. At present most community psychiatric nurses (CPNs) are attached to hospital based psychiatric teams and can seek advice from psychiatrists and psychologists on the multidisciplinary team when need arises: it seems likely that in future changing professional roles, and increasing amounts of counselling and behavioural therapy given by non-medical professionals in primary care settings will call for new patterns of professional relationships between primary and secondary care services.

At present there is little cohesion between the various professional groups jockeying for position in the primary care arena, and lines of communication and responsibility for supervision are poorly co-ordinated. Thus although the family doctor and psychiatrist each cling to ideas of themselves as spiders in the centres of their respective webs, social workers, psychologists, and CPNs each look to more senior members of their respective professions for supervision, while the nurse therapists appear to feel the need for no supervision at all. But even if the spider's webs are not to be completely swept away, they are certain to be pulled into new shapes, and it behoves to us to plan for the future. The family doctor is secure in the middle of his web – at least in developed countries – but it seems likely that he will be relating to a far more complex web of other professionals at a secondary level. It seems likely that psychiatric services, psychological services, and social services will each represent their own webs, and it will be necessary to decide how they relate to one another in a co-ordinated service, and to what extent non-medical professionals working in primary care settings should be free to ask for their help directly rather than channelling requests for specialist help through the family doctor. The role of CPNs is likely to be especially critical as professionals who could move freely between family doctors, psychiatrists, and psychologists; but at present much remains to be done in defining their professional roles *vis-à-vis* other professionals and deciding to whom they should turn for supervision of their work.

While present-day CPN training tends to emphasize the value to the patient and his family of long-term care as well as including a basic knowledge of psychiatric disorders, both of these tend to be played down in most basic social work training courses. For example, only a small proportion of time on most Certificate of Qualification in Social Work (CQSW) courses is given to the study of the handicaps which result from schizophrenia. The main difficulty with basic CQSW training is that it cannot include the detailed study of all client groups, and in recognition of this, programmes of post-qualifying studies have been developed to enable social workers to develop specific areas of knowledge and skill.

A post-qualifying course in work with psychiatrically ill adults and children can only produce small numbers of social workers with special skills in this field, so that it seems important to ensure that such individuals are able to disseminate their skills and to influence the development of services to the mentally ill in the community, rather than being the member of the social work team to whom all the 'specialized' psychiatric work is referred. Whether a social worker is engaged on community tasks or is attached to a multidisciplinary team, an understanding of the major forms of psychiatric disorder will continue to be necessary. Basic CQSW training courses will therefore have to continue to teach about the nature of psychiatric disorders which are encountered in community settings, as well as about the social factors which influence the pathway to psychiatric care.

References

Advancedata (1978) *Office visits to psychiatrists: National Ambulatory Care Survey, United States 1975-6.* Issue 38, August 25, 1978. US Department of Health Education and Welfare: Public Health Service.

Allen, P. (1972) *An Assessment of Psychiatric Social Work Help.* M.Sc. Thesis. University of Manchester.

Andrews, G., Schonell, M., and Tennant, C. (1977) The Relationship between Physical, Psychological and Social Morbidity in a Suburban Community. *American Journal of Epidemiology* **105**: 324-29.

Andrews, G., Tennant, C., Hewson, D. and Schonell, M. (1978) The Relation of Social Factors to Physical and Psychiatric Illness. *American Journal of Epidemiology* **108**: 27-35.

Babigian, H.M. (1977) The Impact of Community Mental Health Centres on the Utilisation of Services. *Archives of General Psychiatry* **34**: 385-94.

Bahn, A., Chandler, C., Issenberg, L. (1961) Diagnostic and demographic characteristics of patients seen in outpatient psychiatric clinics for an entire state (Maryland): Implications for the psychiatrist and Mental Health Programme Planner. *American Journal of Psychiatry* **117**: 769-78.

Bahn, A., Gardner, E., Alltop, L., Knatterud, G. and Solomon, M. (1966) Comparative Study of Rates of Admission and Prevalence for Psychiatric Facilities in Four Register Areas. *American Journal of Public Health* **56**: 2033-46.

Bain, S. (1974) A geographer's approach in the epidemiology of psychiatric disorder. *Journal of Biosocial Science* **6**: 195-220.

Bechofer, F. (1969) Occupations. In M. Stacey (ed.), *Comparability in Social Research.* London: Heinemann.

Bender, M.P. (1976) *Community Psychology.* London: Methuen.

Bird, J., Marks, I.M., and Lindley, P. (1979) Nurse Therapists in Psychiatry – Developments, Controversies and Implications. *British Journal of Psychiatry* **135**: 321-30.

Birley, J. and Hailey, A. (1972) Emergency services. In Wing and Hailey (eds) *Evaluating a Community Psychiatric Service.* London: Oxford University Press.

Bland, R. (1979) Measuring Social Class. *Sociology* **9**: 283-91.

Broadhurst, A. (1977) What part does general practice play in community clinical psychology? *Bulletin of the British Psychological Society* **30**: 305-9.

Brown, G.W. (1959) Experiences of Discharged Chronic Schizophrenic Mental Hospital Patients in Various Types of Living Group. *Milbank Memorial Fund Quarterly* **37**: 101-31.

—————— (1976) Social Causes of Disease. In D. Tuckett (ed.) *An Introduction to Medical Sociology*: 291-33. London: Tavistock Publications.

Brown, G.W. and Birley, J.L.T. (1970) Social precipitants of severe psychiatric disorders. In E.H. Hare and J.K. Wing (eds), *Psychiatric Epidemiology*. London: Oxford University Press.

Brown G.W., Birley, J.L.T. and Wing, J.K. (1972) Influence of family life on the course of schizophrenic disorders : A replication. *British Journal of Psychiatry* **121**: 241-58.

Brown, G.W., Carstairs, G.M., and Topping, G. (1958) Post-hospital adjustment of chronic mental patients. *The Lancet* **2**: 685-89.

Brown G.W., Davidson S., Harris T., Maclean U., Pollock S., and Prudo R. (1977) Psychiatric Disorder in London and North Uist. *Social Science and Medicine* **11**: 367-77.

Brown, G. and Ginsberg, S. (1979) Personal communication to the author, based on a follow-up survey of cases of depressions seen in the Camberwell Survey by Dr S. Ginsberg.

Brown, G.W. and Harris, T. (1978) *Social Origins of Depression*. London: Tavistock Publications.

Brown G.W., Monck E.M., Carstairs G.M. and Wing, J.K. (1962) Influence of family life on the course of schizophrenic illness. *British Journal of Preventive and Social Medicine*, **16**: 55-68.

Brown G.W., Ni Bhrolchain M., and Harris, T.P. (1975) Social class and Psychiatric Disturbance Among Women in an Urban Population. *Sociology* **9**: 225-54.

Brown, G.W. and Rutter, M. (1966) The measurement of family activities and relationships. *Human Relations* **19**: 239-63.

Byrne, P.S. and Long, B.E. (1976) *Doctors Talking to Patients*. London: HMSO.

Campbell, N. (1952) *What is Science?* New York: Dover.

Cartwright, A. and O'Brien, M. (1976) Social Class Variations in Health Care and in the Nature of General Practitioner Consultations. In M. Stacey (ed.), *The Sociology of the NHS*. Sociological Review Monograph 22, University of Keele.

Carey, K. and Kogan, S. (1971) Exploration of factors influencing physician decisions to refer patients to mental health services. *Medical Care* **9**: 55-66.

Challis, D.J. (1978) *The Measurement of Outcome in Social Care of the Elderly*. PSSRU report, University of Kent.

Chancellor, A., Mant, A. and Andrews, G. (1977) The general practitioner's identification and management of emotional disorders. *Australian Family Physician* **6**. Research Report.

Cicourel, A.V. (1964) *Method and Measurement in Sociology*. London: Collier-Macmillan.

Clare, A.W. and Cairns, V.E. (1978) Design, development and use of a standardized interview to assess social maladjustment and dysfunction in community studies. *Psychological Medicine* **8**: 589-604.

Clausen, J. and Yarrow, M.R. (1955) The Impact of Mental Illness on the Family. *Journal of Social Issues* **11**(4).

Cohen, J. (1960) A coefficient of agreement for nominal scales. *Education and Psychological Measurement* **20**: 37-46.

Coleman J.V. (1979) Treatment of emotional problems by primary physicians in an HMO. In Institute of Medicine Conference Report 1 *Mental Health Services in General Health Care*. Washington D.C.: National Academy of Sciences.

Coleman, J.V. and Patrick, D.L. (1976) Integrating Mental Health Services with Primary Medical Care. *Medical Care* 14: 654-61.

Colvin, B.T., Aston, C., Davis, G., Jenkins, G.C., and Dormandy, K.M. (1977) Regional co-ordinator for haemophilia in domicilliary practice. *British Medical Journal* 2: 814-15.

Commission on Chronic Illness (1957) *Chronic Illness in a Large City. Chronic Illness in the USA.* Volume 4. Cambridge, Massachusetts: Harvard University Press.

Cooper, B. (1966) Psychiatric Disorder in Hospital and General Practice. *Social Psychiatry* 1: 7-10.

—— (1971) Social Work in General Practice: the Derby Scheme. *The Lancet*, March 13: 395-402.

—— (1972) Social correlates of psychiatric illness in the community. In McLachlan, G. (ed.) *Approaches to Action: A symposium on services for the mentally ill and handicapped.* London: Oxford University Press.

Cooper, B. Eastwood M.R., and Sylph, J. (1970) Psychiatric morbidity and social adjustment in a general practice population. In E.H. Hare and J.K. Wing (eds), *Psychiatric Epidemiology.* London: Oxford University Press.

Cooper, B., Harwin, C.B.G., Depla, C., and Shepherd, M. (1975) Mental Health Care in the Community: An evaluative study. *Psychological Medicine* 5(4): 372-81.

Cooper, B. and Sylph, J. (1973) Life events and the onset of neurotic illness: an investigation in general practice. *Psychological Medicine* 3: 421-35.

Corney, R.H. and Briscoe, M.E. (1977a) Social workers and their clients: a comparison between primary health care and local authority setting. *Journal of the Royal College of General Practitioners* 27(178): 289-93.

—— (1977b) Investigation into different types of attachment schemes. *Social Work Today* 9(15): 10-14.

Cronbach, L. (1951) Coefficient alpha and the internal structure of tests. *Psychometrika* 16: 297-334.

Cummings, N. and Follette, W. (1968) Psychiatric services and medical utilisation in prepaid Health Plan setting: Part II. *Medical Care* 8: 31-41.

Dalgard, O.S. (1979) Mental Health, Neighbourhood and Related Social Variables in Oslo. Paper delivered to 2nd European Symposium on Social Psychiatry, Aarhus, Denmark. (Abstract to appear in *Acta Psychiatrica Scandinavica* 1979.)

Davidson A.F. (1977) Clinical Psychology and General Practice: a preliminary enquiry. *Bulletin of the British Psychological Society* 30: 337-38.

Department of Health and Social Security (1971) *In-patient statistics from the mental health enquiry for England 1976.* London: HMSO.

—— (1977) *The facilities and services of mental illness and mental handicap hospitals in England 1975.* London: HMSO.

Dilling, H. (1980) Psychiatry and primary health services: Results in a field study. *Acta Psychiatrica Scandinavica* (in press).

Dimascio, A., Weissman, M.M., Prusoff B.A., Neu C., Zwilling M. and Klerman G.L. (1979) Differential symptom reduction by drugs and psychotherapy in acute depression. *American Journal of Psychiatry* 136(48): 555.

Dinitz, S., Lefton, M., Angrist, S., and Pasamanick, B. (1961) Psychiatric and social attributes as predictions of outcome in mental hospitalization. *Social Problems* **8**: 322-28.

Dohrenwend, B. and Dohrenwend, B. (1969) *Social Status and Psychological Disorder*. New York: John Wiley and Sons.

_____ (1974) Social and cultural influences on psychopathology. *Annual Review of Psychology* **25**: 417-52.

Dohrenwend, B., Oksenberg, L., Shrout, P., Dohrenwend, B. and Cook, D. (1979) What psychiatric screening scales measure in the general population. Part 1: Jerome Frank's concept of demoralisation. Mimeographed manuscript available from Dr Dohrenwend, Columbia University, New York.

Dohrenwend, B., Yager, T.J., Egri, G. (1978). The psychiatric status schedule as a measure of dimensions of psychopathology in the general population. *Archives of General Psychiatry* **35**: 731-37.

Duncan, O.D. (1961) A socioeconomic index for all occupations. In A.J. Reiss *et al. Occupations and Social Status*. Glencoe: Free Press.

Duncan-Jones, P. and Henderson, S. (1978) The Use of a Two-Phase Design in a Prevalence Survey. *Social Psychiatry* **13**: 231-37.

Eastwood, M.R. (1975) *The Relation Between Physical and Mental Illness*. Toronto: University of Toronto Press.

Eastwood, M.R. and Trevelyan, M.H. (1972) Relationship between physical and psychiatric disorder. *Psychological Medicine* **2**: 363-72.

Engel, G.L. (1977) The need for a new medical model. A challenge for biomedicine. *Science* **196**: 129-36.

Epson, J.E. (1969) The Mobile Health Clinic : An interim report on a preliminary analysis of the first 1000 patients to attend. Mimeo. London: London Borough of Southwark Health Department.

Essen Moller, E. (1956) Individual Traits and Morbidity in a Swedish Rural Population. *Acta Psychiatrica*. Second Supplement 100, Lund, Sweden.

Exner, J.E. and Murillo, L. (1975) Early prediction of post-hospitalization relapse. *Journal of Psychiatric Research* **12**: 231-37.

Fahy, T.J. (1974) Depression in hospital and in general practice: A direct clinical comparison. *British Journal of Psychiatry* **124**: 240-42.

Fink, R., Goldensohn, S., Shapiro, S. and Daily, E. (1967) Treatment of patients designated by family doctors as having emotional problems. *American Journal of Public Health* **57**: 1550-64.

_____ (1969) Changes in family doctor services for emotional disorders after addition of psychiatric treatment to a prepaid group practice programme. *Medical Care* **7**: 209-24.

Fink, R. and Shapiro, S. (1966) Patterns of medical care relating to mental illness. *Journal of Health and Human Behaviour* **7**: 98-105.

Fink, R. Shapiro, S. Goldensohn, S. and Daily, E. (1969) The Filter-Down Process to Psychotherapy in a Group Practice Medical Care Program. *American Journal of Public Health* **59**: 245-60.

Fink, R., Shapiro S., and Goldensohn, S. (1970) Family Physician Referrals for the Consultation and Pt Initiation in Seeking Care. *Social Science and Medicine* **4**: 273-91.

Finlay-Jones, R.A. and Burvill, P.W. (1977) The Prevalence of Minor Psychiatric Morbidity in the Community. *Psychological Medicine* **7**: 474-89.

Finlay-Jones, R.A. and Murphy, E. (1979) Severity of psychiatric disorders and the 30-item General Health Questionnaire. *British Journal of Psychiatry* **134**: 609-16.

Fitzgerald, R. (1978) The classification and recording of social problems. *Social Science and Medicine* **12**: 253-63.

Foulds, G. (1976) *The Hierarchial Nature of Personal Illness.* London and New York: Academic Press.

Freeman, H.E. and Simmons, O.G. (1958) Mental patients in the community: family settings and performance levels. *American Sociological Review* **23**: 147-54.

Freeman, H.E. and Simmons, O.G. (1959) Social class and posthospital performance levels. *American Sociological Review* **24**: 345-51.

Gardiner, E., Miles, H., A. Bahn, and Romano, J. (1963) All psychiatric experience in a community. *Archives of General Psychiatry* **9**: 369-78.

Gardiner, A., Petersen, J., and Hall, D. (1974) A survey of general practitioners' referrals to a psychiatric out-patient service. *British Journal of Psychiatry* **124**: 536-41.

Gibbons, J.S., Butler, J., Unwin, P., and Gibbons, J.L. (1978) Evaluation of a Social Work Service for Self-poisoning Patients. *British Journal of Psychiatry* **133**: 111-18.

Giel, R. and Van Luijk, J.N. (1969) Psychiatric morbidity in a small Ethiopian town. *British Journal of Psychiatry* **115**: 149-63.

Gillis, L.S. and Keet, M. (1965) Factors underlying the Retention in the Community of Chronic Unhospitalized Schizophrenics *British Journal of Psychiatry* **111**: 1057-67.

Gillis, L., Lewis, J. Slabbert, M. (1968) Psychiatric disorder amongst the coloured people of the Cape Peninsula: an epidemiological study. *British Journal of Psychiatry* **114**: 1575-87.

Glasser, M., and Duggan, T., (1969) Prepaid psychiatric care experience with UAW members. *American Journal of Psychiatry* **126**: 675-81.

Glasser, M.A., Duggan, T.J., and Hoffman, W. (1975) Obstacles to Utilisation of Prepaid Mental Health Care. *American Journal of Psychiatry,* **132**: 710-15.

Goldberg, D. (1970) A psychiatric study of patients with diseases of the small intestine. *Gut* **11**: 459-65.

_____ (1972) *The Detection of Psychiatric Illness by Questionnaire.* Maudsley Monograph No. 21. London: Oxford University Press.

_____ (1978) *Manual of the General Health Questionnaire.* Slough: National Foundation for Educational Research.

_____ (1979) *Training primary care physicians to recognise psychiatric disorder.* Institute of Medicine Publication 79-004. Washington: National Academy of Sciences.

_____ (1979) Detection and assessment of emotional disorder in a primary care setting. *International Journal of Mental Health.* In press.

Goldberg, D. and Blackwell, B. (1970 Psychiatric illness in general practice. A detailed study using a new method of case identification. *British Medical Journal* **2**: 439-43.

Goldberg, D., Cooper, B., Eastwood, M., Kedward, H., and Shepherd, M. (1970) A Psychiatric Interview suitable for using in Community Surveys.*British Journal of the Society of Preventive Medicine* **24**: 18-26.

Goldberg, D. and Hillier, V. (1978) A scaled version of the General Health Questionnaire. To be submitted to *Psychological Medicine.*

Goldberg, D., Kay, C. and Thompson, L. (1976) Psychiatric Morbidity in General Practice and the Community. *Psychological Medicine* **6**: 565-9.

Goldberg, D. and Kessel, N. (1975) Psychiatric research in general practice. In P. Sainsbury and N. Kreitman (eds) *Methods of Psychiatric Research.* London: Oxford University Press.

Goldberg, D., Rickels, K., Downing, R., and Hesbacher, P. (1976) A comparison of two psychiatric screening tests. *British Journal of Psychiatry* **129**: 61-67.

Goldberg, D., Steele, J.J., and Smith, C. (1980) Teaching Psychiatric Interview Techniques to Family Doctors.*Acta Psychiatrica Scandinavica.* (In press.)

Goldberg, D., Steele, J., Smith, C. and Spivey, L. (1980) *Training family practice residents to recognise psychiatric disturbances.* Final report, Contract Number ADAMHA 278-78-003 (DB), Department of Psychiatry, Biometrics and Family Practice, Medical University of South Carolina.

Goldberg, E.M. (1966) Hospital, work and family : A four year study of young mental hospital patients. *British Journal of Psychiatry* **122**: 177-96.

_____ (1976) Towards accountability in social work. A case review system for social workers. *British Journal of Social Work* **6**(1): 3-22.

Goldberg, E.M. and Neil, J.E. (1972) *Social Work in General Practice.* London: George Allen and Unwin.

Goldberg, E.M., Warburton, R.W., McGuiness, B. and Rowlands, J.H. (1977) Towards accountability in social work : one year's intake to an Area Office. *British Journal of Social Work* **7**(3): 257-84.

Goldberg, I., Babigian, H.M., Locke, B., and Rosen, B. (1974) Role of non-psychiatrist physicians in the delivery of mental health services: Implications from three studies. *Public Health Reports* **93**: 240-45.

Goldensohn, S., Fink, R., Shapiro, S. (1969). Referral, utilisation, and staffing patterns for the mental health service in a prepaid group practice programme in New York. *American Journal of Psychiatry* **126**: 689-97.

Goldthorpe, J.H. and Hope, K. (1974) *The social grading of occupation, a new approach and scale.* Oxford: Clarendon Press.

Grad, J. (1976) Social factors in mental illness. In *Recent Advances in Clinical Psychiatry,* No.2: 114-46 Ed. K. Granville Grossman. Churchill Livingstone.

Grad, J. and Sainsbury, P. (1966) Evaluating the Community Psychiatric Service in Chichester: Results. *Milbank Memorial Fund Quarterly* **XLIV**(1): 246-77.

_____ (1968) The effects that patients have on their families in a community care and a control psychiatric service – a two year follow-up. *British Journal of Psychiatry* **114**: 265-78.

Greenley, J. and Mechanic, D. (1976) Social selection in seeking help for psychological problems. *Journal of Health and Social Behaviour* 17 (3) 249-62.

Greunberg, E.M. (1963) A review of mental health in the Metropolis. *Milbank Memorial Fund Quarterly* **41**: 77-8.

Gurland, B.J., Yorkstone, N.J., Stone, A.F., and Frank, J.D. (1972) The

176 *Mental Illness in the Community*

structured and social interview to assess maladjustment (SSIAM) 1. Description, rationale and development. *Archives of General Psychiatry.***27**: 259-64.

Hafner, H. and Klug, J. (1979) First evaluation of the Mannheim Community Mental Health Service. *Acta Psychiatrica Scandinavica.* (In press.)

Hagnell, O. (1966) *A Prospective Study of the Incidence of Mental Disorder.* Svenska Bokforlaget Bonniers.

Hall J. and Jones, D.C. (1950) Social Grading of Occupations. *British Journal of Sociology* **1**(1): 31-55.

Hankin, J. and Oktay, J.S. (1979) *Mental disorder and primary medical care: An analytical review of the literature.* National Institute of Mental Health Series D, No. 5.

Hankin, J. and Shapiro, S. (1979) The demand for medical services by persons under psychiatric care. In Wing and Robins (eds) *Social Consequences of Mental Disorder.* New York: Springer.

Hannay, D.R. (1979) Factors associated with formal symptom referral. *Social Science and Medicine* **13A**: 101-104.

Harries S. (1976) In M.A.A. Baker (ed), *Comprehensive Psychiatric Care.* London: Blackwell.

Harris, M. and Solomon, K. (1977) Roles of the Community Health Nurse JPN and Mental Health Services, 15(2), 35-9.

Harvey-Smith E.A. and Cooper B. (1970) Patterns of neurotic illness in the community. *Journal of the Royal College of General Practitioners* **19**: 132-39.

Hawk, A.B., Carpenter, W.J. Jr., Strauss, J.S. (1975) Diagnostic criteria and five year outcome in schizophrenia : A report from the International Pilot Study of Schizophrenia. *Archives of General Psychiatry* **32**: 343-47.

Helgason, T. (1964) Epidemiology of Mental Disorders in Iceland. *Acta Psychiatrica Scandinavica*, Supplement 173.

———— (1978) Prevalence and incidence of mental disorders estimated by health questionnaire and a psychiatric case register. *Acta Psychiatrica Scandinavica* 258-66.

Henderson, S., Byrne, D.G., Duncan-Jones, P., Scott, R. and Adcock, S. (1980) Social Relationships, Adversity and Neurosis : A Study of Associations in a General Population Sample. *British Journal of Psychiatry.* (In press.)

Henderson, S., Duncan-Jones, P., Byrne, D., Scott, R. and Adcock, S. (1980) Psychiatric disorder in Canberra: a standardised study of prevalence. *Acta Psychiatrica Scandinavica* 1980. (In press.)

Henderson, S., Duncan-Jones, P., McAuley, H. and Ritchie, K. (1978) The patient's primary group. *British Journal of Psychiatry* **132**: 74-86.

Hesbacher, P.T., Rickels, K., and Goldberg, D. (1975) Social factors and neurotic symptoms in family practice. *American Journal of Public Health* **65**: 148-55.

Hoenig, J. and Hamilton, M.W. (1969) *The desegregation of the mentally ill.* London: Routledge and Kegan Paul.

Hoeper, E.W., Nycz, G.R. and Cleary, P. (1979) The quality of mental health services in an organised primary health care setting. Final Report, NIMH contract number: DBE-77--0071. Marshfield Medical Foundation, Marshfield, Wisconsin.

Hollingshead, A.B. and Redlich, F.C. (1953) Social stratification and psychiatric disorders. *American Sociological Review* **18**: 163-9.

Hood, J.E. and Farmer, R.D.T. (1974) A comparative study of frequent and infrequent attenders at a general practice. *International Journal of Nursing* 11: 147-53.

Hopkins, P. and Cooper, B. (1969) Psychiatric referral from a general practice. *British Journal of Psychiatry* 115: 1163-74.

Horwitz, A. (1977) The pathways into psychiatric treatment. Some differences between men and women. *Journal of Health and Social Behaviour* 18: 169-78.

_____ (1978) Family, kin and friend network in psychiatric help-seeking. *Social Science and Medicine* 12(4A): 297-304.

Howe, D. (1979) *A preliminary report on the nature of Area Social Workers' Caseloads*. University of East Anglia. Unpublished.

Hughes, B.J. (1978) *Social and clinical factors associated with burden in the families of schizophrenic patients*. M.Sc. thesis, University of Manchester.

Hulka, B.S. (1972) Determinants of physician utilization. *Medical Care* 10: 300.

Hunter, P. (1978) *Schizophrenia and Community Psychiatric Nursing*. National Schizophrenia Fellowship Survey.

Hurry, J., Tennent, C. and Bebbington, P. (1980) Selective factors leading to psychiatric referral. *Acta Psychiatrica Scandinavica*. (In press.)

Huxley, P.J. (1973) *Clinical versus social prediction in psychiatry*. M.Sc. Thesis. University of Manchester.

_____ (1978) *Social versus clinical prediction in minor psychiatric disorders*. Ph.D. thesis, University of Manchester.

_____ (1980) The relationship provisions of self-poisoning patients. Unpublished.

Huxley, P.J. and Goldberg, D.P. (1975) Social versus clinical prediction in minor psychiatric disorder. *Psychological Medicine* 5: 96-100.

Huxley, P.J., Goldberg D.P., Maguire P., and Kincey, V. (1979) The prediction of the course of minor psychiatric disorders. *British Journal of Psychiatry* 135: 535-43.

Ingham, J.G. and Miller, P.M. (1976) The determinants of illness declaration. *Journal of Psychosomatic Research* 20(4): 309-16.

Ingham, J., Rawnsley, K., and Hughes, D. (1972) Psychiatric Disorder and its Declaration in Contrasting Areas of South Wales. *Psychological Medicine* 2: 281-92.

Innes, G., and Sharp, G. (1962) The study of psychiatric patients in North East Scotland. *Journal of Mental Science* 108: 447-56.

Institute of Medicine (1979) Conference Report: *Mental Health Services in General Care*. National Academy of Sciences Publication 10M-79-004.

Johnson D. (1973a) An analysis of out-patient services. *British Journal of Psychiatry* 122: 301-306.

_____ (1973) Treatment of Depression in General Practice. *British Medical Journal* 2: 18-20.

_____ (1974) A Study of the Use of Antidepressant Medication in General Practice. *British Journal of Psychiatry* 125: 186-92.

Johnstone, A. and Goldberg, D. (1976) Psychiatric Screening in General Practice. *Lancet* 1: 605-608.

Kadushin, C. (1969) *Why People Go to Psychiatrists*. New York: Atherton.

Kaeser, A. and Cooper, B. (1971) The psychiatric patient, the general practitioner, and the outpatient clinic: An operational study and a review. *Psychological Medicine* 1: 312-25.

Katz, M.M. and Lyerly, S.B. (1963) Methods for measuring adjustment and social behaviour in the community, 1: Rationale, description, discriminative validity and scale development. *Psychological Reports* 13: 503-35.

Kedward, H. (1969) The outcome of neurotic illness in the community. *Social Psychiatry* 4(1):1-4.

Kedward, H.B. and Cooper B. (1969) Neurotic disorders in urban practice: A three-year follow-up. *Journal of the College of General Practitioners* 12: 148-63.

Kedward, H.B., and Sylph, J. (1974) The social correlates of chronic neurotic disorder. *Social Psychiatry* 9(3):91-8.

Kelner, R. (1963) *Neurotic ill-health in a general practice on Deeside.* Unpublished MD thesis. University of Liverpool.

Kessel, N. (1960) Psychiatric morbidity in a London general practice. *British Journal of Preventive and Social Medicine* 14: 16-22.

_____ (1963) Who ought to see a psychiatrist? *Lancet* 1092-95.

Kessel, N. and Shepherd, M. (1965) The health and attitudes of people who seldom consult a doctor. *Medical Care* 3: 6-10.

Kincey, J. (1974) General practice and clinical psychology – some arguments for a closer liaison. *Journal of the Royal College of General Practitioners* 24: 882-88.

Kohn, M.L. (1968) Social class and schizophrenia: a critical review. In D. Rosenthal and S.S. Kety (eds), *The Transmission of Schizophrenia*. Oxford: Pergamon Press.

Lawson, A. (1972) *The Recognition of Mental Illness in London*. London: Oxford University Press.

Leighton, A.H. (1963) *Psychiatric disorder among the Yoruba*. Ithaca: Cornell University Press.

_____ (1976) In B.H. Caplan, R.N. Wilson and A.H. Leighton (eds) *Further Explanations In Social Psychiatry*. New York: Basic Books.

Leighton, A.H. and Leighton, D.C. (1959) *My Name is Legion*. New York: Basic Books.

Leighton, D.C., Harding, J.C., Macklin, D.B., Macmillan, A.M., and Leighton, A.H. (1963) *The Character of Danger*. New York: Basic Books.

Leopold, R., Goldberg, D., Schein, L. (1971) Emotional disturbance among non-psychiatric physicians in an urban neighbourhood. Final Report, Contract No. NIMH-HSM-46-69-79.

Lesser, A. (1976) *The Family Physician, The Psychiatrist and the Patient – Can they work together?* Paper read at the Symposium on Common Neurotic Problems in Medical Practice. University of West Ontario.

Lesser, A. and Wakefield, J. (1975) Using the Psychiatrist: A Different Approach to Consultation. *Canadian Family Physician*. 79-85.

Liem, R. and Liem, J. (1978) Social class and mental illness reconsidered: the role of economic stress and social support. *Journal of Health and Social Behaviour* 19: 139-56.

Locke, B., Finucane, D., and Hassler, F. (1967) Emotionally disturbed patients under the care of private non-psychiatric physicians. In R. Munroe, G. Klee, E. Brody (eds), *Psychiatric Epidemiology in Mental Health Planning.* American Psychiatric Association Research Report Number 22.

Locke, B.Z. and Gardner, E.A. (1969) *Psychiatric disorders among the patients of general practitioners and internists.* Public Health Reports **84**: 167-73.

Locke, B.Z., Krantz, G., and Kramer, M. (1965) Psychiatric need and demand in a prepaid group practice programme. *American Journal of Public Health* **56**: 895-904.

Logan, W. and Brooke, E. (1957) *The Survey of Sickness 1943-52.*Studies on Medical and Population Subjects. No. 12. London: HMSO.

Logan, W. and Cushion, A. (1958) *Morbidity Statistics in General Practice.* (General) Studies on Medical and Population Subjects. No 14. London: HMSO.

Maguire, P., Roe, P., Goldberg, D., Jones, S., Hyde, C. and O'Dowd, T. (1978) The value of feedback in teaching interviewing skills to medical students. *Psychological Medicine* **8**: 695-705.

Marks, I.M., Hallam, R.S., Philpott, R., and Connolly, J. (1977) *Nursing in Behavioural Psychotherapy.* Research Series of Royal College of Nursing, London.

Marks, J., Goldberg, D.P., and Hillier, V.F. (1979) Determinants of the Ability of General Practitioners to Detect Psychiatric Illness. *Psychological Medicine* **9**: 337-53.

Martin, F., Brotherstone, J., and Chave, S. (1957) Incidence of Neurosis in a New Housing Estate. *British Journal of Preventive and Social Medicine* **11**: 196-202.

May, A. and Gregory, E. (1968) Participation of General Practitioners in Psychiatry. *British Medical Journal* **2**: 168-71.

Maxwell, A.E. (1977) Coefficients of agreement between observers and their interpretation. *British Journal of Psychiatry* **130**: 79-83.

McAllister, T.A. and Phillip, A.E. (1975) The clinical psychologist in a health centre: one year's work. *British Medical Journal* **4**: 513-14.

McCulloch, J.W. and Philip, A.E. (1967) Social variables in attempted suicide. *Acta Psychiatrica Scandinavica* **43**: 341-46.

Mechanic, D. (1977) Illness behaviour, social adaptation, and the management of illness. A comparison of educational and medical models. *Journal of Nervous Mental Disorder* **165**(2): 79-87.

Mezey, A. and Evans, E. (1971) Psychiatric in-patients and out-patients in a London Borough. *British Journal of Psychiatry* **118**: 609-16.

Michaux, W.W., Katz, M., and Kurland, A. (1969) *The First Year Out.* Baltimore: John Hopkins Press.

Miller, P. McC. and Ingham, J.G. (1976) Friends, Confidants and Symptoms. *Social Psychiatry* **11**: 51-8.

Morrison, T.L. (1976) The Psychologist in the Paediatrician's Office: One Approach to Community Psychology. *Community Mental Health Journal* **12**(3): 306-12.

Murphy, H.M.B. (1976) Which neuroses need specialist care? *Canadian Medical Associations Journal* **115**: 540-43.

Murphy, E. and Brown, G.W. Life events, psychiatric disturbance and physical illness. *British Journal of Psychiatry* **136**: 326-38.

Ndetei, D.M. and Muhangi, J. (1979) The prevalence and clinical presentation of psychiatric illness in a rural setting in Kenya. *British Journal of Psychiatry* **135**: 269-72.

Office of Population Censuses and Surveys (OPCS) (1970) *Classification of Occupations*. London: HMSO.

_____ (1973) *The General Household Survey*. London: HMSO.

_____ (1974) *Morbidity statistics from General Practice. Second National Study 1970-71*. Studies on Medical and Population Subjects No. 26. London: HMSO.

Orley, J. and Wing, J. (1979) Psychiatric disorders in two African villages. *Archives of General Psychiatry* **36**: 513-20.

Osborn, A.F. and Morris, T.C. (1979) The rationale for a composite index of social class and its evaluation. *British Journal of Sociology* **30**(1): 39-60.

Pasamanick, B., Roberts, D., Lemkau, P. (1956) A survey of mental disease in an urban population. *American Journal of Public Health* **47**: 923-29.

Paykel, E.S. (1978) Contribution of life events to causation of psychiatric illness. *Psychological Medicine* **8**: 245-53.

Queen's Nursing Institute (1974) *A seminar on Psychiatric Nursing in the Community held at the Queen's Nursing Institute on 27th March*. Mimeographed booklet.

Querido, A. (1959) Forecast and follow-up. An investigation into the clinical, social and mental factors determining the results of hospital treatment. *British Journal of Preventitive Medicine* **13**: 33-49.

Rawnsley, K. and Loudon, J. (1962) The Attitudes of General Practitioners to Psychiatry. In P. Halmos (ed.), *Sociology and Medicine*. Sociological Review Monograph No. 5. University of Keele.

Rawnsley, K., Loudon, J., Miles, M. (1962) Factors influencing the referral of patients by general practitioners. *British Journal of Preventive and Social Medicine* **16**: 174.

Regier, D., Goldberg, I.D., Taube, C. (1978) The De Facto US Mental Health Services System: A Public Health Perspective. *Archives of General Psychiatry* **35**: 685-93.

Reid, D. (1960) *Epidemiological methods in the study of mental disorder*. Geneva: WHO.

Reid, W.J. and Shyne, A.W. (1969) *Brief and Extended Casework*. New York: Columbia University Press.

Richards, C., Gildersleeve, C., Fitzgerald, R., and Cooper, B. (1976) The health of clients of a Social Service Department. *Journal of the Royal College of General Practitioners* **26**: 237-43.

Robertson, N. (1971) *Some personal and social factors associated with marital adjustment*. Ph.D. Thesis. University of Aberdeen.

_____ (1979) Variations in referral pattern to the psychiatric services by general practitioners. *Psychological Medicine* **9**: 355-64.

Rogan, W. and Gladen, B. (1978) Estimating prevalence from the results of a screening test. *American Journal of Epidemiology* **107**: 71-6.

Rosen, B.M., Locke, B.Z., Goldberg, I.D., Babigian, H.M. (1972) Identification of emotional disturbance in patients seen in industrial dispersaries. *Mental Hygiene* **54**: 271-79.

Rosen, J.C. and Wiens, A.N. 1979 Changes in medical problems and use of medical services following psychological intervention. *American Psychologist* **34**(5): 420-31.

Royal College of General Practitioners : Office of Population Censuses and Surveys, DHSS (1979) *Morbidity Statistics from General Practice* 1971-72 Second National Study. Studies on Medical and Population Subjects No. 36. London: HMSO.

Rutter, M. and Brown, G.W. (1966) The reliability and validity of measures of families containing a psychiatric patient. *Social Psychiatry* **1**: 38-53.

Sartorius, N., Jablensky, A. and Shapiro, R. (1977) Two year follow-up of the patients in the WHO International Pilot Study of Schizophrenia. *Psychological Medicine* **7**: 529-41.

Schien, L. (1977) *Psychiatric Illness in General Practice: Agreement and Disagreement on the Affirmation of Illness*. Ph.D. Dissertation. Ann Arbor, Michigan: University Microfilms International.

Shepherd, M. (1980) Psychiatric aspects of primary care in seventeenth-century England. *Acta Psychiatrica Scandinavica*. (In press.)

Shepherd, M., Cooper, B., Brown, A.C. and Kalton, G.W. (1966) *Psychiatric Illness in General Practice*. London: Oxford University Press.

Shortell, S. and Daniel, R. (1974) Referral relationships between internists and psychiatrists in fee-for-service practice: An empirical examination. *Medical Care* **12**: 229-40.

Sims, A.C.P. and Salmon, P.H. (1975) Severity of symptoms of psychiatric outpatients: Use of the general health questionnaire in hospital and general practice patients. *Psychological Medicine* **5**: 62-6.

Skuse, D.H. (1975) Attitudes to the Psychiatric Out-patient clinic. *British Medical Journal* **3**: 469-71.

Spitzer, R.L., Endicott, J., Robins, E. (1978) Research diagnostic criteria: Rationale and reliability. *Archives of General Psychiatry* **35**: 773-82.

Srole, L., Langner, T., Michael, S., Opler, M., Rennie, T. (1962) *Mental Health in the Metropolis*. New York: McGraw-Hill.

Stewart, M.A., McWhinney, I.R., Buck, C.W., (1975) How illness presents: a study of patient behaviour. *Journal of Family Practitioners* **2**(6): 411-4.

Stevens, B.C. (1972) Dependence of schizophrenic patients on elderly relations. *Psychological Medicine* **2**:17-32.

Stoeckle, J.D. and Twaddle, A.C. (1974) Non-physician health workers: some problems and prospects. *Social Science and Medicine* **8**: 71-6.

Strauss, J.S. and Carpenter, W.T. (1972) The prediction of outcome in schizophrenia. *Archives of General Psychiatry* **27**: 739-46.

———— (1974a) Evaluation of the outcome in schizophrenia. In D.F. Ricks, A. Thomas, and M. Roff (eds). *Life History Research in Psychopathology 3*. Minneapolis: University of Minnesota Press.

———— (1974b) The Prediction of Outcome in Schizoprenia II. Relationships between predictor and outcome variables. Report from WHO international pilot study of schizophrenia. *Archives of General Psychiatry* **32**(1): 37.

———— (1977) The Prediction of Outcome in Schizophrenia III. Five Year Outcome and its Predictors. *Archives of General Psychiatry* **34**: 159-63.

Suchman, E.A. (1965) Stages of Illness and Medical Care. *Journal of Health and*

182   *Mental Illness in the Community*

Human Behaviour **6**: 115.

Surtees, P.G. and Kendell, R.E. (1979) The hierarchy model of psychiatric symptomatology: An investigation based on Present State Examination ratings. *British Journal of Psychiatry* **135**: 438-43.

Tanner, J., Weissman, M.M., and Prusoff, B. (1975) Social adjustment and clinical relapse in depressed outpatients. *Comprehensive Psychiatry* **16**(6): 547-56.

Tantam, D. and Burns, B. (1979) An international comparison of two systems of community health care. *Psychological Medicine* **9**: 541-50.

Tessler, R., Mechanic, D. and Dimond, M. (1976) The Effect of Psychological Distress on Physician Utilization : A Prospective Study. *Journal of Health and Social Behaviour* **17**: 353-64.

Thomas, K.B. (1974) Temporarily dependent patient in general practice. *British Medical Journal* **1**: 625-26.

Tischler, G.L., Henisz, J.E., Myers, J.K. and Boswell, P.C. (1975a) Utilisation of Mental Health Services. *Archives of General Psychiatry* **32**: 411-15.

_____ (1975b) Utilisation of mental health services, II: Mediators of service allocation. *Archives of General Psychiatry* **32**: 416-18.

Vaughn, C.E. and Leff, J.P. (1976) The influence of family and social factors on the course of psychiatric illness. *British Journal of Psychiatry* **129**: 125-37.

Venables, P.H. (1960) The effect of auditory and visual stimulation on the potential response of schizophrenics. *Brain* **83**: 77-92.

Verby, J.E., Holden, P., and Davis, R.H. (1979) Peer Review of Consultations in Primary Care: The use of audiovisual recordings. *British Medical Journal* **ii**: 1686-88.

Wadsworth, M., Butterfield, W.J.H. and Blaney, R. (1971) *Health and Sickness : The Choice of Treatment*. London: Tavistock Publications.

Watts, C.A.H. (1958) *Morbidity statistics from general practice*. Vol. III Studies on Medical and Population Subjects. No. 14. London: HMSO.

Weinberg, W. (1925) Meth. Tech. Stat. Vol. 1, 138-49: and see D. Reid (1960).

Weiss, R.S. (1974) The provisions of social relationships. In *Doing Unto Others*. Z. Rubin (ed.). New Jersey: Prentice Hall.

Weissman, M.M. and Klerman, G.L. (1977) Sex Differences and the Epidemiology of Depression. *Archives of General Psychiatry* **34**: 98-111.

Weissman, M.M. and Klerman, A.L. (1978) Epidemiology of mental disorders. *Archives of General Psychiatry* **35**: 703-15.

Weissman, M.M. and Myers, J.K. (1978) Rates and risks of depressive disorders in a US suburban community. *Acta Psychiatrica Scandinavica* **57**: 219-31.

Weissman, M.M., Myers, J.K. and Harding, P.S. (1978) Psychiatric Disorders in a US Urban Community: 1975/1976 *American Journal of Psychiatry* **135**: 459-62.

_____ (1978) Rates and risks of depression symptoms in a US urban community. *Acta Psychiatrica Scandinavica* **57**: 219-31.

Weissman, M.M., Neu, C., Rounsaville, B.J., Dimascio, A., Prusoff, B.A. and Klerman, G.L. (1979) Short-term interpersonal psychotherapy (IPT) for depression : Description and efficacy. Unpublished manuscript from Depression Research Unit, Yale University.

Weissman, M.M. and Paykel, E. (1974) *The Depressed Woman : A study of social relationships*. Chicago: University of Chicago Press.

Wing, J.K. (1972) The Statistical Context: comparisons with national local statistics. In J.K. Wing and A. Hailey (eds) *Evaluating a Community Psychiatric Service.* London: Oxford University Press.

———— (1976) Preliminary Communication : a technique for studying psychiatric morbidity in in-patient and out-patient series and in general population samples. *Psychological Medicine* **6**: 665-71.

———— (1980) The use of the Present State Examination in general population surveys. *Acta Psychiatrica Scandinavica* (In press).

Wing, J.K., Birley, J.L.T., Hailey, A.M. (1972) Out-patient facilities. In Wing and Hailey (eds) *Evaluating a Community Psychiatric Service.* London: Oxford University Press.

Wing, J.K. and Bransby, R. (1970) *Psychiatric case registers.* DHSS Statistical Report Series No. 8. London: HMSO.

Wing, J.K. and Brown, G. (1970) *Institutionalism and Schizophrenia.* Cambridge: Cambridge University Press.

Wing, J.K., Carstairs, G.M., Monck, E. and Brown, E.W. (1964) Morbidity in the community of schizophrenic patients discharged from London Mental Hospitals in 1959. *British Journal of Psychiatry* **110**: 10.

Wing, J.K., Cooper, J. and Sartorius, N. (1974) *The measurement and classification of psychiatric symptoms.* Cambridge: Cambridge University Press.

Wing, J.R. and Fryers, T. (1976) *Statistics from the Camberwell and Salford psychiatric case registers 1964-74.* Published privately: Department of Community Medicine, University of Manchester.

Wing, J.K., Hailey, A.M. (1972) Reported prevalence. In Wing and Hailey (eds) *Evaluating a Community Psychiatric Service,* London: Oxford University Press.

———— (1972b) Use of hospital beds. In Wing and Hailey (eds) *Evaluating a Community Psychiatric Service.* London: Oxford University Press.

Wing, J.K., Hailey, A. Bransby, E. and Fryers, T. (1972) The statistical context: Comparisons with national and local statistics. In Wing and Hailey (eds) *Evaluating a Community Psychiatric Service.* London: Oxford University Press.

Wing, J.K., Nixon, J.M. and Leff, J.P. (1977) Reliability of the PSE (ninth edition) used in a population study. *Psychological Medicine* **7**: 505-16.

Wing, J.K., Mann, S.A., Leff, J.T., and Nixon, J.N. (1978) The concept of a case in psychiatric population surveys. *Psychological Medicine* **8**: 203-219.

Wing, L., Wing, J., Hailey, A., Bahn, A., Smith, H., and Baldwin, J. (1967) The use of psychiatric services in three urban areas: an international case register study. *Social Psychiatry* **2**: 158-66.

Wittenborn, J.R., McDonald, D.C., and Maurer, H.S. (1977) Persisting symptoms in schizophrenia predicted by background factors. *Archives of General Psychiatry* **34**: 1057-61.

World Health Organization. *Schizophrenia: An International Follow-up Study.* Chichester: John Wiley.

———— (1961) *The Undergraduate Teaching of Psychiatry and Mental Health Promotion.* Geneva: WHO. (Technical reports series 208.)

———— (1974) *Glossary of Mental Disorders and Guide to their Classification.* Geneva: WHO.

Name Index

Subject Index

Prediction
  clinical, 39n, 40n
  social, 39n, 40n, 122-6
Present State Examination (PSE), 2, 10,
  15n 17n, 23, 26, 27, 28, 35, 36, 63, 89,
  157, 158
Prevalence, 3, 7, 8, 9, 10, 12, 23, 25, 32,
  69, 86, 87n, 90n, 104, 107n, 119, 157,
  lifetime, 22, 32
  period, 6, 9, 10, 20n, 22, 23, 24, 25
  point, 6, 10, 22, 23, 25, 158
  probable, 87
Primary care physicians, 2, 4, 5, 7, 10, 13,
  20n, 28, 29, 47, 55n, 57ff, 85, 98-114
Primary group, 35
Provisional validation of sickness, 48
Psychiatric,
  associated illness, 9
  hospital beds, *see* Hospital beds
  illness (definition), 1
  social work, 149, 150
  status schedule, 16n
Psychologist, 9, 93n, 120, 144, 150-53
Psychomotor retardation, 28, 37n
Psychoses, 5, 24, 28, 59, 111, 129
Psychotherapy, 48, 50-1, 99-101, 109, 121,
  143, 149
Psychotic symptoms, 12, 16n
Psychotropic drugs, 64, 100, 107n, 113,
  168

Qualifications, 66
Questionnaires, self report, 13

Random samples, 3, 4, 6, 10, 16, 22, 24,
  26, 29, 33, 34, 35, 51, 54, 55, 112,
  158, 161, 164
Referral, 1, 4, 9, 11
Registrar General's Classification of
  Occupations, 30, 42n, 43n, 84
Reliability, 29, 37n, 38n, 39n, 103
Renard Interview, 16n

Salford, 8
Sampling, stratified, 18n
Schedule for affective disorders and
  schizophrenia (SADS), 15n, 16n, 23,
  26, 27, 64
Schizophrenia, 2, 16n, 20n, 28, 96, 97,
  118, 119, 124, 125, 128, 129, 132, 134,
  135n, 154, 155, 161, 164, 165
Screening instruments, 2, 16n, 24, 29, 35,
  50, 61, 83, 85, 86n, 98
Selection processes, 4

Self-poisoning, 150
Self-rating scales, 24, 26
Services, 115n, 119, 159
Severity,
  of illness, 28, 36n, 111, 113, 159
  of symptoms, 17n, 29, 49, 115n
Sex differences in rates of disorder, 24, 29,
  37n, 51-3, 56n, 83, 131, 132, 135n
Sexual dysfunction, 152
Sick role, 52
Sleep disturbance (insomnia), 2, 26, 27,
  59
Social Adjustment Schedule, 40n
Social,
  affiliations, 35
    inadequacy of, 33, 164
  class, 30, 32, 33, 41n, 42n, 84, 101, 104,
    112, 124, 132, 133, 164
  correlates, 1, 32
  dysfunction, 30, 40n
  factors, 4, 29, 30, 31, 51-3, 101-4, 122,
    131, 161, 163, 164
  functioning, 39n, 102
  Index Score, 43n
  integration, 35
  Interview Schedule (SIS), 39n, 40n,
    103-4, 149
  isolation, 52, 54, 155
  mobility, 32-3
  network, 35, 41n, 52
  problems, classification of, 30, 40n, 41n
      measurement of, 37-41n, 43n
  Services Departments, 40n, 145, 147
  workers, 39n, 40n, 55, 101, 102, 121,
    143, 144-52
Sociocultural disintegration, 31
Socioeconomic status, *see* Social Class
Somatic symptoms, 28, 57, 60, 165
Spearman's Rank Order Correlation
  Coefficient, 64, 71-3, 75, 77, 79, 80,
  90n, 91n, 93n
Standardized psychiatric interview, 2
Statistical Package for the Social Sciences
  (SPSS), 90n
Stigma, 59
Stirling County, 30-32, 36n, 56n
Structured and Social Interview to Assess
  Maladjustment (SSIAM), 40n
Surveys of sickness, 56
Symptom Checklist (SCL-90), 93n
Syndromes of disorder, 96

Task-oriented casework, 147
Taxonomy (psychiatric), 15n